Beginning JavaScript Syntax

Understanding Syntactical Rules and Structures for Better JavaScript Programming

Sonu Kapoor

Apress®

Beginning JavaScript Syntax: Understanding Syntactical Rules and Structures for Better JavaScript Programming

Sonu Kapoor
Brampton, ON, Canada

ISBN-13 (pbk): 979-8-8688-1459-4 ISBN-13 (electronic): 979-8-8688-1460-0
https://doi.org/10.1007/979-8-8688-1460-0

Copyright © 2025 by Sonu Kapoor

This work is subject to copyright. All rights are reserved by the Publisher, whether the whole or part of the material is concerned, specifically the rights of translation, reprinting, reuse of illustrations, recitation, broadcasting, reproduction on microfilms or in any other physical way, and transmission or information storage and retrieval, electronic adaptation, computer software, or by similar or dissimilar methodology now known or hereafter developed.

Trademarked names, logos, and images may appear in this book. Rather than use a trademark symbol with every occurrence of a trademarked name, logo, or image we use the names, logos, and images only in an editorial fashion and to the benefit of the trademark owner, with no intention of infringement of the trademark.

The use in this publication of trade names, trademarks, service marks, and similar terms, even if they are not identified as such, is not to be taken as an expression of opinion as to whether or not they are subject to proprietary rights.

While the advice and information in this book are believed to be true and accurate at the date of publication, neither the authors nor the editors nor the publisher can accept any legal responsibility for any errors or omissions that may be made. The publisher makes no warranty, express or implied, with respect to the material contained herein.

Managing Director, Apress Media LLC: Welmoed Spahr
Acquisitions Editor: Anandadeep Roy
Editorial Assistant: Jessica Vakili

Cover designed by eStudioCalamar

Distributed to the book trade worldwide by Springer Science+Business Media New York, 1 New York Plaza, New York, NY 10004. Phone 1-800-SPRINGER, fax (201) 348-4505, e-mail orders-ny@springer-sbm.com, or visit www.springeronline.com. Apress Media, LLC is a Delaware LLC and the sole member (owner) is Springer Science + Business Media Finance Inc (SSBM Finance Inc). SSBM Finance Inc is a **Delaware** corporation.

For information on translations, please e-mail booktranslations@springernature.com; for reprint, paperback, or audio rights, please e-mail bookpermissions@springernature.com.

Apress titles may be purchased in bulk for academic, corporate, or promotional use. eBook versions and licenses are also available for most titles. For more information, reference our Print and eBook Bulk Sales web page at http://www.apress.com/bulk-sales.

Any source code or other supplementary material referenced by the author in this book is available to readers on GitHub. For more detailed information, please visit https://www.apress.com/gp/services/source-code.

If disposing of this product, please recycle the paper

To my wonderful wife, Jyoti, whose unwavering love and support have been the foundation of my journey. Your belief in me has been my greatest strength.

To my amazing daughters, Jasmine, Kareena, and Isha - you inspire me every day with your curiosity, kindness, and boundless energy. This book is a testament to the lessons I hope to pass on to you and to all those eager to learn.

With all my love, this book is for you.

Table of Contents

About the Author .... **xxi**

About the Technical Reviewer .... **xxiii**

Preface .... **xxv**

Introduction .... **xxvii**

Chapter 1: Introduction to JavaScript Syntax **1**
    Objective 1
    What Is Syntax? 2
    Why Syntax Is Essential in Programming 3
    Syntax Across Programming Languages 4
    Syntax Errors and Debugging 5
    The Syntax–Logic Connection 5
    JavaScript Syntax and Interpreted Execution 6
    Summary 7

Chapter 2: How JavaScript Works in Web Development **9**
    Objective 9
    JavaScript As an Interpreted Language 10
    The Role of JavaScript in Web Development 10
    JavaScript and the Document Object Model (DOM) 11
    JavaScript Events and User Interaction 13
    JavaScript in Front-End and Back-End Development 14

TABLE OF CONTENTS

JavaScript and Asynchronous Programming 14
Why Understanding JavaScript's Role Matters 16
Summary 16

Chapter 3: Setting Up the Environment 19
Objective 19
Choosing a Code Editor 20
    Setting Up Visual Studio Code 21
Setting Up a Web Browser for Development 22
    Using Chrome Developer Tools (DevTools) 22
Setting Up Node.js (Optional) 23
Setting Up a Basic HTML Template 24
Using Online Playgrounds (Optional) 25
Setting Up Your Environment for Exercises 26
    1. Create an HTML File 26
    2. Create a JavaScript File 27
    3. Run Your Code 28
    4. Organizing Your Exercises 28
    5. Additional Tools (Optional) 28
    6. Tips for Success 29
Summary 29

Chapter 4: The Evolution of JavaScript 31
Objective 31
ECMAScript 3 (1999) 31
    Regular Expressions 32
    Error Handling with try/catch 32
    String and Array Methods 33

TABLE OF CONTENTS

ECMAScript 4: The Version That Never Was 34
Why It Matters 35
ECMAScript 5 (2009) 35
use strict 36
Array Methods 37
JSON 39
Why It Matters 41
Getter and Setter Methods 41
Object.create() 42
Object.defineProperty() and Object.defineProperties() 42
Array.prototype.indexOf() 43
Function.prototype.bind() 44
ECMAScript 6 (2015) 44
let and const for Safer Variable Declarations 45
Arrow Functions: Concise Syntax for Functions 46
Classes: A Syntactic Sugar Over Prototypes 47
Modules: Native Support for Modular Codebases 48
Template Literals: Easier String Interpolation 48
Destructuring Assignment 49
Example Combining ES6 Features 50
ECMAScript 7 (2016) 51
Array.prototype.includes() 51
Exponentiation Operator (**) 52
Combining Features of ES7 53
ECMAScript 8 (2017) 53
Async/Await 54
Object.entries() and Object.values() 56
Combining ES8 Features 58

vii

TABLE OF CONTENTS

Smoother and More Intuitive Development 58

ECMAScript 9 (2018) 59

Rest/Spread in Objects 59

Promise.finally() 60

Asynchronous Iteration with for-await-of 62

Regular Expression Enhancements 63

ECMAScript 10 (2019) 64

Optional Catch Binding 65

Array.prototype.flat() 65

Array.prototype.flatMap() 66

String.prototype.trimStart() and trimEnd() 67

Object.fromEntries() 68

Well-Formed JSON Strings in JSON.stringify() 68

ECMAScript 11 (2020) 69

Nullish Coalescing Operator (??) 70

Optional Chaining (?.) 70

BigInt 72

ECMAScript 12 (2021) 74

Logical Assignment Operators 74

Numeric Separators 75

String.prototype.replaceAll() 75

Promise.any() 76

WeakRefs and FinalizationRegistry (Experimental) 77

Array.prototype.at() 77

Promise.allSettled() 78

ECMAScript 13 (2022) 79

Top-Level Await 79

Enhanced Error Handling 80

TABLE OF CONTENTS

    Numeric Separator (_) in Numbers 81

    Private Methods and Fields in Classes 81

    Record and Tuple Types 82

  Summary 83

Chapter 5: The Role of JavaScript in Modern Web Development 85

  Objective 85

  Dynamic Content and Interactivity 85

  Single-Page Applications (SPAs) 87

    Benefits of SPAs 87

  Server-Side JavaScript 88

    Why Node.js? 88

  Frameworks and Libraries 90

    What Are Frameworks and Libraries? 90

  Progressive Web Apps (PWAs) 93

    Why PWAs Matter 93

  Real-Time Applications 96

    WebSockets 96

  JavaScript in Mobile Development 98

    React Native 98

    Ionic 100

  The JavaScript Ecosystem 102

    Package Management 102

    Build Tools 103

    Linting and Formatting 104

  Challenges in Modern Web Development 105

    Browser Compatibility 106

    Performance Issues 106

TABLE OF CONTENTS

Security Risks 107

The Future of JavaScript 108

    Zoneless Frameworks 108

    WebAssembly (Wasm) 108

    AI and ML Integration 109

Summary 110

Chapter 6: The Role of Transpilers and Polyfills 113

Objective 113

What Are Transpilers? 113

    Transpiler vs. Compiler 115

    Example Arrow Functions 115

    Transpiler Example: ES6 Classes to ES5 116

    Conclusion 120

Pollyfills 120

    How the Polyfill Works 121

Transpilers vs. Polyfills 124

When to Use Transpilers vs. Polyfills 125

Why Use Transpilers and Polyfills Together? 126

Challenges and Best Practices 126

    Best Practices 127

Future of Transpilers and Polyfills 128

Summary 128

Chapter 7: Debugging JavaScript in the Browser 129

Objective 129

Introduction to Browser Developer Tools (DevTools) 129

    Key Features of DevTools 130

Console Logging: The Most Basic Debugging Tool 131

TABLE OF CONTENTS

Best Practices for console.log 131
Setting Breakpoints in the Sources Panel 132
    How to Set Breakpoints 132
    Types of Breakpoints 133
Stepping Through Code 133
    Example: Setting Breakpoints in Action 134
Using the Call Stack to Trace Execution 136
    Example: Understanding the Call Stack in Action 137
    Step-by-Step Debugging Guide 137
    Call Stack Execution Flow Diagram 139
    Why This Is Useful 140
Debugging Asynchronous JavaScript 140
    Using console.log() with Asynchronous Code 140
    Using Breakpoints with Asynchronous Code 141
Debugging with debugger Statement 141
Performance and Memory Debugging 142
Debugging Tools in Popular Frameworks 142
Summary 143

Chapter 8: Building Blocks of JavaScript 145

Objective 145
Variables: var, let, and const 145
    Declaring Variables with var 146
    Declaring Variables with let 146
    Declaring Constants with const 147
Problems with var in JavaScript 148
    Function Scope vs. Block Scope 148
    Hoisting and Accidental Use of Undefined Variables 150

TABLE OF CONTENTS

- Redeclaration and Accidental Overwrites 151
- Global Variables and the Window Object 152
- Comments and Code Readability 154
  - Single-Line Comments 154
  - Multi-line Comments 154
- Using Operators: Arithmetic, Assignment, Comparisons and Operator Precedence 155
  - Arithmetic Operators 155
  - Assignment Operators 156
  - Comparison Operators 156
  - Operator Precedence 156
  - Common Operator Precedence 157
  - Parentheses for Clarity 158
  - Associativity 158
- Constants and Immutability in JavaScript 158
  - 1. Understanding const and Immutability 159
  - 2. Why Use const? 160
  - 3. Immutability with Primitive Types 160
  - 4. Immutability with Objects and Arrays 161
  - 5. Achieving Immutability: Object.freeze() 161
  - 6. When to Use const 162
  - 7. Practical Use Cases for const 162
  - Conclusion 163
- Performance Implications of const 164
  - Immutability and Performance 164
  - Optimization Techniques for Immutability 166
  - When to Choose Mutability Over Immutability 167

Summary..167
Full Solutions 168

Chapter 9: Working with Strings and Numbers 171
Objective 171
String Literals and Template Strings...171
    String Literals 172
    Template Strings..172
    Tagged Template Literals..173
    When to Use Which?..174
    String Methods, Manipulation, and Comparison............................175
Working with Numbers: Math Operations and Methods 180
    Basic Math Operations 180
Type Coercion and Equality...182
    What Is Type Coercion? 183
    When == Makes Sense 187
    Why Is This Useful? 188
    Conclusion 189
Implicit String and Number Conversion 190
Precision Limitations with Floating-Point Numbers............................191
The NaN Type and Its Unusual Properties 192
Falsy and Truthy Values...193
    Why Falsy and Truthy Matter 193
The Strange Case of typeof null 200
Summary..201
Full Solutions 202

xiii

TABLE OF CONTENTS

Chapter 10: Control Flow in JavaScript 209
Objective 209
if and else Statements 209
    Using else with if 211
    else if and Multiple Conditions 212
    Ternary Operator...214
    Why It Matters 216
Switch Statements..218
    Why Use a Switch Statement? 219
    Switch vs. if...else 220
Loops in JavaScript...221
    For Loop..222
    While Loop..226
    Do...While Loop..230
    forEach Loop..232
    for...of Loop..237
    Where to Use for...of vs. forEach 240
Using Break and Continue Statements 241
    Break Statement...241
    Continue Statement..242
    Why Use Break and Continue? 243
    When to Use Break and Continue 244
Why Loops Matter 244
    Key Benefits of Loops...245
    Real-World Use Cases 246
Nullish Coalescing Operator (??)..246
    How It Works 247
    Why It Matters 249

Logical Nullish Assignment (??=) 249
    How It Works 249
    Why It Matters 252
Comparing Control Flow Mechanisms 253
Summary...255
Full Solutions 257

Chapter 11: Functions and Scope 261

Objective 261
Defining Functions: function Keyword 261
    Function Declaration 261
    Function Expressions 262
    Function Hoisting...263
    Function Parameters and Return Values 263
    Returning Values from Functions 276
    Validating Function Arguments..279
    Arrow Functions 283
The this Keyword: Understanding Context 286
    What Is this?..287
    this in Methods..287
    this in Regular Functions..288
    this in Arrow Functions...288
    Binding this with .bind(), .call(), and .apply()..289
    this in Constructors and Classes 290
    this in Classes 291
    this in Event Handlers...291
    Conclusion 292

TABLE OF CONTENTS

- Scope: Global vs. Local Variables 293
  - Global Scope 293
  - Local Scope 294
  - Block Scope 295
  - Lexical Scope 296
- Currying in JavaScript 298
  - What Is Currying? 298
  - Key Takeaways 314
- Immediately Invoked Function Expressions (IIFEs) 316
  - Why Use an IIFE? 317
- Closures 326
  - Basic Closure 326
  - Basic Account Closure 328
  - When to Use Closures 331
- Higher-Order Functions 335
  - Array Methods (map) 336
  - Custom Higher-Order Function 337
  - When to Use Higher-Order Functions 338
  - Conclusion 342
- Summary 343
- Full Solutions 344

Chapter 12: Objects and Arrays 347

- Objective 347
- Introduction to Objects and Arrays 347
- What Are Objects in JavaScript? 348
  - Why Use Objects? 348
  - Methods for Creating Objects 349

Adding Methods to Objects 358

Dynamic Object Properties and Computed Property Names 359

Summary of Object Creation Methods.. 360

Arrays: Creation, Accessing, and Methods 361

What Are Arrays in JavaScript? 361

Prototypes and Prototypal Inheritance.. 372

Understanding Prototypes 372

Classes and Their Relation to Prototypes 377

Summary.. 381

Full Solutions 382

Chapter 13: Error Handling 385

Objective 385

Introduction to Error Handling... 385

Types of Errors in JavaScript.. 386

try, catch, and finally Blocks... 388

Creating Custom Errors.. 390

Using the Error Class 391

Advanced Error Handling with ??= Operator for Fallbacks......................... 393

Adding Methods to Objects 393

Error Handling with async and await 394

Using try/catch with async/await 395

Handling Multiple Asynchronous Calls 396

Global Error Handling... 398

Graceful Degradation vs. Failing Fast... 400

Summary.. 401

Full Solutions 401

TABLE OF CONTENTS

Chapter 14: Working with ES6+ Syntax 409

Objective 409

Template Literals 410

    Multi-line Strings 410

    Interpolation 411

    Tagged Templates 411

    Limitations of Template Literals 412

    Best Practices 413

Destructuring Arrays and Objects 414

    Array Destructuring 414

    Object Destructuring 414

Spread and Rest Operators 416

    Spread Operator 417

    Rest Operator 418

Default Parameters 419

    Basic Defaults 420

    Dynamic Defaults 420

Optional Chaining 421

Nullish Coalescing Operator (??) 422

Enhanced Object Literals 422

    Shorthand Property Names 423

    Computed Properties 423

    Method Definitions 423

Classes 424

    Basic Syntax 424

    Inheritance 424

Iterators and Generators 425

TABLE OF CONTENTS

Custom Iterators 425

Generators 428

Promises and Async/Await 433

    Callback Hell and Why Promises Are Better 433

    Chaining Promises 435

    Async/Await 436

    Do's and Don'ts of Promises and Async/Await 436

Sets and Maps 437

    Set: Unique Value Storage 437

    Map: Efficient Key–Value Storage 438

    Performance Comparison: Map vs. Set vs. Object vs. Array 439

    Key Takeaways 439

Proxy and Reflect 440

    What Are Proxies? 440

    Reflect: A Companion to Proxy 441

    Practical Scenarios for Proxies and Reflect 443

    Advantages of Using Proxy and Reflect 444

    Limitations 444

Summary 445

Full Solutions 446

Index **451**

About the Author

Sonu Kapoor is a seasoned web developer, technical writer, and recognized expert in JavaScript and Angular. He is a Google Developer Expert (GDE) in Angular, a Microsoft MVP in Developer Technologies, and a member of the exclusive Angular Collaborators program. Previously, he was a Microsoft MVP in ASP.NET for six consecutive years.

Sonu is an active contributor to the Angular ecosystem, with notable open source contributions that have influenced the framework. He is the core maintainer of ngx-layout, a popular library for responsive Angular applications, which receives over 20,000 downloads per day and has garnered 200+ stars on GitHub.

Beyond code, he shares his expertise through technical articles, international conference talks, and podcasts. With a passion for teaching and simplifying complex topics, he has helped countless developers master modern web technologies.

About the Technical Reviewer

With over a decade of technical expertise in the San Francisco Bay Area, **Mohit Menghnani** brings a strong track record of architecting and scaling full-stack solutions using modern JavaScript technologies, including React, Node.js, and GraphQL. His experience spans leading cross-functional teams, driving digital transformation at Fortune 500 companies and startups, and shaping enterprise-grade applications in telecommunications, subscription commerce, and enterprise planning. Passionate about innovation and mentorship, he provides strategic insights into emerging trends and best practices in JavaScript development.

Preface

Welcome to *Beginning JavaScript Syntax*! This book is designed to help you navigate the fundamental building blocks of JavaScript, one of the most widely used and versatile programming languages in the world. Whether you're a newcomer to programming or looking to solidify your understanding of JavaScript, this guide will give you a strong foundation for your journey into web development. By breaking down complex topics into easy-to-understand chapters, this book ensures that you'll be well-equipped to write clean, efficient code and build interactive web applications.

The journey begins with understanding the concept of syntax in programming, which is the set of rules that govern how we write code. In *Chapter 1*, we'll explore why syntax is essential for writing correct and readable JavaScript. We'll also dive into how JavaScript functions in the context of web development in *Chapter 2*, where you'll learn how it powers interactive web pages both on the client side and server side.

Setting up your development environment is the next critical step, and in *Chapter 3*, you'll get hands-on guidance for choosing and configuring the tools you need. As we progress, *Chapter 4* will take you through the evolution of JavaScript, showing how the language has transformed from a simple browser scripting tool to the backbone of modern web applications. In *Chapter 5*, we'll discuss the role of JavaScript in today's web development ecosystem, emphasizing its importance in creating rich, dynamic user experiences.

Along the way, you'll encounter tools like transpilers and polyfills, which allow you to write modern JavaScript code that runs seamlessly across various environments, covered in *Chapter 6*. Debugging is a crucial

PREFACE

skill for every developer, and in *Chapter 7*, we'll teach you how to use the browser's built-in developer tools (DevTools) to find and fix errors in your JavaScript code.

As we move deeper into the language itself, *Chapters 8—12* will cover essential topics such as working with JavaScript's core building blocks – variables, data types, and operators. You'll also learn to manipulate strings and numbers, control the flow of your programs with conditionals and loops, and work with objects and arrays to store and manipulate data.

In *Chapter 13*, we'll tackle error handling, covering best practices for catching and managing errors in your code, while *Chapter 14* will introduce you to the latest JavaScript syntax improvements from ES6 onward. These features, like arrow functions, promises, and async/await, will help make your code cleaner, more efficient, and easier to maintain.

Throughout this book, each chapter includes explanations, practical examples, and exercises that will reinforce your learning and give you hands-on experience with JavaScript. Whether you are just starting out or looking to deepen your existing knowledge, *Beginning JavaScript Syntax* will provide the tools and confidence you need to become proficient in JavaScript and web development.

Let's get started!

Introduction

JavaScript is the language that powers the Web, bringing interactivity, responsiveness, and engagement to millions of websites and applications used daily. As one of the "big three" languages in web development alongside Hypertext Markup Language (HTML) and Cascading Style Sheets (CSS), JavaScript plays a critical role in transforming a basic web page into an interactive experience. While HTML provides structure and CSS adds styling, JavaScript is what enables dynamic interactions: everything from drop-down menus and image sliders to complex data visualizations and web-based applications. Learning JavaScript opens the door to a vast range of possibilities in web development and beyond.

However, starting to learn JavaScript syntax can feel challenging. If you've ever come across JavaScript code, you might have noticed that it looks different from human languages. Understanding JavaScript means learning a new way to communicate with computers using specific syntax rules. Like learning any new language, the journey begins with the basics. Syntax refers to the set of rules that define the combinations of symbols that are considered a correctly structured program in JavaScript. Think of syntax as the grammar and vocabulary of the language. Understanding these building blocks is the foundation upon which you'll build your programming skills.

Why Learn JavaScript Syntax First?

Learning syntax is essential because it enables you to read, write, and debug code. Syntax is like learning the alphabet before forming words or sentences. Without a solid understanding of JavaScript syntax, you'll struggle to write code that the computer can interpret or to understand the code that others have written. When you know the syntax, you can start solving problems, building projects, and confidently creating web applications.

In addition, learning syntax well will help you avoid common pitfalls and improve your code's readability, maintainability, and efficiency. Clean and correct syntax makes code easier for others (and your future self) to read and understand, and it helps avoid errors that can lead to hours of debugging. A strong grasp of syntax also allows you to write code that performs efficiently, enabling you to build applications that run smoothly across devices and browsers.

What Makes JavaScript Unique?

JavaScript is unique among programming languages because it runs on virtually every device that has a web browser. Originally developed as a client-side scripting language to run directly within web browsers, JavaScript has since expanded to include server-side capabilities with platforms like Node.js. This versatility means that JavaScript developers can write code that runs both in the browser and on the server, allowing for an end-to-end development experience that was once uncommon.

Another unique feature of JavaScript is that it is an interpreted language, not a compiled one. This means JavaScript code is executed line by line by the browser as the code runs, making it flexible and dynamic. While there are many types of programming languages, each with different rules and uses, JavaScript's unique design allows it to run instantly on most devices and browsers, making it the go-to language for web development.

JavaScript also includes many modern features thanks to regular updates to the language keeping it powerful and adaptable to current development needs. As you progress, you'll find that JavaScript syntax has evolved significantly over the years, and while this book focuses on the core syntax, you'll also be introduced to modern syntax and features.

How to Use This Book

Each chapter in *Beginning JavaScript Syntax* is dedicated to a specific part of the language's syntax, beginning with foundational concepts and advancing to more complex topics. Throughout this book, you'll find

- **Step-by-Step Explanations**: Each concept is broken down into clear, manageable sections, with examples and explanations to help solidify your understanding.
- **Real-World Examples**: Concepts are illustrated with real-world examples to show you how syntax applies in practical scenarios.
- **Practice Exercises**: At the end of each chapter, you'll have the opportunity to practice what you've learned with exercises that reinforce your understanding and help you gain hands-on experience.
- **Syntax Best Practices**: You'll learn techniques to write clean, efficient, and maintainable code by following best practices in syntax and code structure.

Each chapter builds on the last, so by following along in order, you'll develop a strong foundation in JavaScript syntax. That said, each chapter is also self-contained, so if you already know some concepts, you're welcome to jump around or use this book as a reference.

Who Is This Book For?

This book is for anyone who wants to start learning JavaScript from the ground up. No prior programming experience is necessary, although familiarity with HTML and CSS may be beneficial. *Beginning JavaScript Syntax* is also a useful resource for developers from other programming backgrounds who want to learn the syntax and conventions specific to JavaScript. Whether you're a student, aspiring web developer, or hobbyist, this book provides a comprehensive introduction to JavaScript syntax that will prepare you for further learning and development.

What You Will Learn

By the end of this book, you'll be able to

- Understand and use JavaScript's core syntax elements, such as variables, operators, and expressions

- Write conditional logic and use loops to control the flow of your program

- Define and use functions, understanding the nuances of scope

- Manipulate strings, numbers, arrays, and objects to create functional, dynamic code

- Implement error handling techniques to write robust and reliable code

- Leverage modern JavaScript syntax and conventions, including ES6+ features that simplify and enhance code readability

- Develop a foundation in best practices to write clean, maintainable code

Conclusion

Learning JavaScript syntax is a rewarding journey that opens doors to endless possibilities. As you master the syntax and fundamentals, you'll gain confidence in building interactive and dynamic web applications. Once you're familiar with the syntax, you'll be well-equipped to explore more advanced JavaScript topics; dive into frameworks like React, Vue, or Angular; or take on full-stack development with Node.js.

Whether you want to create your first web application or enhance your existing skills, *Beginning JavaScript Syntax* is your guide to understanding and using JavaScript effectively.

CHAPTER 1

Introduction to JavaScript Syntax

Objective

The objective of this chapter is to introduce the concept of syntax in programming, specifically within JavaScript, and explain its importance in ensuring code clarity and functionality. By understanding syntax, readers will gain insight into how JavaScript "speaks" to the computer, laying the foundation for writing error-free and effective code.

JavaScript is one of the most widely used programming languages in the world, integral to creating interactive, dynamic web applications. It's the language of the browser, enhancing HTML and CSS to enable modern, responsive, and feature-rich websites. For anyone stepping into the world of programming, learning JavaScript syntax is a powerful starting point. The syntax forms the building blocks of how JavaScript programs are written and how they operate.

This chapter introduces what syntax is, why it's important, and how it affects programming in JavaScript. We'll also cover JavaScript's role in web development and provide guidance on setting up your development environment.

CHAPTER 1   INTRODUCTION TO JAVASCRIPT SYNTAX

What Is Syntax?

Syntax is a concept fundamental to programming, yet its significance often goes overlooked by new developers. In programming, syntax refers to the set of rules that dictate how code must be written to be understood by the computer. Just as in human language, syntax is essentially the "grammar" of a programming language. When you write code, each line, character, and command must follow these syntax rules, ensuring the computer can parse and execute it correctly. Even a small deviation, like a missing bracket or incorrect punctuation, can cause errors and prevent your code from running as intended.

At its core, syntax defines the structure and form of commands in a programming language. For example, in JavaScript, creating a variable typically follows the syntax

```
let variableName = value;
```

Here, `let` is a keyword, `variableName` represents the name of the variable, and `value` is the assigned data. This exact structure is crucial; changing the order, omitting keywords, or skipping semicolons may produce syntax errors, stopping the code from running correctly. Syntax acts as a bridge between the programmer's intentions and the computer's understanding, transforming human-readable commands into machine-executable instructions.

However, if the syntax is incorrect, the JavaScript engine will throw an error. For example, missing the let keyword results in

```
variableName = value; // ✗ ReferenceError: variableName is
                            not defined
```

Or using an invalid assignment operator results in

```
let variableName == value; // ✗ SyntaxError: Unexpected
                                        token '=='
```

Proper syntax ensures that the code runs without errors and behaves as expected.

Why Syntax Is Essential in Programming

In the early stages of programming, focusing on syntax might feel tedious, especially when errors arise. However, it's crucial to understand that syntax is the foundational aspect of writing effective and correct code. If syntax represents the grammar of a language, then learning syntax is akin to learning how to construct sentences that make sense. Only when you understand syntax well can you begin creating complex and meaningful code.

Programming languages like JavaScript have specific syntax rules that govern everything from declaring variables and defining functions to constructing loops and handling conditions. Knowing these syntax rules lets you write code that works reliably and performs as expected. Without a strong understanding of syntax, even a simple task can become challenging, as syntax errors can cause programs to behave unpredictably or even crash.

Another reason syntax is essential is for code readability. Developers often work in teams, and writing code with correct syntax makes it easier for others (and your future self) to read, understand, and modify your work. Well-structured syntax leads to clean, maintainable code, which is crucial when multiple developers are collaborating on a project. In addition to readability, syntax plays a direct role in the efficiency and performance of your code. Correct syntax ensures that the JavaScript engine can parse and execute the code optimally, reducing the risk of slow execution due to unnecessary error handling or re-parsing. For example, using proper loop syntax avoids infinite loops that can freeze execution, and correctly structured function calls prevent unexpected scope issues that might lead to excessive memory usage. Well-formed syntax also allows JavaScript engines to apply optimizations like Just-In-Time (JIT) compilation, leading to faster execution.

Syntax Across Programming Languages

Each programming language has its unique syntax, designed to suit specific purposes and computational needs. For example, the syntax in JavaScript is different from that in Python, C++, or HTML. While JavaScript has optional semicolons to end statements, Python uses indentation to structure code, and HTML relies on tag structures. These syntax differences reflect the goals of each language. JavaScript is optimized for web interactivity, Python for readability, and HTML for document structure.

JavaScript syntax has evolved significantly over the years. Initially created for adding simple interactions on websites, JavaScript syntax now includes features that support complex applications. The language continues to adapt, with each version introducing new syntax to keep it efficient and versatile. In Chapter 4, you'll see how these changes have shaped the language from its inception in 1995 through to 2022. Understanding syntax deeply not only helps you grasp these changes but also makes it easier to transition between programming languages, as the core principles of structure and organization remain consistent, even if the rules differ.

CHAPTER 1   INTRODUCTION TO JAVASCRIPT SYNTAX

Syntax Errors and Debugging

Syntax errors are among the most common issues faced by beginner programmers. A syntax error occurs when a line of code breaks the language's syntax rules, making it unreadable by the computer. For instance, forgetting to close a bracket and misspelling a keyword are common syntax errors in JavaScript that result in error messages when you try to run your code. Since computers require exact instructions, even a minor syntax error can cause a program to fail.

Learning to debug syntax errors is an essential skill for any programmer. JavaScript, as an interpreted language, often provides detailed error messages that can guide you to the source of the problem. For example, if you forget a closing parenthesis, JavaScript might display an error message like "Unexpected token" or "Syntax error," along with the line number. Debugging involves reading these error messages, identifying the issue, and correcting the syntax. As you practice, you'll become familiar with common syntax errors and develop an intuition for troubleshooting them quickly.

The Syntax–Logic Connection

Understanding syntax also lays the groundwork for grasping programming logic. Syntax alone doesn't make a program functional; it must be coupled with logical flow and design. Think of syntax as the building blocks, while logic dictates how you assemble these blocks to solve a problem. Mastering syntax is the first step toward creating logical, error-free code, as syntax errors can often mask larger issues with your logic.

For instance, let's say you're writing a JavaScript function that calculates the average of a list of numbers. If your syntax is incorrect perhaps due to a misplaced bracket or missing semicolon, the program will fail to run, making it difficult to verify your logic. Once the syntax is correct, you can focus on the logic, ensuring that your function calculates the average accurately. Clear syntax allows you to implement complex algorithms and structures with confidence.

JavaScript Syntax and Interpreted Execution

JavaScript is an interpreted language, which means it is executed line by line by the browser as it runs, rather than being compiled into machine code beforehand. This gives JavaScript a high level of flexibility and enables developers to see their code's effects immediately. However, it also makes understanding syntax even more critical. Since JavaScript interprets code in real time, a syntax error on one line can prevent subsequent lines from executing, interrupting the program's flow.

To address this challenge, tools like TypeScript have gained popularity. TypeScript is a superset of JavaScript that introduces static typing and compiles to JavaScript. It catches many syntax and type-related issues during the development process, reducing the risk of runtime errors. While JavaScript allows you to experiment and resolve errors as they occur, TypeScript provides an additional layer of safety and predictability.

As you write JavaScript code, you'll see how the interpreter reacts to different syntax structures, offering instant feedback on whether your syntax is correct. This real-time interaction is especially beneficial for learning, as it encourages experimentation and immediate error resolution. By understanding JavaScript's syntax and being aware of tools like TypeScript, you can write code that runs smoothly without being interrupted by syntax-related issues, fully leveraging JavaScript's interpreted nature.

Summary

Mastering JavaScript syntax is your gateway to writing effective, functional code. With a clear grasp of syntax rules, you'll be able to communicate your ideas clearly to the computer, avoid common errors, and create readable, maintainable code. Syntax knowledge also forms the foundation for learning more advanced programming concepts, as it provides the structure upon which logical and creative problem-solving can be built.

In the next chapters, we'll begin exploring JavaScript syntax in detail, starting with the basics of variables and data types. Each chapter will provide hands-on examples, exercises, and explanations to ensure that you gain confidence with JavaScript syntax, setting you on a path toward becoming a skilled programmer.

CHAPTER 2

How JavaScript Works in Web Development

Objective

The objective of this chapter is to explain JavaScript's function and structure in web development, exploring how it interacts with HTML, CSS, and the Document Object Model (DOM). Readers will learn the basic principles behind JavaScript's role as an interpreted language, its event-driven nature, and its evolution into a full-stack tool. This knowledge will provide the context necessary to understand JavaScript's syntax and capabilities more deeply in the chapters to come.

JavaScript is a unique language designed specifically for the Web, giving developers the power to create interactive, dynamic websites that respond to user actions in real time. Its role in web development has expanded significantly since its creation, growing from a language used primarily for simple animations and effects to an essential tool for building robust enterprise applications that operate smoothly across devices. In this chapter, we'll explore what makes JavaScript integral to web development and discuss how it interacts with HTML and CSS to bring web pages to life.

CHAPTER 2   HOW JAVASCRIPT WORKS IN WEB DEVELOPMENT

JavaScript As an Interpreted Language

Unlike compiled languages, where code is converted into machine language before it runs, JavaScript is an **interpreted language**. This means JavaScript code is read and executed line by line directly by the browser's JavaScript engine as it's loaded on the web page. Interpreted lwwanguages tend to be more flexible and forgiving than compiled languages, making them ideal for rapid development and real-time debugging. However, this also means that JavaScript can be affected by syntax errors in real time, potentially causing parts of the code to fail if even a minor error is detected.

When you load a web page containing JavaScript, the browser downloads the HTML, CSS, and JavaScript files from the server. The JavaScript code is then processed and executed by the browser's JavaScript engine. Each browser has its own engine such as V8 in Google Chrome, SpiderMonkey in Firefox, and JavaScriptCore in Safari. These engines optimize and execute JavaScript code, allowing for fast, responsive interactions on the page. Understanding this process helps developers write efficient, error-free code that can run smoothly across various browsers and devices.

The Role of JavaScript in Web Development

JavaScript works in tandem with HTML and CSS, forming the foundational trio of front-end web development. Each of these technologies has a distinct role:

- HTML (Hypertext Markup Language) provides the structure of the page. It defines elements like headings, paragraphs, links, images, and other content.
- CSS (Cascading Style Sheets) defines the style of the page. It controls the layout, colors, fonts, and overall visual presentation.

- JavaScript is responsible for making the page interactive and dynamic. It allows developers to modify HTML and CSS in real time, respond to user actions, fetch data from servers, and more.

Together, these technologies create the web experience we know today. HTML lays out the content, CSS styles it, and JavaScript brings it to life. For instance, when you click a "Submit" button on a form, JavaScript can validate the input, send it to the server, and provide feedback to the user all without needing to reload the entire page. This seamless interaction is a core feature of modern web applications.

JavaScript and the Document Object Model (DOM)

One of JavaScript's primary functions is interacting with the **Document Object Model (DOM)**. The DOM is an in-memory representation of an HTML document structured as a hierarchical tree. Each element in HTML, such as a `<div>`, `<p>`, or `<img>`, is represented as a node within the DOM tree. This structure allows JavaScript to access and manipulate page elements, making it possible to dynamically alter content, layout, and style in response to user actions.

For example, if a user clicks a button to open a menu, JavaScript can be used to modify the DOM by changing the button's CSS classes, hiding or showing certain elements, or even adding new elements entirely. This ability to update the DOM in real time is one of JavaScript's defining features and enables web pages to behave more like applications rather than static documents.

Some common DOM-related tasks that JavaScript can perform include

- **Selecting Elements**: Using functions like `document.getElementById()` or `document.querySelector()`, JavaScript can access specific elements in the DOM.

CHAPTER 2 HOW JAVASCRIPT WORKS IN WEB DEVELOPMENT

- **Modifying Elements**: JavaScript can change an element's properties, such as updating its text content, changing its CSS styles, or modifying its attributes.

- **Creating and Deleting Elements**: JavaScript can add new elements to the DOM, such as creating a new div or button, and it can also remove elements that are no longer needed.

- **Event Handling**: JavaScript can listen for events, such as clicks, keyboard input, or page loads, and perform specific actions in response.

Below is a simplified diagram of the DOM tree, which includes two buttons and a div element.

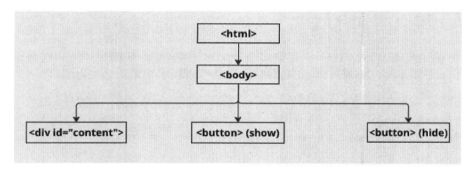

The workflow that follows depends on which button is clicked. In the first row, the user interface (UI) is shown in its initial state. When the "Hide" button is clicked (second row), the onclick event handler is triggered. This event adds a display: none style to the div, effectively hiding it from the UI. In the third row, the "Show" button is clicked, and the display: block style is applied to the div, making it visible again.

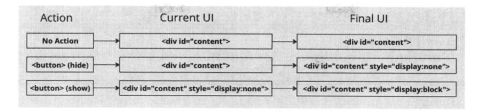

JavaScript Events and User Interaction

One of JavaScript's core strengths is handling **events**. Events are actions that occur in the browser, such as mouse clicks, key presses, or the completion of a data load. By "listening" for these events, JavaScript can respond to user input in real time. This allows for smooth, engaging user experiences, like real-time form validation, dynamic animations, or updating page content without reloading the page.

Event handling is crucial for building interactive web applications. In JavaScript, developers use methods like addEventListener() to attach functions, known as event handlers, to specific events on HTML elements. Here's a simple example:

```
const button = document.querySelector('button');
button.addEventListener('click', () => {
  alert('Button clicked!');
});
```

In this example, JavaScript waits for the user to click a button on the page. When the click event occurs, it triggers a function that displays an alert. This simple interaction demonstrates how JavaScript can connect user actions with custom behavior, creating a dynamic experience.

JavaScript in Front-End and Back-End Development

Though JavaScript was originally designed for front-end development running in the browser to interact with the DOM, it has evolved to become a **full-stack language** capable of running on both the client (browser) and server (back end).

On the client side, JavaScript enables interactive web pages, user input handling, and the manipulation of HTML and CSS. It's the language behind modern front-end frameworks like **React**, **Angular**, and **Vue.js**, which help developers build complex, single-page applications (SPAs) that offer a seamless user experience without page reloads.

In 2009, the introduction of **Node.js** extended JavaScript's reach to server-side development. Node.js is a runtime environment that allows JavaScript code to execute outside of the browser, opening up new possibilities. With Node.js, developers can use JavaScript to handle back-end logic, connect to databases, serve APIs, and manage server resources. JavaScript's versatility as a full-stack language has made it one of the most widely used programming languages globally, powering applications from simple websites to large-scale platforms like Netflix, LinkedIn, and PayPal.

JavaScript and Asynchronous Programming

One of JavaScript's standout features is its asynchronous capabilities, which allow it to perform tasks in parallel without blocking other operations. This is particularly important for web applications, where waiting for data from an external server can cause delays. Through asynchronous programming, JavaScript can fetch data, load images, or interact with APIs while allowing the rest of the page to remain responsive.

JavaScript achieves this through mechanisms like callbacks, promises, and async/await. For example, if you're building a news app that fetches articles from an API, JavaScript can request the data and continue to load other parts of the page without making users wait. When the data arrives, JavaScript can dynamically update the DOM to display the articles, providing a smoother user experience. This asynchronous behavior underpins many of the interactive features seen in modern web applications.

Here's an example of how this could work with async/await:

```
async function fetchArticles() {
  try {
    // Make an asynchronous request to fetch the articles
    from an API
    const response = await fetch('https://api.example.com/
    articles');
    const articles = await response.json();

    // Dynamically update the DOM with the fetched articles
    const articleContainer = document.getElementById
    ('article-container');
    articles.forEach(article => {
      const articleElement = document.createElement('div');
      articleElement.textContent = article.title;
      articleContainer.appendChild(articleElement);
    });
  } catch (error) {
    console.error('Error fetching articles:', error);
  }
}
// Call the function to fetch articles
fetchArticles();
```

In this example, the fetchArticles function asynchronously retrieves article data from an API. While waiting for the data, the rest of the page remains interactive. Once the data is received, the DOM is updated with the article titles, enhancing the user experience by keeping the UI responsive.

Why Understanding JavaScript's Role Matters

Knowing how JavaScript operates within web development is essential for anyone looking to create interactive websites and applications. JavaScript's unique position as the only language that runs natively in browsers makes it indispensable for front-end development, and understanding its interactions with HTML, CSS, and the DOM is the foundation of effective web development.

Furthermore, grasping JavaScript's strengths such as event handling, asynchronous programming, and cross-platform capability will allow you to build efficient, user-friendly web applications that function well across a variety of devices and environments. The more you understand how JavaScript works, the better you'll be at troubleshooting, optimizing, and writing code that delivers seamless, dynamic experiences for users.

Summary

In this chapter, we explored JavaScript's essential role in web development, highlighting how it works as an interpreted language within browsers to create interactive, dynamic websites. JavaScript complements HTML and CSS by handling tasks that require real-time user interaction, leveraging the Document Object Model (DOM) to modify page elements on the fly. We also touched on JavaScript's event-driven nature, allowing it to respond seamlessly to user actions, and its evolution into a full-stack language capable of powering both front-end and back-end applications through environments like Node.js. Finally, we discussed the importance of asynchronous programming for creating responsive applications, especially when working with APIs or other external data sources. Understanding these aspects of JavaScript's functionality is fundamental for any web developer, as it paves the way for mastering the language's syntax, logic, and best practices in the upcoming chapters.

CHAPTER 3

Setting Up the Environment

Objective

The objective of this chapter is to guide you through the setup of a working environment for JavaScript programming. By the end, you will be able to install and configure essential tools like code editors, browsers, and basic developer tools. This foundation will enable you to effectively write, run, and troubleshoot JavaScript code as you progress through the book.

Starting a journey in JavaScript programming requires a properly configured environment. Having the right tools can make a significant difference in learning efficiency and ease, especially for beginners. In this chapter, we'll cover the essential elements you need to set up to begin coding confidently in JavaScript.

CHAPTER 3   SETTING UP THE ENVIRONMENT

Choosing a Code Editor

A code editor is where you'll spend a lot of time writing and debugging your JavaScript code. Many editors are available, each offering unique features to suit different programming needs. Here are a few popular ones that are particularly beginner-friendly:

- **Visual Studio Code (VS Code)**: A free, open source editor developed by Microsoft, VS Code is a favorite among developers due to its extensive library of extensions, ease of use, and efficient debugging tools. VS Code also integrates seamlessly with AI tools like **GitHub Copilot**, which offers real-time code suggestions and can significantly speed up development. Copilot is free for personal use in VS Code, making it a great choice for beginners and professionals alike.

- **Sublime Text**: Known for its speed and responsiveness, Sublime Text offers a straightforward interface that is well-suited for beginners, though it lacks some of the built-in tools available in VS Code.

- **Atom**: Atom, originally developed by GitHub, is another free and open source editor with a strong community. It's highly customizable, although it may not perform as well with larger codebases compared with VS Code.

- **WebStorm**: A premium Integrated Development Environment (IDE) developed by JetBrains, WebStorm is tailored for JavaScript, TypeScript, and front-end development. It offers advanced features like intelligent code completion, integrated version control, and seamless debugging tools. WebStorm also supports AI-powered assistance through JetBrains' **Code With Me** for collaborative development and third-party AI plugins that integrate with JetBrains IDEs. While it's a paid tool, many developers find its robust features and enhanced productivity worth the investment.

Setting Up Visual Studio Code

1. **Download and Install VS Code**: Visit the official VS Code website and download the installer for your operating system.

2. **Install Extensions**: For JavaScript, the following extensions can improve your coding experience:

   - **Prettier** for consistent formatting
   - **ESLint** to check for syntax and style issues
   - **JavaScript (ES6) code snippets** to simplify coding with predefined snippets

3. **Configure Settings**: You can modify settings within VS Code by navigating to File ➤ Preferences ➤ Settings. Here, you can adjust font size, enable autosave, and configure other settings that personalize your environment.

CHAPTER 3   SETTING UP THE ENVIRONMENT

Setting Up a Web Browser for Development

JavaScript primarily runs within web browsers, so having a developer-friendly browser is essential. Here are a few commonly used browsers with strong developer support:

- **Google Chrome**: Known for its powerful developer tools (DevTools), Chrome is often the first choice for JavaScript development.
- **Firefox**: Firefox also provides an extensive set of developer tools and is a strong choice, especially if you're interested in cross-browser compatibility testing.
- **Microsoft Edge**: Edge shares many features with Chrome, as both are built on the Chromium engine. It includes a comprehensive set of tools for debugging.

Using Chrome Developer Tools (DevTools)

DevTools is an integrated suite of tools within Chrome that allows you to inspect and debug JavaScript code directly in the browser. Here's how to access and use DevTools for JavaScript:

1. **Open DevTools**: Right-click any web page, select **Inspect**, or press F12. This will open the DevTools panel.
2. **Use the Console Tab**: The Console tab is a critical area for JavaScript development. You can enter JavaScript commands here to test code or debug errors in real time.

3. **Sources Tab**: This tab is useful for viewing and setting breakpoints within your code, helping you step through JavaScript line by line.

4. **Network Tab**: The Network tab displays all network activity, which is particularly helpful for monitoring API calls and performance.

5. **Use Lighthouse for Performance Audits**: The Lighthouse tab in DevTools allows you to run performance audits on your web page. It provides insights on performance, accessibility, search engine optimization (SEO), and best practices. You can generate a report by clicking the "Generate report" button, which will give you a detailed analysis and suggestions for improving the performance and user experience of your website.

Setting Up Node.js (Optional)

While JavaScript is typically associated with browser-based environments, many developers also use it outside the browser with Node.js. Node.js is a JavaScript runtime built on Chrome's V8 engine that allows JavaScript to run on the server side. Although Node.js is optional for basic JavaScript learning, it opens up new possibilities, such as running JavaScript locally on your machine.

To install Node.js

1. **Download Node.js**: Visit the Node.js website and choose the LTS (Long-Term Support) version, as it's more stable for development.

2. **Verify Installation**: After installing, open a terminal and type

   ```
   node -v
   ```

   If the installation was successful, you should see the version number of Node.js displayed.

3. **Installing npm Packages**: Node.js comes with npm (Node Package Manager), which is useful for installing libraries and frameworks. For instance, you can install popular JavaScript libraries with

   ```
   npm install <package-name>
   ```

Setting Up a Basic HTML Template

In this book, we will primarily run JavaScript directly within the browser using an HTML file as the container. Setting up a basic HTML template allows you to write and test JavaScript in a real web environment. Below is a simple HTML template for embedding JavaScript:

1. **Create an HTML File**: Open your code editor and create a new file named `index.html`.

2. **Add Basic HTML Structure**:

   ```html
   <!DOCTYPE html>
   <html lang="en">
   <head>
       <meta charset="UTF-8">
       <meta name="viewport" content="width=device-width, initial-scale=1.0">
       <title>JavaScript Practice</title>
   </head>
   ```

```
<body>
    <h1>Welcome to JavaScript Programming!</h1>
    <script src="script.js"></script>
</body>
</html>
```

3. **Create a JavaScript File**: In the same directory, create a file named `script.js`. This is where you will write your JavaScript code.

4. **Run Your HTML File in the Browser**: Open `index.html` in your browser to see your page. You can use the Console in DevTools to observe any JavaScript output.

Using Online Playgrounds (Optional)

For quick JavaScript testing, online playgrounds are a fantastic option. These platforms let you write and run JavaScript code without the need for a full environment setup. They are particularly useful for experimentation, prototyping, and sharing code snippets. Here are some popular choices:

- **JSFiddle**: A long-standing favorite for testing and sharing code that combines HTML, CSS, and JavaScript. It's simple to use and allows you to quickly experiment with different ideas.

- **CodePen**: Ideal for front-end development and widely used by designers and developers to create and share interactive code snippets. CodePen supports live previews and offers a vibrant community where you can explore examples and learn from others' work.

- **Replit**: A collaborative online IDE that supports JavaScript and many other languages. It allows real-time collaboration, making it great for pair programming or working on small projects with others.

- **StackBlitz**: A powerful option tailored for modern web development. It provides an online environment for JavaScript, TypeScript, and even full Angular, React, or Vue projects. StackBlitz mimics a local development setup, supports npm packages, and integrates well with GitHub, making it a great tool for more advanced testing and prototyping.

These tools provide a convenient way to practice coding and explore concepts without setting up local files. However, as you progress, setting up a local development environment will be essential for working on larger projects and understanding the complete development workflow.

Setting Up Your Environment for Exercises

This book contains numerous exercises designed to help you practice and solidify your understanding of JavaScript. Programming is best learned by doing, and these exercises provide an opportunity to apply the concepts you learn as you progress through the chapters.

To get started with these exercises, you'll need to set up a basic HTML and JavaScript environment. Don't worry, this setup is simple and quick, even for beginners. Let's walk through the steps.

1. Create an HTML File

The HTML file serves as the foundation for your exercises. Follow these steps:

CHAPTER 3   SETTING UP THE ENVIRONMENT

1. Open a text editor or Integrated Development Environment (IDE).

2. Create a new file and save it with the name index.html (or any name of your choice) with the .html extension.

3. Add the following boilerplate code to your file:

```html
<!DOCTYPE html>
<html lang="en">
<head>
    <meta charset="UTF-8">
    <meta name="viewport" content="width=device-width, initial-scale=1.0">
    <title>JavaScript Exercises</title>
</head>
<body>
    <script src="script.js"></script>
</body>
</html>
```

This code sets up a basic HTML page that links to a JavaScript file named script.js. You can use this file to run all your exercises.

2. Create a JavaScript File

The JavaScript file is where you'll write the code for the exercises.

1. In the same folder as your index.html file, create a new file named script.js.

2. You can use this file to write all your exercises or create a new .js file for each exercise (e.g., exercise1.js, exercise2.js).

If you decide to use separate files, remember to update the `<script>` tag in your HTML file to reference the corresponding JavaScript file, for example:

```
<script src="exercise1.js"></script>
```

3. Run Your Code

Once your HTML and JavaScript files are ready, you can test your code:

1. Open the `index.html` file in a web browser by double-clicking it or dragging it into the browser window.

2. Open the browser's developer tools (usually accessible by pressing `F12` or `Ctrl + Shift + I`).

3. Navigate to the **Console** tab, where you can see the output of your JavaScript code or any errors.

4. Organizing Your Exercises

You have two options for managing your exercise files:

- **Single JavaScript File**: Use one `script.js` file for all exercises. This approach keeps things simple and requires minimal setup, but you may need to comment out older code as you progress.

- **Multiple JavaScript Files**: Create a separate `.js` file for each exercise. This keeps your exercises organized and makes it easier to revisit individual tasks.

5. Additional Tools (Optional)

While not required, you might find these tools helpful:

- **Online Code Editors**: Platforms like CodePen, JSFiddle, or Replit allow you to write and run JavaScript directly in your browser without setting up files locally.

- **Live Server Extension**: If you're using Visual Studio Code, consider installing the Live Server extension to automatically refresh your browser whenever you make changes.

6. Tips for Success

- Save your work frequently.

- Experiment with the code; don't be afraid to break things and debug them.

- Add comments in your JavaScript code to explain what each part does. This helps reinforce your understanding.

Summary

In this chapter, we covered the essential setup required for starting your JavaScript development journey. We discussed how to choose a suitable code editor, focusing on Visual Studio Code and its helpful extensions, and examined popular web browsers for debugging, particularly Google Chrome and its DevTools. Additionally, we explored optional setups like Node.js for running JavaScript outside the browser and online playgrounds for quick testing. By setting up a basic HTML and JavaScript structure, you now have a foundation for writing and testing code as you progress through this book. With your environment in place, you're ready to dive into JavaScript syntax and begin programming.

CHAPTER 4

The Evolution of JavaScript

Objective

JavaScript has undergone a remarkable transformation since its inception in 1995. With each new version of the ECMAScript (ES) standard – the official specification for JavaScript - JavaScript has grown more powerful, efficient, and versatile. Understanding these versions helps developers appreciate the modern features of JavaScript while learning about its historical growth. Below, we explore ECMAScript versions from ES3 to ES13, showcasing their significant contributions.

ECMAScript 3 (1999)

The third version of ECMAScript, released in 1999, established the foundational features that contributed to JavaScript's widespread adoption, particularly in the browser environment. This version laid the groundwork for the dynamic and interactive web applications we build today. Key features of ES3 are as follows.

Regular Expressions

ECMAScript 3 introduced powerful support for regular expressions (regex), making it easier to perform string pattern matching and manipulate text. Regular expressions (/hello/i) allow developers to define search patterns using special characters, making tasks like validation, text extraction, and data processing simpler and more efficient.

Example:

```
let pattern = /hello/i;
console.log(pattern.test("Hello, world!")); // true
```

Why It Matters

Regular expressions allow developers to search, validate, and manipulate strings with great flexibility. They are particularly useful for tasks like validating user input (e.g., email addresses), performing complex string searches, or replacing text patterns. Mastery of regular expressions is essential for efficient text processing and data validation in web applications.

Error Handling with try/catch

One of the most important features introduced in ECMAScript 3 was the try/catch block for robust error handling. Before this, JavaScript lacked structured error handling, meaning that errors would stop the execution of code entirely. The introduction of the try/catch construct allowed developers to gracefully handle exceptions that might occur during the execution of JavaScript code, making applications more reliable. The try/catch construct wraps code that might throw an error, enabling the developer to manage and report issues without crashing the application.

Example:

```
try {
  let result = riskyOperation();
} catch (error) {
  console.error("An error occurred:", error.message);
}
```

Why It Matters

Proper error handling is critical for building resilient and user-friendly applications. The `try/catch` mechanism allows developers to manage errors without crashing the application, providing a smoother user experience. Without error handling, uncaught exceptions could lead to unexpected behaviors, bugs, and poor application stability.

String and Array Methods

ECMAScript 3 brought several new built-in methods that enhanced string manipulation and array handling. These included `split()`, `join()`, `slice()`, and `push()`. These methods facilitated common tasks like splitting strings into arrays, joining arrays into strings, extracting parts of arrays, and modifying their contents.

Why It Matters

String and array methods are foundational for data manipulation in JavaScript. They simplify common tasks like searching through text, splitting strings, sorting arrays, or transforming data. By using these methods, developers can write cleaner, more readable, and more efficient code when working with textual and array data.

Example:

```
let str = "apple, banana, mango";
let fruits = str.split(", ");
console.log(fruits); // ["apple", "banana", "mango"]

let numbers = [1, 2, 3, 4];
numbers.push(5);
console.log(numbers); // [1, 2, 3, 4, 5]
```

ECMAScript 3 was a pivotal release that not only improved JavaScript's feature set but also increased its versatility as a language, helping it to become the cornerstone of modern web development. It provided the essential tools and syntax that developers still use today, making it possible to create dynamic and interactive web applications.

ECMAScript 4: The Version That Never Was

While ES4 was never officially released, it holds a unique place in the history of JavaScript. Initially proposed in the early 2000s, ES4 aimed to introduce groundbreaking features like

- **Classes**: A more structured way to define objects and inheritance
- **Type Annotations**: Adding optional static typing to JavaScript
- **Namespaces and Packages**: To better organize code in larger applications
- **Block Scoping**: Similar to `let` and `const`, later introduced in ES6
- **Destructuring**: To easily unpack values from arrays or objects

However, the proposal was deemed overly complex, and disagreements among stakeholders – primarily browser vendors like Microsoft (Internet Explorer), Mozilla (Firefox), and Apple (Safari) – led to its eventual abandonment. Instead, the JavaScript community shifted its focus to creating a simpler, more incremental update ES3.1, which was eventually released as **ES5**.

Why It Matters

The ES4 proposal represents a pivotal moment in JavaScript's development. Although it failed, its ambitious vision set the stage for many features that became integral parts of the language in later versions, particularly in ES6. For example, ES4's concept of classes influenced the class syntax introduced in ES6, block scoping (via let and const) was inspired by the block-scoping ideas in ES4, and destructuring was also part of ES4's proposal. By understanding ES4, readers can appreciate the careful balance between innovation and simplicity that guides JavaScript's ongoing evolution.

ECMAScript 5 (2009)

ECMAScript 5 (ES5), released in 2009, introduced several features that enhanced JavaScript's flexibility and error handling. It introduced **strict mode** for stricter syntax rules; new **array methods** like forEach, map, filter, and reduce; and **JavaScript Object Notation (JSON) support** for easier data parsing. **Getter and setter methods** allowed for more controlled property access, while **Object.create()** and **Object.defineProperty()** improved object creation and property management. Additionally, **indexOf()** simplified array searches, and **bind()** provided better control over the this context. These updates formed the backbone of modern JavaScript, which we will explore in detail in this chapter.

CHAPTER 4 THE EVOLUTION OF JAVASCRIPT

use strict

The "use strict"; directive was introduced in ES5 as a way to enforce stricter parsing and error handling in JavaScript. When a script or function runs in strict mode, it helps you write cleaner code by identifying bad practices and preventing certain types of errors that JavaScript might otherwise ignore.

Strict Mode: Enforces cleaner code by throwing errors for bad practices

Example:

```
"use strict";
x = 10; // ReferenceError: x is not defined
```

Here's what's happening:

1. **Strict Mode Activation**: The "use strict"; directive at the beginning of the code enables strict mode for the script. This ensures that JavaScript will enforce stricter rules for the code that follows.

2. **Undeclared Variable Assignment**: In non-strict mode, JavaScript allows variables to be assigned without declaring them first using var, let, or const. For example, x = 10; would implicitly create a global variable x.

3. **Error in Strict Mode**: However, in strict mode, such assignments without declaration are not allowed. Since x is not declared (e.g., let x; or var x;), JavaScript throws a ReferenceError.

This behavior helps developers avoid bugs caused by accidentally creating global variables, which can lead to unintended side effects in larger programs.

Why It Matters

Strict mode prevents accidental errors, like creating global variables or using reserved keywords. It improves security by disallowing potentially unsafe actions. It also paves the way for future versions of JavaScript to introduce new features without breaking older code.

By enforcing strict mode, your code becomes more predictable, easier to debug, and less prone to silent failures. This is why strict mode has become a best practice in modern JavaScript development.

Array Methods

ES5 introduced several new array methods that make it easier to manipulate arrays. These methods allow developers to iterate over arrays, transform data, and filter elements with clean, functional code. Let's dive into the map() method using the provided example.

Example:

```
let numbers = [1, 2, 3, 4];
let doubled = numbers.map((num) => num * 2);
console.log(doubled); // [2, 4, 6, 8]
```

Explanation:

1. **The Original Array:**

    The array numbers contains the values [1, 2, 3, 4].

2. **The map() Method:**

    - map() is used to create a new array by applying a transformation function to each element of the original array.
    - The original array remains unchanged, as map() does not modify it directly.

3. **The Callback Function**:
   - The arrow function (num) => num * 2 is the callback function that map() executes on every element in the array.
   - It takes one argument (num), which represents the current element of the array, and returns num * 2.
4. **Result**:
   - For each number in numbers, the function multiplies it by 2 and adds the result to the new array.
   - The new array, stored in doubled, becomes [2, 4, 6, 8].
5. **Logging the Output**:
   - console.log(doubled); prints [2, 4, 6, 8] to the console, showcasing the transformed array.

Why Use map()?

- **Declarative Style**: It allows you to express *what* you want to do (double the numbers) rather than *how* to iterate and transform elements.
- **Immutability**: The original array is untouched, promoting safer practices when working with data.
- **Chaining**: map() can be chained with other methods like filter() and reduce() for more complex operations.

CHAPTER 4   THE EVOLUTION OF JAVASCRIPT

Best Use Cases for map():

- Transforming data, such as converting an array of objects to an array of specific values

- Applying a uniform operation to all elements in an array, like scaling numbers or formatting strings

By using methods like map(), developers write cleaner, more expressive, and more maintainable JavaScript code.

JSON

Before ES5, working with JSON (JavaScript Object Notation) required external libraries or manual implementations, which were cumbersome and error-prone. ES5 introduced JSON as a global object, providing standardized methods for parsing JSON strings into JavaScript objects and serializing JavaScript objects into JSON strings.

Key Methods in the JSON Object:

1. JSON.parse():

   - Converts a JSON string into a JavaScript object.

   - Automatically handles string-to-type conversion, making it easier to work with server responses or stored data.

2. **JSON.stringify()**:

   - Converts a JavaScript object into a JSON string.

   - This string can be transmitted over a network or saved for later use.

Example:

```
// JSON String
let jsonString = '{"name": "Alice", "age": 25}';

// Parsing JSON into a JavaScript Object
let user = JSON.parse(jsonString);
console.log(user.name); // Alice
console.log(user.age);  // 25

// Serializing a JavaScript Object into a JSON String
let userObject = { name: "Bob", age: 30 };
let serialized = JSON.stringify(userObject);
console.log(serialized); // {"name":"Bob","age":30}
```

Explanation:

1. **Parsing with `JSON.parse()`:**

   - The JSON string {"name": "Alice", "age": 25} is parsed into a JavaScript object: { name: "Alice", age: 25 }.

   - Once parsed, properties of the object can be accessed using dot notation or brackets.

2. **Serializing with `JSON.stringify()`:**

   - The JavaScript object { name: "Bob", age: 30 } is converted into a string: {"name":"Bob","age":30}.

   - This format is ideal for transmitting data in APIs or saving objects as text.

CHAPTER 4   THE EVOLUTION OF JAVASCRIPT

Why It Matters

The introduction of `JSON.parse()` and `JSON.stringify()` in ES5 standardized the handling of JSON data in JavaScript. Before this, developers had to rely on custom libraries or implement their own solutions to work with JSON, which could be error-prone and inconsistent across projects. By providing native methods, ES5 made it easier to parse JavaScript objects into JSON strings and serialize JSON strings back into objects. This was especially crucial as JSON became the de facto standard for data exchange in APIs, enabling seamless communication between client-side JavaScript and back-end services. These functions remain fundamental to modern web development, powering everything from HTTP requests to local storage operations.

Getter and Setter Methods

ES5 introduced getter and setter methods, allowing developers to define custom behavior when accessing or modifying object properties. These methods are defined using get and set syntax within object definitions.

Example:

```
const person = {
  firstName: "John",
  lastName: "Doe",
  get fullName() {
    return `${this.firstName} ${this.lastName}`;
  },
  set fullName(name) {
    [this.firstName, this.lastName] = name.split(' ');
  }
};
```

Why It Matters

Getter and setter methods provide a way to define custom logic for reading and writing object properties. This enables more controlled access to object data, allowing for validation, calculation, or other logic when a property is accessed or modified. They also promote better encapsulation, helping prevent direct manipulation of object state.

Object.create()

Object.create() allows you to create a new object with a specified prototype. This method provides more control over object inheritance and is an alternative to using constructor functions or new Object().

Example:

```
const personProto = { greet: function() { console.
log("Hello!"); } };
const person = Object.create(personProto);
person.greet(); // "Hello!"
```

Why It Matters

Object.create() allows for more flexible and controlled object inheritance, letting you create an object with a specified prototype. It provides a cleaner alternative to using constructor functions or class inheritance, offering a simpler and more explicit way to set an object's prototype.

Object.defineProperty() and Object.defineProperties()

These methods allow you to add or modify object properties with more fine-grained control, such as making properties read-only, adding descriptors, or defining properties with specific getter/setter functions.

Example:

```
const obj = {};
Object.defineProperty(obj, "name", {
  value: "John",
  writable: false,
  configurable: true,
  enumerable: true
});
```

Why It Matters

These methods allow developers to define or modify object properties with more control. You can specify attributes like `writable`, `enumerable`, and `configurable`, making it possible to enforce immutability, create computed properties, or prevent accidental changes to important values. This enables more robust and flexible object management.

Array.prototype.indexOf()

This method allows you to search for an element within an array and returns the first index where the element is found. If the element is not found, it returns -1. It's a cleaner alternative to manually looping through the array.

Example:

```
const arr = [1, 2, 3, 4];
console.log(arr.indexOf(3)); // 2
```

Why It Matters

`indexOf()` simplifies searching for an element within an array. It eliminates the need for manually iterating through the array and checking each value. This method enhances code readability and efficiency, making it easier to work with arrays in a clean, concise manner.

Function.prototype.bind()

The bind() method allows you to create a new function that, when called, has its this value set to a specific context. It's useful for ensuring that the correct context is used in event handlers or callback functions.

Example:

```
const person = {
  name: "Alice",
  greet: function() {
    console.log(`Hello, ${this.name}`);
  }
};
const greetAlice = person.greet.bind(person);
greetAlice(); // "Hello, Alice"
```

Why It Matters

The bind() method ensures that a function retains the correct this context, especially in asynchronous code or event handlers. It enables more predictable behavior when passing functions around as callbacks, making it easier to manage context in complex applications.

ECMAScript 6 (2015)

Often regarded as the most transformative update in JavaScript's history, ES6 (also known as ES2015) introduced a comprehensive set of features, enhancing the language's usability, readability, and scalability. These updates catered to both beginners and advanced developers by addressing common pain points in JavaScript and introducing modern programming paradigms. The key features of ES6 are as follows.

let and const for Safer Variable Declarations

Before ES6, var was the only way to declare variables in JavaScript. However, var's function scope and susceptibility to hoisting led to bugs and confusion. ES6 introduced let and const, which use block scoping and eliminate many pitfalls associated with var.

- **let**: Allows mutable variables, ensures block-scoped behavior, and permits reassignment but not redeclaration within the same block.
- **const**: Prevents both reassignment and redeclaration, ensuring the variable's value remains constant. However, it does not make objects immutable - only the reference to the object is constant, not the object's internal properties.

Example:

```
if (true) {
  let blockScoped = "I'm block scoped!";
  const immutable = "I cannot be changed!";
  console.log(blockScoped); // Works
  console.log(immutable); // Works
}
// console.log(blockScoped); // ReferenceError
// console.log(immutable); // ReferenceError
```

Why It Matters

The introduction of let and const helps eliminate the issues related to var (like scoping problems). let allows for block-level scoping, reducing errors in loops and conditionals, while const ensures that variables that shouldn't change remain constant. Together, they promote safer and more predictable code, making it easier to manage variables' lifetimes and behaviors.

Arrow Functions: Concise Syntax for Functions

Arrow functions (=>) introduced a shorthand syntax for defining functions. They also bind this lexically, solving issues with context in callbacks.

Example:

```
// Traditional function
const add = function (a, b) {
  return a + b;
};

// Arrow function
const addArrow = (a, b) => a + b;

console.log(add(2, 3)); // 5
console.log(addArrow(2, 3)); // 5
```

Why It Matters

Arrow functions offer a shorter and more expressive way to write functions. They automatically bind the this context lexically, which eliminates confusion around how this behaves in traditional function expressions. Unlike traditional functions, arrow functions do not have their own this context but instead inherit this from the surrounding lexical scope. This behavior is particularly useful in event listeners and object methods, where traditional functions may cause unexpected behavior due to their dynamic this binding. As a result, arrow functions lead to cleaner, more predictable code, especially in callbacks, event handlers, and array methods.

Classes: A Syntactic Sugar Over Prototypes

JavaScript's prototypal inheritance model was powerful but unintuitive. ES6 introduced the class keyword to provide a more familiar, object-oriented programming syntax, making JavaScript accessible to developers coming from languages like Java or C#.

Example:

```
class Animal {
  constructor(name) {
    this.name = name;
  }
  speak() {
    console.log(`${this.name} makes a noise.`);
  }
}

class Dog extends Animal {
  speak() {
    console.log(`${this.name} barks.`);
  }
}
let dog = new Dog("Buddy");
dog.speak(); // Buddy barks.
```

Why It Matters

Classes provide a more intuitive and familiar syntax for object-oriented programming in JavaScript, making it easier to work with inheritance and methods. While JavaScript still uses prototypes behind the scenes, classes simplify the process of defining and extending objects. This makes it easier for developers from other object-oriented languages to work with JavaScript and improves code readability and structure.

Modules: Native Support for Modular Codebases

ES6 introduced import and export keywords to natively support modules, replacing the need for tools like CommonJS or AMD. This promotes better organization and maintainability in large codebases.

Example math.js:

```
export const add = (a, b) => a + b;
export const subtract = (a, b) => a - b;
```

Example app.js:

```
import { add, subtract } from './math.js';

console.log(add(5, 3)); // 8
console.log(subtract(5, 3)); // 2
```

Why It Matters

Native support for modules in JavaScript allows for cleaner, more maintainable code by breaking up large applications into smaller, reusable pieces. With import and export, developers can easily share functionality between files, making the codebase easier to organize, test, and scale. It also improves dependency management, preventing global namespace pollution and reducing the risk of naming conflicts.

Template Literals: Easier String Interpolation

Template literals allow embedded expressions in strings, making string manipulation more intuitive.

Example:

```
let name = "Alice";
let greeting = `Hello, ${name}! Welcome to ES6.`;
console.log(greeting); // Hello, Alice! Welcome to ES6.
```

Why It Matters

Template literals simplify string interpolation by allowing expressions to be embedded directly within strings using backticks (`` ` ``). This makes string concatenation more readable and less error-prone, especially when working with complex expressions or multi-line strings. It enhances code clarity and efficiency, making string manipulation a much smoother process.

Destructuring Assignment

Destructuring assignment provides a concise syntax for extracting values from arrays and objects. It helps avoid repetitive code, making it easier to work with data structures by allowing direct assignment of variables from complex structures. This feature enhances code readability and simplifies operations like swapping variables, handling function parameters, and working with deeply nested objects.

Example:

```
const user = { name: "Alice", age: 25 };
const { name, age } = user;

console.log(name); // Alice
console.log(age); // 25
```

Why It Matters

Destructuring assignment provides a concise syntax for extracting values from arrays and objects. It helps avoid repetitive code, making it easier to work with data structures by allowing direct assignment of variables from complex structures. This feature enhances code readability and simplifies operations like swapping variables, handling function parameters, and working with deeply nested objects.

Example Combining ES6 Features

```
class Person {
  constructor(name, age) {
    this.name = name;
    this.age = age;
  }
  introduce() {
    console.log(`Hi, I'm ${this.name}, and I'm ${this.age}
    years old.`);
  }
}
const person = new Person("Alice", 25);
person.introduce(); // Hi, I'm Alice, and I'm 25 years old.

// Using let, const, and arrow functions
const names = ["Bob", "Charlie"];
let greetings = names.map((name) => `Hello, ${name}!`);
console.log(greetings);

// Using destructuring
const { name, age } = person;
console.log(`${name} is ${age} years old.`);
```

ES6 fundamentally transformed JavaScript, setting the foundation for modern frameworks and tooling. By introducing more readable and powerful constructs, ES6 improved developer productivity and code maintainability, marking a significant leap in JavaScript's evolution.

ECMAScript 7 (2016)

Although a smaller update compared with its predecessor, ES7 introduced a couple of impactful features that enhanced JavaScript's simplicity and expressiveness. These updates were specifically designed to reduce boilerplate code and improve readability in common use cases.

Array.prototype.includes()

The includes() method was introduced to simplify the task of checking whether an array contains a specific element. Prior to ES7, this was typically done using the indexOf() method, which could be unintuitive and verbose.

- **indexOf Limitation**: Returns -1 if the element is not found, which requires extra checks for clarity
- **includes Advantage**: Provides a clean, readable boolean return value (true or false)

Example:

```
let fruits = ["apple", "banana", "mango"];

// Using includes
console.log(fruits.includes("banana")); // true
console.log(fruits.includes("grape")); // false

// Before ES7, using indexOf
console.log(fruits.indexOf("banana") !== -1); // true
```

Why It Matters

The includes() method provides a more readable and expressive way to check if an array contains a specific element, eliminating the need for manual loops or indexOf() checks. This improves code clarity, making it easier to understand the intent behind the operation, and helps avoid common errors like incorrect index-based searches.

Exponentiation Operator (**)

The exponentiation operator (**) provides a more intuitive and concise syntax for power calculations. Before ES7, developers relied on the Math.pow() function, which was less readable in arithmetic expressions.

Example:

```
// Using the exponentiation operator
console.log(2 ** 3); // 8
console.log(5 ** 2); // 25

// Equivalent pre-ES7 syntax using Math.pow
console.log(Math.pow(2, 3)); // 8
console.log(Math.pow(5, 2)); // 25
```

Why It Matters

The ** exponentiation operator simplifies the process of performing exponentiation (raising a number to a power) in JavaScript. It makes the code more concise and readable compared with using Math.pow(), allowing developers to express mathematical operations in a more natural way. This enhances both developer experience and code clarity, especially when dealing with mathematical computations.

Combining Features of ES7

The following example combines the includes method and the exponentiation operator for practical use.

Example:

```
let numbers = [1, 2, 3, 4, 5];

// Check if a number exists in the array
if (numbers.includes(3)) {
  console.log(`The square of 3 is ${3 ** 2}`);
  // The square of 3 is 9
}

// Checking a number that doesn't exist
if (!numbers.includes(6)) {
  console.log("6 is not in the array.");
  // 6 is not in the array.
}
```

While ES7 had fewer features compared with its predecessor, the introduction of includes() and the exponentiation operator demonstrated a continued effort to streamline and modernize JavaScript. These features may appear minor but significantly improve the language's ease of use in everyday scenarios.

ECMAScript 8 (2017)

ES8 focused on improving the developer experience by introducing powerful features for asynchronous programming and utility methods to work with objects. These additions reduced boilerplate code and made JavaScript cleaner and more intuitive.

Async/Await

One of the most impactful features of ES8 was the introduction of **async/await**. This syntax simplifies asynchronous programming by making asynchronous code look and behave like synchronous code. Before its introduction, handling asynchronous operations typically involved using Promises with .then() or callback functions, leading to complicated and nested code often referred to as "callback hell." With **async** and **await**, this challenge is significantly reduced, as developers can write asynchronous logic that reads much more clearly and flows like traditional synchronous code.

The async keyword is used to define a function that will always return a **Promise**, allowing you to use await within it. The await keyword pauses the execution of the function until the Promise resolves, making the asynchronous process easier to follow. If an async function throws an error, it is automatically wrapped as a rejected Promise, which can be caught in a catch block, eliminating the need for chaining .then() or handling Promise resolution manually. By making async code easier to understand and manage, **async/await** greatly enhances developer productivity and code maintainability, particularly when dealing with operations like network requests, file I/O, or interacting with APIs. It reduces cognitive load and leads to cleaner, more concise code that is easier to debug and reason about.

Example Fetching Data Using Async/Await:

```
async function fetchData() {
  try {
    let response = await fetch("https://api.example.com/data");
    // Waits for the fetch to complete
    let data = await response.json();
    // Waits for JSON parsing to complete
    console.log(data); // Logs the fetched data
```

```
  } catch (error) {
    console.error("An error occurred:", error);
  }
}
// Call the asynchronous function
fetchData();
```

Explanation:

1. **async Function**: Declares that the function contains asynchronous operations. It always returns a `Promise`.

2. **await Keyword**: Pauses the execution of the function until the `Promise` is resolved or rejected.

3. **Error Handling**: Use `try/catch` for cleaner error management compared with chaining `.catch()`.

Why It's Important:

- Dramatically improves code readability compared with chaining `.then()` methods

- Makes JavaScript's asynchronous nature more accessible for developers unfamiliar with Promises

Why It Matters

Async/await simplifies handling asynchronous code by allowing developers to write code that looks and behaves like synchronous code, making it easier to read and maintain. Instead of chaining `.then()` and dealing with callback hell, `async` and `await` allow for cleaner code, reducing the complexity of working with Promises. Additionally, async and await make the stack trace for debugging easier to follow, which is crucial for identifying and resolving issues in asynchronous code. This makes asynchronous logic much more intuitive and less error-prone, which is essential for modern web applications that rely heavily on asynchronous operations like data fetching and I/O.

Object.entries() and Object.values()

Another powerful addition in ES8 was the introduction of **Object.entries()** and **Object.values()**. These methods simplify working with objects by providing convenient ways to extract the keys, values, or key–value pairs of an object, which can be very useful for tasks like iteration, transformation, or filtering.

Object.entries() returns an array of an object's own enumerable string-keyed property [key, value] pairs. This makes it easy to loop through both the keys and values of an object simultaneously, which is a common requirement when manipulating data. In contrast, previous methods like Object.keys() or Object.values() only returned either the keys or the values, respectively, requiring additional logic to access both.

Object.values() returns an array of all the values in an object, which simplifies operations where you need to process just the values of an object. This is especially useful when dealing with objects representing collections of data where the key isn't as important as the value itself.

These methods enhance the ability to manipulate object data concisely and intuitively. They reduce the need for manual iteration (such as using for...in loops) and help avoid verbose solutions. Additionally, Object.values() is generally faster than for...in loops in many cases, as it directly returns an array of values, avoiding the need to traverse the object's prototype chain. While the performance difference might be minimal for small objects, Object.values() is more efficient when working with larger datasets or in performance-sensitive applications. They are particularly useful when dealing with object transformations or when performing operations like mapping or filtering. Overall, **Object.entries()** and **Object.values()** bring efficiency, readability, and flexibility to working with objects in JavaScript.

Example Using Object.entries():

```
let user = { name: "Alice", age: 25, role: "Developer" };

// Iterate over key-value pairs
for (let [key, value] of Object.entries(user)) {
  console.log(`${key}: ${value}`);
}

// Output:
// name: Alice
// age: 25
// role: Developer
```

Example Using Object.values():

```
let user = { name: "Alice", age: 25, role: "Developer" };

// Get all values
let values = Object.values(user);
console.log(values); // ["Alice", 25, "Developer"]
```

Why It Matters

These methods make it easier to work with objects by providing a cleaner and more efficient way to iterate over their keys, values, or both. Object.entries() and Object.values() simplify the process of transforming object data into arrays for operations like mapping or filtering.
They enhance the flexibility of working with objects and are a more straightforward solution compared with manually iterating with for...in loops or using Object.keys().

Combining ES8 Features

You can combine async/await with Object.entries() for powerful, readable code.

Example Fetch and Process Object Data:

```
async function fetchAndProcessData() {
  try {
    let response = await fetch("https://api.example.com/user");
    let user = await response.json();

    // Log all user properties using Object.entries()
    for (let [key, value] of Object.entries(user)) {
      console.log(`${key}: ${value}`);
    }
  } catch (error) {
    console.error("Error fetching user data:", error);
  }
}

fetchAndProcessData();
```

Smoother and More Intuitive Development

With features like async/await, Object.entries(), and Object.values(), ES8 continued JavaScript's evolution toward clean and modern programming. These additions enhanced both readability and functionality, especially for tasks involving asynchronous operations and object manipulations.

ECMAScript 9 (2018)

ECMAScript 2018 (ES9) introduced a set of important features that enhanced both the functionality and usability of JavaScript. Among the most significant changes were the improvements to how we handle objects, promises, and asynchronous operations. **Rest/spread in objects** allowed for more efficient manipulation of object properties, while **Promise.finally()** gave developers a more elegant way to handle final steps in Promise chains. Asynchronous code became even more powerful with the addition of **asynchronous iteration** using for-await-of, making it easier to work with asynchronous data streams. Additionally, **regular expression enhancements** provided more robust patterns and matching capabilities. These new features collectively brought more flexibility and control to JavaScript development, streamlining common tasks and improving code readability.

Rest/Spread in Objects

The **rest** and **spread** operators in JavaScript revolutionized the way we handled arrays in ES6, but in ES9, these operators were extended to support objects as well. This extension was crucial for developers managing complex data structures, enabling simpler and more efficient code for copying, merging, and destructuring objects. Before this, developers had to rely on more verbose techniques, such as Object.assign(), to achieve similar outcomes. By integrating rest and spread into object manipulation, ES9 made object handling more concise and expressive, aligning with the cleaner, more functional style that modern JavaScript promotes.

- **Rest Operator (...)**: Collects remaining properties into a new object
- **Spread Operator (...)**: Spreads properties from one object into another

Example Cloning and Extending Objects:

```
let user = { name: "Alice", age: 25 };
// Clone and add a new property
let userCopy = { ...user, city: "Paris" };
console.log(userCopy);
// Output: { name: "Alice", age: 25, city: "Paris" }
```

Why It Matters

The addition of **rest/spread in objects** allows for more concise and readable code when dealing with object manipulation. The spread operator (...) enables easy copying of object properties or merging objects, while the rest operator (...) simplifies extracting properties into a new object. These features reduce the need for boilerplate code, making object operations more intuitive and less error-prone. They also enable a functional programming style where immutability is preferred, allowing you to handle state changes more efficiently without directly modifying objects.

Promise.finally()

Promises in JavaScript provided a powerful way to manage asynchronous tasks, but developers often struggled with ensuring that certain code, like cleanup actions, was executed regardless of whether a promise resolved or rejected. Prior to ES9, repeating cleanup logic in both .then() and .catch() blocks was cumbersome and error-prone. **Promise.finally()** was introduced to simplify this process by allowing developers to define a final block of code that runs after the promise has settled, independent of its outcome. This feature was a natural progression in JavaScript's approach to handling asynchronous workflows, adding more convenience and clarity to promise-based code.

Example Using **Promise.finally()** for Cleanup:

```
function fetchData() {
  return new Promise((resolve, reject) => {
    setTimeout(() => resolve("Data fetched!"), 1000);
  });
}

fetchData()
  .then((data) => {
    console.log(data); // Logs: "Data fetched!"
  })
  .catch((error) => {
    console.error("Error:", error);
  })
  .finally(() => {
    console.log("Cleanup or follow-up action.");
  });
// Output:
// "Data fetched!"
// "Cleanup or follow-up action."
```

Why It Matters

Promise.finally() provides a way to execute cleanup code after a Promise has been resolved or rejected, regardless of the outcome. Before its introduction, developers had to repeat cleanup logic in both the .then() and .catch() handlers. With finally(), this code is run just once, improving code clarity and reducing redundancy. It is especially useful for tasks like closing file streams, stopping loaders, or clearing up resources in an elegant, less error-prone way, regardless of whether the operation succeeded or failed.

CHAPTER 4   THE EVOLUTION OF JAVASCRIPT

Asynchronous Iteration with `for-await-of`

Working with asynchronous data sources like streams or APIs was challenging before ES9, as it often involved managing Promises manually within traditional loops. ES9 introduced the `for-await-of` loop, which simplifies asynchronous iteration by allowing developers to iterate over asynchronous data sources just like synchronous ones. This new syntax is especially valuable when dealing with asynchronous generators or scenarios where data is fetched sequentially, such as reading files or processing API responses one at a time. With this feature, asynchronous code became much easier to write and read, eliminating the need for verbose chaining or handling Promises manually within loops.

Example Asynchronous Iteration:

```
async function* fetchData() {
  yield "Data chunk 1";
  yield "Data chunk 2";
  yield "Data chunk 3";
}
(async () => {
  for await (let chunk of fetchData()) {
    console.log(chunk);
  }
})();

// Output:
// "Data chunk 1"
// "Data chunk 2"
// "Data chunk 3"
```

Why It Matters

Asynchronous iteration with for-await-of simplifies working with asynchronous data sources like streams, file reading, or APIs that return data over time. This feature makes it possible to use for-of loops with asynchronous operations, avoiding the need for explicit .then() chains or handling asynchronous logic within async functions. It makes your code cleaner and more readable, reducing the complexity of managing multiple asynchronous operations. It's especially useful when dealing with iterable objects that return Promises or asynchronous data streams, such as those from API calls or file systems.

Regular Expression Enhancements

With the rise of more sophisticated string manipulation needs in modern JavaScript applications, regular expressions (regex) were enhanced in ES9 to offer greater functionality and flexibility. Prior to these updates, regex in JavaScript was powerful but lacked certain features that could make pattern matching and text manipulation more efficient. ES9 introduced several improvements, including the ability to work with named capture groups, which allow developers to refer to captured groups by name rather than by number, as well as the dotAll flag to enable the dot (.) to match newline characters. These enhancements made regular expressions more intuitive, enabling cleaner, more readable code and reducing the complexity of pattern matching in more advanced text-processing scenarios.

- **s (dotAll) Flag**: Allows the dot (.) to match newline characters
- **Named Capture Groups**: Provides descriptive names for capturing groups in regular expressions

Example Named Capture Groups:

```
let dateRegex = /(?<year>\d{4})-(?<month>\d{2})-(?<day>\d{2})/;
let match = dateRegex.exec("2023-12-14");
console.log(match.groups);
// Output: { year: "2023", month: "12", day: "14" }
```

Why It Matters

Regular expression enhancements introduced in ES9 bring new capabilities for pattern matching, making it easier to work with text processing and validation. Features like named capture groups, lookbehind assertions, and the dotAll flag enhance the flexibility of regular expressions, allowing for more complex matching without resorting to workarounds. This makes regular expressions more powerful and expressive, reducing the need for manual string manipulation or complex parsing logic. Developers can write cleaner and more efficient code for validating input, extracting information from strings, and performing advanced text-processing tasks.

ECMAScript 10 (2019)

ECMAScript 2019 (ES10) introduced several enhancements that improved code readability, simplified common tasks, and added more powerful features for modern JavaScript development. Among the most notable additions were improvements to arrays, string handling, and JSON manipulation. ES10 brought us more streamlined ways to deal with data structures and string manipulation, as well as cleaner code through optional catch bindings. These features significantly enhanced JavaScript's ability to handle complex tasks while reducing boilerplate code and improving performance.

Optional Catch Binding

ES10 introduced **optional catch binding**, which allows developers to omit the error parameter in a catch block when it's not needed. This change was particularly useful for situations where the error object isn't necessary for handling the exception, making the code cleaner and more readable. Before ES10, developers had to define a catch parameter even if it was unused, which could clutter the code and make it harder to follow.

Example Catch Without Binding:

```
try {
  performTask();
} catch {
  console.log("An error occurred.");
}
```

Why It Matters

Optional catch binding helps reduce unnecessary boilerplate code and enhances readability when the error information is not required for error handling. It encourages more concise and focused error-handling logic.

Array.prototype.flat()

The **flat()** method was introduced in ES10 to simplify the process of flattening arrays. It allows you to reduce the depth of nested arrays into a single-level array. For example, an array of arrays can be flattened into a single array, and this process is done recursively to any depth specified. The default depth is 1 if no argument is provided.

Example Flattening Arrays:

```
let arr = [1, [2, 3], [4, [5]]];
// Flatten to a depth of 1
console.log(arr.flat());
// Output: [1, 2, 3, 4, [5]]

// Flatten to a depth of 2
console.log(arr.flat(2));
// Output: [1, 2, 3, 4, 5]
```

Why It Matters

Before ES10, developers had to manually flatten arrays using loops or libraries. With flat(), flattening is now built into JavaScript, making the code cleaner and improving performance when working with nested data structures, especially in cases like processing user input or working with APIs that return nested arrays.

Array.prototype.flatMap()

ES10 also introduced **flatMap()**, a combination of the map() and flat() methods. This method first maps each element using a function and then flattens the result into a new array. It is particularly useful when applying transformations to arrays and ensuring that the result is flat.

Example Using flatMap():

```
let phrases = ["hello world", "welcome to ES10"];
let words = phrases.flatMap((phrase) => phrase.split(" "));
console.log(words);
// Output: ["hello", "world", "welcome", "to", "ES10"]
```

Why It Matters

This method provides a more efficient and concise way to transform and flatten arrays in a single step, reducing the need for nested operations like map() followed by flat(). It simplifies code and increases performance, particularly for operations that need both mapping and flattening simultaneously.

String.prototype.trimStart() and trimEnd()

In ES10, two new methods were added to strings: **trimStart()** and **trimEnd()**. These methods are similar to trim(), but instead of trimming whitespace from both ends of the string, they specifically trim whitespace from the start or end of the string, respectively.

Example:

```
let str = "   Hello World!   ";
console.log(str.trimStart()); // "Hello World!   "
console.log(str.trimEnd());   // "   Hello World!"
```

Why It Matters

Before ES10, developers had to use more complex methods to trim only one end of a string (like using regular expressions). These new methods simplify the process and improve clarity, making string manipulation easier and reducing the risk of errors when dealing with spaces at the beginning or end of a string.

Object.fromEntries()

The **Object.fromEntries()** method was introduced in ES10 to transform a list of key-value pairs into an object. It is essentially the reverse of `Object.entries()`, which turns objects into arrays of key-value pairs. This method is useful when working with Map objects or converting arrays into objects more easily.

Example:

```
let entries = [["name", "Alice"], ["age", 25]];
let obj = Object.fromEntries(entries);
console.log(obj);
// Output: { name: "Alice", age: 25 }
```

Why It Matters

Before ES10, creating an object from an array of key-value pairs was less straightforward. `Object.fromEntries()` streamlines this process and enables more efficient transformations, particularly when working with Map objects or other iterable data sources. It also improves code readability when converting collections into objects.

Well-Formed JSON Strings in JSON.stringify()

ES10 improved **JSON.stringify()** to ensure it always produces well-formed JSON strings. Specifically, it prevents invalid or broken UTF-8 sequences from being included in the resulting string. This is particularly important for data exchange across systems or APIs, as malformed JSON could lead to errors or data corruption.

Example:

```
console.log(JSON.stringify("\uD800"));
// Output: "\"\\ud800\"" (correctly escaped)
```

Why It Matters

Prior to ES10, `JSON.stringify()` could produce problematic strings if the input contained invalid or non-standard UTF-8 characters. This improvement ensures that JavaScript handles JSON serialization correctly, making it safer for developers working with APIs or transferring data between systems. It reduces errors and ensures consistent output, improving data integrity and reliability.

ECMAScript 11 (2020)

ECMAScript 2020 (ES11) introduced a series of new features that enhanced JavaScript's ability to handle edge cases, work with large numbers, and improve code readability. The addition of the **nullish coalescing operator** and **optional chaining** simplified common operations, making code more concise and resilient to errors. **BigInt** was also introduced to provide support for arbitrarily large integers, addressing the limitations of the `Number` type for certain applications, such as dealing with financial data or cryptography. These features further modernized JavaScript and made it more adaptable to the needs of developers working on complex applications.

CHAPTER 4   THE EVOLUTION OF JAVASCRIPT

Nullish Coalescing Operator (??)

The **nullish coalescing operator** (??) was introduced in ES11 to provide a more precise way to handle default values. It checks if a value is null or undefined and returns the right-hand operand if it is. Unlike the logical OR operator (||), which returns the right-hand operand for falsy values (like 0, false, or ' '), the nullish coalescing operator only triggers for null or undefined. This makes it ideal for scenarios where 0, false, or an empty string is a valid value, but you still want to provide a fallback for null or undefined.

Example:

```
let name = null;
console.log(name ?? Guest); // Guest
```

Why It Matters

Before the nullish coalescing operator, developers had to use workarounds (like combining || with additional checks) to handle cases where falsy values such as 0 or false should not trigger a fallback. This operator simplifies these scenarios, allowing developers to specify defaults only when a value is truly null or undefined. It improves code readability, reduces the chance of errors, and makes working with default values more intuitive.

Optional Chaining (?.)

ES11 introduced **optional chaining** (?.), a feature that allows developers to safely access deeply nested properties of an object without having to check each level for null or undefined values. With optional chaining, if a reference is null or undefined, it will short-circuit and return undefined instead of throwing an error. This feature is incredibly useful when dealing with complex object structures, such as working with APIs or large data models. Optional chaining also works with function calls, allowing you to safely call methods on potentially null or undefined objects without causing runtime errors.

CHAPTER 4   THE EVOLUTION OF JAVASCRIPT

Example:

```
const user = {
  name: 'Alice',
  address: { city: 'Wonderland' },
  getProfile(): () => ({ name: 'Alice', age: 30})
};

// Accessing nested properties
console.log(user?.address?.city); // "Wonderland"
console.log(user?.contact?.email); // undefined (no error)

// Function call with optional chaining
console.log(user?.getProfile?.().name); // "Alice" - safely
calls getProfile()
console.log(user?.getProfle?.().email); // undefined -
getProfile() is called, but email does not exist

// Using optional chaining with function calls inside
   the object
const person = {
  name: 'Bob',
  greet: (message) => `Hello, ${message}`
};

console.log(person?.greet?.('World'));
// "Hello, World" - safely calls greet()
console.log(person?.greet?.())
// "Hello, undefined" - greet() still works

// Example with an undefined function
const personWithoutGreet = { name: 'Eve' };
console.log(personWithoutGreet?.greet?.('World'));
// undefined - no error, greet is not defined
```

```
// Optional chaining in arrays or method calls
const books = [{title: 'Book 1'}, {title: 'Book 2'}];
console.log(books?.[0]?.title); // "Book 1" - safely accesses array element and property
console.log(books?.[2]?.title); // undefined - no error, index 2 doesn't exist
```

Additionally, optional chaining can improve performance in some cases by avoiding unnecessary checks. In traditional code, you might need to manually check for null or undefined at every level, which can become repetitive and impact readability and performance. With optional chaining, you reduce the number of checks, making your code cleaner and potentially improving execution speed in cases where deep checks are involved.

Why It Matters

Before optional chaining, accessing deeply nested properties in JavaScript required verbose checks for null or undefined at each level of the chain. This added complexity and clutter to the code, often leading to repetitive patterns. Optional chaining significantly reduces the need for these checks, making code more concise, readable, and error-resistant. It simplifies data access, especially when dealing with complex objects or when the structure of the data may vary.

BigInt

BigInt was introduced in ES11 to address the limitations of the Number type in JavaScript. The Number type can represent only integers within a certain range, which can be problematic when working with very large numbers, such as in financial calculations, cryptography, or scientific computing. BigInt allows developers to work with integers larger than $2^{53} - 1$, making it possible to handle arbitrarily large numbers with ease. You can create a BigInt by appending an n to the end of an integer literal or by using the BigInt() constructor.

Example:

```
const largeNumber = 12345678901234567890n;
const anotherBigInt = BigInt(12345678901234567890);
console.log(largeNumber); // 12345678901234567890n
```

Why It Matters

Before BigInt, JavaScript could only represent integers within a limited range. This was fine for many everyday uses, but not sufficient for operations requiring extremely large numbers, like cryptography or high-precision scientific calculations. BigInt provides a way to represent arbitrarily large integers, which expands the capabilities of JavaScript in fields that require high numerical precision. With BigInt, developers no longer have to worry about precision loss when working with large numbers.

Example:

```
const bigIntValue = 9007199254740992n + 1n;
console.log(bigIntValue); // 9007199254740993n
```

Important Considerations: While BigInt is incredibly useful for large number calculations, it cannot be mixed directly with regular Number types in arithmetic operations. You'll need to ensure that both operands are of type BigInt when performing operations like addition, subtraction, or multiplication.

Example:

```
const bigInt1 = 12345678901234567890n;
const bigInt2 = 98765432109876543210n;
const result = bigInt1 + bigInt2;
console.log(result); // 111111111011111111100n
```

ECMAScript 12 (2021)

ECMAScript 2021, or ES12, was officially released in June 2021 and introduced several important features that enhanced the language's performance, usability, and developer experience. While many of the changes were relatively small compared with previous releases, they had a significant impact on everyday JavaScript development. Here are some key features introduced in ES12.

Logical Assignment Operators

ECMAScript 2021 introduced three new logical assignment operators that combine logical operators with assignment, offering a more concise syntax for common patterns. These include

- **&&= (Logical AND Assignment):** Executes the assignment only if the left-hand operand is truthy
- **||= (Logical OR Assignment):** Executes the assignment only if the left-hand operand is falsy
- **??= (Logical Nullish Assignment):** Executes the assignment only if the left-hand operand is `null` or `undefined`

Why It Matters

These operators reduce boilerplate code and make conditional assignments more concise and readable. Instead of using multiple lines to check conditions before assigning a value, these operators streamline the process, improving both code efficiency and clarity.

Example:

```
let a = 5;
let b = 10;
a ||= b;  // a becomes 10 since a is falsy
```

Numeric Separators

This feature allows developers to insert underscores (_) in numeric literals for better readability, particularly in large numbers or in cases of very long integer values. This helps improve clarity when dealing with large numbers, especially when working with values like financial figures or byte sizes.

Why It Matters

Numeric separators make code more readable and easier to maintain. When working with large values, the underscores provide visual separation that prevents errors and enhances the developer's ability to quickly spot and comprehend numbers, such as file sizes or monetary values, without getting lost in a sea of digits.

Example:

```
const oneMillion = 1_000_000;
const bytes = 1_024_000_000;
```

String.prototype.replaceAll()

The `replaceAll()` method is now available in ES12. It allows you to replace all occurrences of a substring in a string without the need for regular expressions.

Why It Matters

This method simplifies string manipulation, particularly when you need to perform global replacements. It reduces the need for regular expressions and makes the code cleaner, easier to read, and less error-prone.

Example:

```
const str = 'foo bar foo';
const newStr = str.replaceAll('foo', 'baz');
console.log(newStr); // "baz bar baz"
```

Promise.any()

Promise.any() was added to allow developers to handle multiple promises in parallel and proceed with the first one that resolves, instead of waiting for all of them to finish. This is particularly useful for scenarios where any successful operation is sufficient, like trying multiple network requests or fallback options.

Why It Matters

Promise.any() is a useful addition for scenarios where speed is more important than completeness. It allows developers to handle the first resolved promise, making it ideal for cases like fallback systems or when multiple parallel operations are competing for the quickest resolution. This improves performance and user experience in asynchronous tasks.

```
const p1 = new Promise((resolve, reject) => setTimeout(reject, 100, 'Failed'));
const p2 = new Promise((resolve, reject) => setTimeout(resolve, 500, 'Success'));

Promise.any([p1, p2]).then(value => console.log(value));
// "Success"
```

WeakRefs and FinalizationRegistry (Experimental)

ES12 introduced WeakRef, a way to create a weak reference to an object, which does not prevent garbage collection. Combined with FinalizationRegistry, developers can track the garbage collection of objects.

Why It Matters

This allows more precise memory management, particularly in complex applications where you want to manage resources carefully. It's useful in caching systems or situations where objects should be cleaned up when no longer in use, without preventing garbage collection. However, this feature is experimental and should be used with caution.

```
let obj = { foo: 'bar' };
const weakRef = new WeakRef(obj);
```

Array.prototype.at()

The at() method was introduced, allowing developers to access elements in an array using negative indices, making it easier to work with the end of an array.

Why It Matters

This method simplifies accessing elements from the end of an array, improving both the readability and maintainability of the code. Negative indices are a common pattern when dealing with arrays, and at() removes the need for complex logic or manual calculations.

```
const arr = [1, 2, 3, 4, 5];
console.log(arr.at(-1)); // 5 (last element)
console.log(arr.at(-2)); // 4 (second-to-last element)
```

Promise.allSettled()

`Promise.allSettled()` is a new method that allows you to handle multiple promises, regardless of whether they resolve or reject. It returns a promise that resolves when all input promises have settled (either fulfilled or rejected), providing a list of their outcomes.

```
const promises = [
  Promise.resolve('Success 1'),
  Promise.reject('Error 1'),
  Promise.resolve('Success 2')
];

Promise.allSettled(promises).then(results => {
  results.forEach((result, index) => {
    if (result.status === 'fulfilled') {
      console.log(`Promise ${index + 1} was fulfilled with
      value: ${result.value}`);
    } else {
      console.log(`Promise ${index + 1} was rejected with
      reason: ${result.reason}`);
    }
  });
});
```

Why It Matters

Prior to `Promise.allSettled()`, you would have to use `Promise.all()` or `Promise.race()`, which either resolves when all promises are fulfilled or rejects when any promise is rejected. `Promise.allSettled()` provides a better way to handle multiple promises where you want to know the result of every promise, regardless of whether they succeeded or failed.

This is particularly useful in scenarios where you need to ensure that all asynchronous operations are finished, but don't want a single failure to affect the rest.

ECMAScript 13 (2022)

ECMAScript 2022 (ES13) introduced features that significantly improved developer experience by simplifying syntax, enhancing class capabilities, and enabling better handling of structured data. The **Top-Level Await** removed unnecessary boilerplate for asynchronous operations, while **enhanced error handling** provided developers with more precise control in managing exceptions. The **Numeric Separator** improved code readability for large numbers, and **private methods and fields in classes** strengthened encapsulation in object-oriented programming. Additionally, the introduction of **record and tuple types** paved the way for immutable data structures, offering new opportunities for efficient and predictable programming patterns. These updates made JavaScript even more powerful, expressive, and modern.

Top-Level Await

The **Top-Level Await** feature allows await to be used outside of an async function, enabling developers to write cleaner asynchronous code at the module level. This eliminates the need for wrapping top-level asynchronous code in an additional async function, making the code simpler and more intuitive.

Example Top-Level Await:

```
let data = await fetch("https://api.example.com/data")
  .then((res) => res.json());
console.log(data);
```

Why It Matters

Before this feature, asynchronous operations at the top level of a module required extra scaffolding, which could clutter code and make it less readable. Top-Level Await simplifies this, especially in scenarios like dynamic imports, fetching configurations, or initializing resources. By making asynchronous programming more straightforward, it enhances developer productivity and reduces boilerplate code.

Enhanced Error Handling

ES13 introduced improvements to error handling, enabling developers to catch and handle specific exceptions more effectively. This feature allows finer-grained control over how errors are caught and processed, reducing the risk of unintended exception handling behavior.

Example Enhanced Error Handling:

```
try {
  // Code that might throw an error
  let result = await someAsyncFunction();
} catch (error) {
  console.error(`Error occurred: ${error.message}`);
  console.error(`Stack trace: ${error.stack}`);
}
```

Why It Matters

Prior to this enhancement, error handling in JavaScript could be overly broad, potentially catching and handling errors that weren't intended. This made debugging and maintaining code challenging. With enhanced error handling, developers can isolate specific error cases, leading to more reliable and maintainable error management.

CHAPTER 4   THE EVOLUTION OF JAVASCRIPT

Numeric Separator (_) in Numbers

The **Numeric Separator** allows developers to use underscores (_) to separate digits in numeric literals, improving readability for large numbers. For example, 1_000_000 is easier to read than 1000000.

   Example:

```
let largeNumber = 1_000_000;
console.log(largeNumber); // Output: 1000000
```

Why It Matters

When working with large numbers, the lack of visual separation between digits made it challenging to read and verify numeric literals. The Numeric Separator addresses this issue, making numeric literals more human-readable and reducing the likelihood of errors in interpreting or transcribing large numbers. This improvement is particularly beneficial in domains like finance, data analysis, or scientific programming.

Private Methods and Fields in Classes

Private methods and fields allow developers to define truly private properties and methods in JavaScript classes, using the # syntax. These members are accessible only within the class itself, providing stronger encapsulation compared with previous approaches.

   Example:

```
class User {
  #password; // private field

  constructor(name, password) {
    this.name = name;
    this.#password = password;
  }
```

81

```
  #validatePassword(input) {
    return input === this.#password;
  }
  login(input) {
    if (this.#validatePassword(input)) {
      console.log("Logged in successfully");
    } else {
      console.log("Invalid password");
    }
  }
}
let user = new User("Alice", "secret");
user.login("wrong"); // Invalid password
user.login("secret"); // Logged in successfully
```

Why It Matters

Before this feature, developers relied on naming conventions or closures to simulate private properties, which were not truly secure and could be accessed from outside the class. Private methods and fields enforce encapsulation at the language level, improving security and ensuring that internal implementation details are hidden from external code. This leads to cleaner, more robust class designs and better adherence to object-oriented principles.

Record and Tuple Types

Record and **tuple types** are immutable and deeply frozen data structures introduced in ES13. A **record** is similar to an object but immutable, while a **tuple** is an immutable version of an array. These structures ensure that their contents cannot be changed once created.

Example:

```
let user = Record({ name: "Alice", age: 25 });
let coordinates = Tuple([40.7128, -74.0060]);
```

Why It Matters

Immutability is a cornerstone of functional programming and contributes to predictable code by eliminating side effects. Previously, developers relied on third-party libraries like Immutable.js to achieve this functionality. With native support for records and tuples, JavaScript now provides efficient and standardized tools for immutable programming. These structures enhance performance and simplify reasoning about code, making them ideal for state management, data sharing, and other use cases requiring immutability.

Summary

ECMAScript has evolved significantly over the years, introducing a series of updates that have enhanced JavaScript's capabilities and developer experience. Starting with ECMAScript 3, which introduced fundamental language constructs like `eval`, `arguments`, and the `with` statement, the language provided a solid foundation. ECMAScript 5 in 2009 revitalized JavaScript with strict mode to enforce cleaner code and new array methods like `forEach()`, `map()`, `filter()`, and `reduce()`, making code more readable and maintainable. ECMAScript 6 marked a major milestone by introducing `let` and `const` for safer variable declarations, arrow functions, classes, and modules, which improved code modularity and syntax clarity. Each subsequent version addressed specific developer needs: ECMAScript 7 added `Array.prototype.includes()` and the exponentiation operator for simpler and more readable code; ECMAScript 8 introduced `async/await` for cleaner asynchronous programming and new object iteration methods; ECMAScript 9 enhanced destructuring capabilities with `Rest/Spread` in objects and added `Promise.finally()` for better promise handling. ECMAScript 10 brought `Optional Catch Binding` and `Array.prototype.flat()` to streamline error handling and flatten nested arrays, while ECMAScript 11 introduced the `Nullish Coalescing Operator` and `Optional Chaining`, which provide safer access to deeply nested properties and default values for null or undefined. The latest versions, including ECMAScript 12 and 13, continue to refine JavaScript's capabilities with features like `Numeric Separator`, `Private Methods and Fields in Classes`, `Record`, and `Tuple` types to enhance data management and security. Each version of ECMAScript has contributed to a more robust, versatile, and expressive JavaScript language, helping developers write more efficient, maintainable, and secure code. As a result, users have gained a deeper understanding of how JavaScript can be used to build dynamic and responsive web applications, enabling them to solve real-world development challenges more effectively.

CHAPTER 5

The Role of JavaScript in Modern Web Development

Objective

JavaScript has become the backbone of the modern Web, transforming static HTML pages into interactive, dynamic experiences. It enables developers to build everything from single-page applications (SPAs) to server-side APIs, mobile apps, and even machine learning tools. In this chapter, we will explore how JavaScript powers modern web development, its ecosystem, and its essential role in creating user-centric applications.

Dynamic Content and Interactivity

JavaScript enables websites to offer more than just static content by allowing them to dynamically respond to user interactions. This interactivity is achieved through manipulating the Document Object Model (DOM), enabling real-time updates without requiring a full page reload. This capability is essential for creating engaging and responsive web applications.

CHAPTER 5   THE ROLE OF JAVASCRIPT IN MODERN WEB DEVELOPMENT

Dynamic Updates Without Reloads: JavaScript is used to dynamically change page content based on user actions. For instance, when a user clicks a button, JavaScript can update the content of a web page without reloading the entire page. This not only improves user experience but also enhances performance by reducing server requests.

Example:

```
document.querySelector("#changeText").
addEventListener("click", () => {
  document.querySelector("#output").textContent = "Text updated dynamically!";
});
```

In this example, a click event listener is attached to an element with the ID changeText. When clicked, it updates the text content of an element with the ID output to display new content dynamically without reloading the page.

Event Handling: JavaScript listens for a variety of user actions, such as clicks, scrolls, and key presses, to trigger interactive behaviors on the web page. This event-driven model allows applications to react instantly to user inputs, making them more intuitive and user-friendly.

Example:

```
document.addEventListener("keydown", (event) => {
  console.log(`You pressed ${event.key}`);
});
```

In this example, a keydown event listener is used to capture when a user presses a key on their keyboard. It responds by logging the key pressed to the console, providing immediate feedback to the user and enabling keyboard navigation and shortcut functionalities in web applications.

Single-Page Applications (SPAs)

Single-page applications (SPAs) have transformed web development by offering a faster, app-like user experience that loads content dynamically. Unlike traditional multi-page websites, SPAs load a single HTML page and update its content using JavaScript and APIs. This dynamic content rendering allows for smoother transitions and more responsive user interactions, making SPAs ideal for modern web applications.

How SPAs Work: SPAs typically load a minimal initial HTML page, and subsequent views or content updates are loaded via JavaScript without requiring full page reloads. This approach minimizes server load and provides faster navigation between views. JavaScript frameworks such as Angular, React, and Vue.js are commonly used to build SPAs, leveraging their component-based architecture to manage UI updates and state efficiently.

Benefits of SPAs

1. **Faster Navigation Between Views**: Users can switch between different sections or pages of the application without experiencing delays or waiting times for page reloading.

2. **Reduced Server Load**: Since only updated content is sent from the server to the client, SPAs reduce server traffic and improve scalability.

3. **Seamless Transitions Without Page Reloads**: SPAs enhance user experience by maintaining a continuous, fluid interaction as users move through the application.

Example (React Component):

```
function Greeting() {
  const [message, setMessage] = React.useState("Hello, User!");
  return (
    <div>
      <h1>{message}</h1>
      <button onClick={() => setMessage("Welcome to SPAs!")}>
      Update Message</button>
    </div>
  );
}
```

In this example, a React component is used to display a greeting message that can be updated dynamically by clicking a button. The React.useState hook is utilized to manage the state of the message, and clicking the button triggers an update without reloading the page. This showcases the responsiveness and interactivity that SPAs can offer to users.

Server-Side JavaScript

With the advent of Node.js, JavaScript broke free from the confines of the browser and entered the server space. This transition marked a significant evolution in JavaScript's utility, allowing it to be used for back-end development just as effectively as for front-end tasks.

Why Node.js?

Built on Chrome's V8 engine, Node.js is fast and lightweight. Its event-driven, non-blocking I/O model makes it highly efficient, ideal for handling multiple connections simultaneously without blocking the server's main thread. This architecture is particularly beneficial for real-time applications where responsiveness and low latency are critical. Node.js leverages JavaScript's versatility and scalability, making it a popular choice for a wide range of server-side tasks.

Use Cases:

- **Building REST APIs**: Node.js excels in creating efficient, scalable RESTful APIs. Its rich ecosystem of libraries and frameworks, such as Express.js, simplifies routing, middleware handling, and response management. For example, an ecommerce application can use Node.js to manage product listings, user authentication, and order processing via REST APIs.

- **Real-Time Applications**: Thanks to its non-blocking nature and asynchronous I/O, Node.js is well-suited for real-time applications like chat apps, live dashboards, and online gaming platforms. For instance, consider a live chat application where users can exchange messages instantly. Node.js ensures that the server can handle a large number of simultaneous connections, pushing updates to all users in real time.

- **Handling File Systems and Databases**: Node.js's efficient handling of file systems and databases is another key advantage. It can read and write files, perform database operations, and manage data streams seamlessly. For example, a content management system (CMS) built with Node.js can quickly access, manipulate, and store large volumes of data from a database or file storage.

CHAPTER 5   THE ROLE OF JAVASCRIPT IN MODERN WEB DEVELOPMENT

Example (Node.js Server):

```
const http = require("http");

http.createServer((req, res) => {
  res.writeHead(200, { "Content-Type": "text/plain" });
  res.end("Hello from the server!");
}).listen(3000);

console.log("Server running at http://localhost:3000/");
```

This code snippet illustrates the simplicity and power of Node.js for building a basic server. By leveraging JavaScript on both the client and server sides, developers can create full-stack applications more efficiently. The use of Node.js enables developers to write server-side code that can handle requests, manage server state, and serve dynamic content, all while maintaining a seamless user experience.

Frameworks and Libraries

JavaScript's versatility is greatly amplified by the abundance of frameworks and libraries, each tailored for specific use cases, making development more efficient and standardized.

What Are Frameworks and Libraries?

Frameworks provide a structured environment with pre-built solutions to common problems. They enforce architectural principles and patterns, which can help maintain code consistency and scalability A **library**, on the other hand, is a collection of utility functions or pre-written code that solves specific tasks. While frameworks offer a high-level structure and enforce best practices, libraries are more about utility providing specific functionality that developers can easily integrate into their applications.

Front-End Frameworks:

1. **React**: React is a popular front-end library known for its component-based architecture. It allows developers to build single-page applications (SPAs) efficiently, by breaking the user interface into reusable components. For example, Facebook's newsfeed is a SPA built using React, where each component (like posts, comments, and likes) can be independently managed and updated without reloading the entire page.

2. **Angular**: Angular is a full-fledged framework that offers a complete solution for building web applications. It comes with built-in dependency injection and routing capabilities, which make it a powerful choice for developing large-scale applications. For instance, Google's web applications use Angular for their high-performance needs, such as Google Maps and Gmail.

3. **Vue.js**: Vue.js is a lightweight and beginner-friendly framework that focuses on the view layer of applications. It's often used for smaller projects or as a stepping stone for developers new to front-end development. For example, Alibaba's Taobao Marketplace uses Vue.js to create a fast, responsive, and smooth user experience.

Back-End Frameworks:

1. **Express**: Express is a minimalist back-end framework for Node.js that makes it simple to build APIs. Its lightweight nature allows developers to set up routes, handle HTTP requests, and manage middleware efficiently. For example, an ecommerce application can use Express to manage product details, user authentication, and order processing.

2. **NestJS**: NestJS is a more full-featured framework built with TypeScript that provides robust support for building scalable server-side applications. It integrates seamlessly with other libraries and frameworks, allowing for a clean, maintainable architecture. For instance, NestJS can be used to build a high-performance API for a large-scale social network or elearning platform.

Testing Libraries:

1. **Jest**: Jest is a popular testing framework for JavaScript that is easy to set up and use, especially in a React or Angular project. It provides built-in mocking and a rich API for testing components and unit tests.

2. **Mocha and Jasmine**: These libraries are often used alongside Node.js for server-side testing. Mocha is known for its flexibility and can run tests in a variety of environments, while Jasmine focuses on behavior-driven development and provides a simple, readable syntax for test descriptions.

These frameworks and libraries provide standardized tools that help developers streamline development processes, ensuring consistency and reducing errors. By using the right framework or library, developers can concentrate on the core functionality of their applications, whether it's building interactive UIs, managing state, handling API requests, or testing the application's performance.

Progressive Web Apps (PWAs)

Progressive Web Apps (PWAs) combine the best features of web and mobile applications, providing a native-like experience with offline capabilities, push notifications, and fast loading speeds. They aim to deliver a seamless user experience across devices and platforms.

Why PWAs Matter

1. **Installable and Offline Capable**: PWAs can be installed on a user's device just like native apps, appearing on the home screen without requiring an app store. This means users can access them without a network connection, allowing offline functionality such as browsing content, reading articles, and using local features.

2. **Responsive and Platform-Independent**: PWAs adapt to different screen sizes and orientations, ensuring a consistent experience across desktops, tablets, and smartphones. They use responsive web design principles to provide an optimal user interface on any device, enhancing usability and accessibility.

CHAPTER 5   THE ROLE OF JAVASCRIPT IN MODERN WEB DEVELOPMENT

Example (Service Worker for Caching):

Service Workers are a key component of PWAs, providing offline support by intercepting network requests, caching resources, and delivering them when the user is offline. This allows PWAs to work even when the network is unavailable, ensuring a consistent experience for users regardless of their connectivity status. In addition to offline functionality, Service Workers also enable background synchronization and push notifications, enhancing the usability of PWAs when the app is not actively being used. Background sync ensures that data is updated or sent to the server when the user regains connectivity, improving the app's reliability. Push notifications allow PWAs to send timely updates to users, even if the app is not open, boosting engagement.

It's important to note that Service Workers require HTTPS for security reasons. This ensures that the data being intercepted and cached by the Service Worker is safe from tampering and provides a secure environment for both the user and the app. HTTPS is a fundamental requirement for PWAs, not just for Service Workers, but for maintaining overall security and reliability.

```
self.addEventListener("install", (event) => {
  event.waitUntil(
    caches.open("app-cache").then((cache) => {
      return cache.addAll(["/index.html", "/styles.css",
        "/app.js"]);
    })
  );
});
```

In this example, a Service Worker is being used to cache essential files (/index.html, /styles.css, /app.js) during the installation phase. Once installed, the Service Worker will handle requests for these resources from the cache, providing a faster load time and improving user experience during offline usage.

1. **Push Notifications**: PWAs can send push notifications to users, just like native apps, to keep them engaged with updates, reminders, and other alerts even when the app is not open. This feature is especially useful for news websites, ecommerce platforms, and social media applications that want to communicate directly with users.

2. **Enhanced Performance**: By leveraging modern web technologies like Service Workers, Web App Manifests, and HTTPS, PWAs can deliver fast loading speeds and smooth interactions. They use features like lazy loading, background synchronization, and optimized resource loading to ensure that users get a responsive experience with minimal latency.

3. **SEO Benefits**: PWAs benefit from search engine optimization (SEO) advantages because they are indexed by search engines like Google. This improves discoverability in search results, potentially driving more organic traffic to the application.

PWAs are a compelling choice for businesses and developers looking to create a single, maintainable application that can deliver a high-quality user experience across multiple platforms without compromising on performance.

CHAPTER 5   THE ROLE OF JAVASCRIPT IN MODERN WEB DEVELOPMENT

Real-Time Applications

Real-time applications such as live chats, notifications, and collaborative tools rely on JavaScript to enable instant communication between clients and servers. Technologies like WebSockets and frameworks like Socket. IO make it possible to build applications that deliver near-instantaneous responses, which are critical for user engagement and experience.

WebSockets

WebSockets provide a powerful mechanism for full-duplex communication between clients and servers. Unlike HTTP, which is request–response based, WebSockets establish a persistent, two-way connection that allows data to be sent and received immediately, as soon as it is available. This makes them ideal for real-time applications that require low-latency interaction, such as live chat, online gaming, and real-time data updates.

One of the key advantages of WebSockets over traditional HTTP polling is efficiency. HTTP polling repeatedly sends requests at regular intervals, increasing server load and network traffic. Each request and response cycle adds overhead, especially for applications that require frequent data updates. In contrast, WebSockets maintain a single open connection between the client and server, significantly reducing overhead and minimizing latency, making them much more efficient for real-time applications.

Example (Socket.IO Chat):

```
const io = require("socket.io")(3000);

io.on("connection", (socket) => {
  console.log("User connected");
  socket.on("message", (msg) => {
    io.emit("message", msg);
  });
});
```

In this example, Socket.IO is used to create a real-time chat application. When a user connects to the server, they can send messages through the `message` event. The server listens for these messages and, when one is received, broadcasts it to all connected clients using `io.emit("message", msg)`. This ensures that all users see the same messages instantly, creating a seamless chat experience.

Use Cases:

- **Live Chat**: Real-time chat functionality enables instant messaging between users without the need to refresh the page. It's commonly used on social media platforms, customer support websites, and collaborative tools.

- **Notifications**: Applications can send instant alerts and updates to users, such as new messages, friend requests, or system alerts, ensuring users stay informed and engaged.

- **Collaborative Tools**: Real-time applications can support multiple users working on documents, code, or other content simultaneously. For instance, collaborative coding platforms or online editing tools rely on WebSockets or Socket.IO to enable real-time synchronization of changes across all users.

Benefits:

- **Improved User Experience**: Real-time updates enhance user experience by providing timely responses, reducing latency, and improving overall interactivity.

- **Scalability**: WebSockets and Socket.IO handle scaling more efficiently compared with traditional request–response models, making them suitable for high-traffic applications.

- **Flexibility**: The bidirectional nature of WebSockets allows developers to build dynamic, responsive applications that can adapt to changing user needs without interrupting the user experience.

By using WebSockets or frameworks like Socket.IO, JavaScript can power real-time applications that are responsive, scalable, and user-friendly, meeting the demands of today's interactive web applications.

JavaScript in Mobile Development

JavaScript frameworks have revolutionized mobile app development, enabling developers to build cross-platform applications that run seamlessly on both iOS and Android devices. This approach not only saves time and effort but also ensures that the app delivers a consistent user experience across different platforms.

React Native

React Native combines JavaScript with native components, allowing developers to build mobile apps that feel natural and perform well on devices. By leveraging React, a popular JavaScript library for building user interfaces, React Native provides a familiar development environment for web developers transitioning to mobile app development. The framework enables direct access to native device APIs and performance optimizations, resulting in high-quality, performant mobile applications.

Example (React Native):

```
import React from "react";
import { View, Text, StyleSheet } from "react-native";

export default function App() {
  return (
    <View style={styles.container}>
      <Text style={styles.text}>Hello, React Native!</Text>
    </View>
  );
}

const styles = StyleSheet.create({
  container: {
    flex: 1,
    justifyContent: "center",
    alignItems: "center",
  },
  text: {
    fontSize: 20,
  },
});
```

In this example, a simple "Hello, React Native!" app is created using React Native. It utilizes native UI components such as View and Text and applies basic styles via the StyleSheet API. This allows the app to render smoothly on mobile devices with a responsive design that adapts to different screen sizes.

Ionic

Ionic, on the other hand, takes a different approach by leveraging web technologies HTML, CSS, and JavaScript to build mobile apps. This cross-platform framework allows developers to maintain a single codebase, reducing development time and ensuring consistency across platforms. Ionic uses Apache Cordova underneath to bridge the gap between web technologies and native mobile app capabilities, enabling access to native device features like camera, GPS, and storage.

Example (Ionic):

```
<!DOCTYPE html>
<html>
<head>
  <title>Ionic App</title>
  <script src="https://unpkg.com/@ionic/core@latest/dist/ionic.js"></script>
</head>
<body>
  <ion-app>
    <ion-header>
      <ion-toolbar>
        <ion-title>Welcome to Ionic</ion-title>
      </ion-toolbar>
    </ion-header>

    <ion-content>
      <ion-button>Click Me!</ion-button>
    </ion-content>
  </ion-app>
</body>
</html>
```

CHAPTER 5   THE ROLE OF JAVASCRIPT IN MODERN WEB DEVELOPMENT

In this Ionic example, a basic mobile app is built using HTML and JavaScript. The `ion-button` element from the Ionic framework provides a standard button UI component that behaves consistently across platforms. By focusing on user interface components and leveraging a shared codebase, Ionic simplifies the development process and allows developers to create feature-rich mobile applications quickly.

Use Cases:

- **React Native**: Ideal for building high-performance, visually rich mobile applications, such as ecommerce apps, social media platforms, and gaming apps. Its ability to integrate smoothly with native device APIs ensures a seamless user experience across different mobile platforms.

- **Ionic**: Suited for projects that require rapid prototyping, simple app interfaces, and minimal native integrations. It's often used for apps like dashboards, forms, and other business-centric applications that benefit from responsive design and cross-platform compatibility.

Benefits:

- **Cost-Effective Development**: By allowing developers to write a single codebase, both React Native and Ionic reduce the time and resources required to build and maintain mobile apps for multiple platforms.

- **Access to Native Features**: Both frameworks provide ways to interact with native device capabilities, such as cameras, GPS, and storage, ensuring that apps have the functionality users expect from native applications.

- **Community and Support**: Both React Native and Ionic have active communities that contribute to libraries, plugins, and extensions, making it easier for developers to find solutions to common problems and stay updated with the latest developments.

JavaScript frameworks like React Native and Ionic have empowered developers to create high-quality mobile applications that deliver consistent user experiences across multiple platforms. These frameworks offer flexibility, performance, and a straightforward path for developers to build apps that meet the demands of modern mobile users.

The JavaScript Ecosystem

JavaScript's ecosystem is vast, dynamic, and constantly evolving, comprising tools, libraries, and frameworks that streamline development and enhance productivity. This interconnected network of resources is integral to building modern web applications and managing large-scale projects efficiently.

Package Management

The cornerstone of JavaScript's ecosystem is **npm** (Node Package Manager), which hosts millions of reusable packages that can be installed and used to accelerate development. Whether you need a utility library, a testing framework, or an entire application framework, npm provides easy access to a vast collection of pre-built solutions. This helps developers avoid reinventing the wheel and speeds up development cycles.

Example (Using npm):

```
npm install lodash
```

This command fetches and installs the latest version of lodash along with its dependencies. The lodash library provides a variety of utility functions that simplify tasks like array manipulation, object iteration, and data transformation making it a staple in many JavaScript projects.

Build Tools

Build tools like Webpack and Vite are essential for managing assets and optimizing code for production. They take care of bundling JavaScript, CSS, HTML, and other assets into efficient packages that can be served to users. These tools can also transpile code, optimize images, and split bundles for faster loading times.

Example (Using Webpack):

```
const path = require("path");

module.exports = {
  entry: "./src/index.js",
  output: {
    filename: "bundle.js",
    path: path.resolve(__dirname, "dist"),
  },
  module: {
    rules: [
      {
        test: /\.js$/,
        exclude: /node_modules/,
        use: ["babel-loader"],
      },
    ],
  },
};
```

In this Webpack configuration, the `entry` property specifies the main file from which the bundling process starts. The `output` property defines where the bundled file will be placed after Webpack processes it. The `module.rules` section tells Webpack how to handle different file types, in this case, transpiling JavaScript files using `babel-loader` to ensure compatibility across browsers.

Linting and Formatting

To maintain clean, readable, and error-free code, **linting** and **formatting** tools like `ESLint` and `Prettier` are indispensable. `ESLint` scans your code for potential errors, stylistic issues, and bugs, providing feedback to developers in the form of warnings or errors. `Prettier` on the other hand, enforces a consistent code style, automatically formatting the code according to predefined rules.

Example (Using ESLint):

```
module.exports = {
  env: { browser: true, es2021: true },
  extends: "eslint:recommended",
  rules: {
    "no-unused-vars": "warn",
    "eqeqeq": "error", // Enforces the use of strict
    equality (===)
    "semi": ["error", "always"], // Requires semicolons at the
    end of statements
  },
};
```

In this configuration, `ESLint` is set up to enforce best practices such as requiring strict equality checks and semicolons. It provides a standardized approach to code quality, which is especially important in large teams or projects with multiple contributors.

Why These Tools Matter:

- **Package Management**: npm simplifies the management of dependencies, ensuring that each package has the correct version compatibility. This reduces conflicts and simplifies dependency resolution.

- **Build Tools**: They improve performance by reducing the size of the code delivered to users and ensuring faster load times. This is crucial for modern web applications that demand quick responsiveness and minimal latency.

- **Linting and Formatting**: These tools help maintain consistent coding standards across a team, which improves code readability and reduces bugs. They also make code reviews more effective by highlighting issues early in the development process.

JavaScript's ecosystem is rich with tools that support every stage of the development lifecycle from managing dependencies and optimizing performance to maintaining code quality and consistency. By integrating these tools, developers can focus more on writing code and less on managing the surrounding logistics, leading to more efficient and maintainable projects.

Challenges in Modern Web Development

Despite JavaScript's versatility and widespread use, it presents several challenges that developers must address to ensure smooth, secure, and performant applications.

Browser Compatibility

JavaScript applications must work across a wide range of browsers each with its own rendering engine and behavior. This can be challenging because not all browsers support the latest JavaScript features in the same way or at the same time. Developers often need to test their applications in multiple browsers and provide fallbacks or polyfills for features that aren't universally supported.

For instance, newer JavaScript syntax such as **async/await** is not fully supported in older browsers like Internet Explorer 11. To make such code work universally, developers might use Babel, a JavaScript compiler that transforms ES6+ code into ES5, ensuring compatibility across all browsers.

Performance Issues

Large JavaScript files can significantly slow down page load times, which is detrimental to user experience. Performance optimization techniques like **tree-shaking** and **code splitting** are crucial in mitigating this. **Tree-shaking** removes unused code during the build process, reducing the file size. **Code splitting** breaks down the JavaScript code into smaller, more manageable chunks that are only loaded when needed, speeding up the loading time for critical parts of the application.

Example (Code Splitting with Webpack):

```
import('./module1').then(module => {
  // Do something with the module
});
```

In this example, `import()` dynamically loads `module1` only when it is required, ensuring that unnecessary code isn't loaded up front, which helps in keeping the initial load time fast.

Security Risks

JavaScript is often a target for security threats, especially when used on the client side. Common security risks include **Cross-Site Scripting (XSS)** attacks, where malicious scripts are injected into web pages viewed by other users. This can happen if user inputs aren't properly sanitized before being added to the DOM.

A common vulnerability is when user-supplied data is rendered directly into a web page without escaping special characters. This can lead to XSS attacks. To mitigate this, developers should use **Content Security Policy (CSP)** headers, input sanitization, and **escaping** to prevent script injection attacks.

Example:

```javascript
function escapeHtml(unsafe) {
  return unsafe
    .replace(/&/g, "&")
    .replace(/</g, "&lt;")
    .replace(/>/g, "&gt;")
    .replace(/"/g, "&quot;");
}
let userInput = "<script>alert('XSS Attack!');</script>";
let safeInput = escapeHtml(userInput);
```

In this example, escapeHtml is a function used to sanitize user input, preventing it from being executed as JavaScript code and thus protecting against XSS attacks.

These challenges underscore the importance of adopting best practices, using appropriate tools, and maintaining up-to-date knowledge of JavaScript standards and browser capabilities. By addressing these issues, developers can build secure, efficient, and user-friendly web applications.

The Future of JavaScript

JavaScript is rapidly evolving to meet the demands of modern web applications and to integrate with emerging technologies.

Zoneless Frameworks

Zoneless frameworks like **Angular's Signals** represent a significant evolution in JavaScript performance. Traditional frameworks manage change detection using a **zone** system, which can be costly in terms of performance. By removing zones, these frameworks like Angular's Signals aim to deliver faster updates and more efficient change detection. This results in smoother user experiences, especially in applications with complex state management and frequent UI updates.

In an Angular application using Signals, updates to the UI can be handled without the performance overhead associated with traditional Angular zones. This makes it ideal for performance-critical applications where speed is crucial, such as real-time dashboards or collaborative tools.

WebAssembly (Wasm)

WebAssembly (Wasm) allows JavaScript to offload performance-critical tasks to low-level, compiled languages like C or Rust. This integration enables JavaScript to handle heavy computations more efficiently, which is crucial for applications requiring fast rendering or real-time data processing, such as 3D graphics or complex simulations.

For instance, a game that requires real-time physics calculations or a data visualization tool handling large datasets can leverage WebAssembly to improve performance. JavaScript can orchestrate the high-level application logic, while Wasm handles the heavy computational tasks, resulting in a seamless and responsive user experience.

Complementing WebAssembly with Service Workers

Service Workers can further optimize the performance of applications using WebAssembly by enabling offline support and caching of Wasm modules. For example, a WebAssembly module for processing 3D graphics can be cached using a Service Worker, ensuring that the module is readily available even when the user is offline. This combination allows for both efficient computation and a smooth, uninterrupted experience, even in low or no network conditions.

AI and ML Integration

JavaScript is increasingly being used in **AI and ML** applications through libraries like **TensorFlow.js**. This enables developers to run machine learning models directly in the browser, bringing AI capabilities to the front end. This not only improves performance by avoiding server latencies but also allows for more interactive and personalized user experiences.

For example, TensorFlow.js can be used for real-time image classification. Imagine a photo editing app where the user uploads a picture, and the app uses TensorFlow.js to classify the objects in the image, such as detecting faces or identifying items like trees or cars. As the user interacts with the image, the model can quickly update, providing real-time feedback on the classification. Here's a simplified example of how TensorFlow.js might be used for image classification in the browser:

```
// Import TensorFlow.js

import * tf from '@tensorflow/tfjs';

// Load a pre-trained model
const model = await tf.loadLayersModel('https://example.com/model.json');

// Select an image from the DOM
```

```
const img = document.getElementById('image');

// Preprocess the image and make predictions
const tensor = tf.browser.fromPixels(img).
resizeNearestNeighbor([224, 224]).toFloat().expandDims();
const prediction = await model.predict(tensor);

// Display the prediction result
prediction.array().then(result => {
  console.log(result); // Log the classification result
});
```

This tight integration of AI and JavaScript opens up new possibilities for creativity and user engagement. By performing computations directly in the browser, TensorFlow.js allows developers to create AI-driven experiences that are both interactive and responsive.

These advancements position JavaScript as a central technology not only for traditional web development but also as a key player in emerging fields like AI, ML, and real-time applications. As JavaScript continues to evolve, it will increasingly serve as a bridge between high-level web applications and low-level performance optimization, ensuring developers can deliver powerful and responsive experiences to users.

Summary

JavaScript has evolved significantly since its inception, continuously adapting to meet the needs of modern web development. From the foundational features of ECMAScript 3 to the transformative updates in ES6, ES7, and beyond, JavaScript has embraced new paradigms like asynchronous programming (with async/await), modular code (using ES modules), and the integration of WebAssembly for performance-critical tasks. Frameworks and libraries like React, Angular, and Node.js have extended JavaScript's capabilities, enabling developers to build dynamic and scalable applications across both front-end and back-end environments. Emerging trends like zoneless frameworks, WebAssembly, and AI/ML integration are pushing JavaScript's boundaries, making it a central technology not only for traditional web applications but also for real-time and performance-critical applications. This evolution ensures JavaScript remains at the forefront of innovation, shaping the future of web and mobile development.

CHAPTER 6

The Role of Transpilers and Polyfills

Objective

As JavaScript evolves through new ECMAScript standards, developers often face the challenge of ensuring their code runs seamlessly across various browsers and environments. Not all browsers immediately support the latest JavaScript features, creating a gap between cutting-edge syntax and practical compatibility. This is where **transpilers** and **polyfills** come into play, enabling developers to leverage modern JavaScript features while maintaining compatibility with older platforms.

What Are Transpilers?

A **transpiler** (short for "source-to-source compiler") converts code written in one version of JavaScript (or a different language altogether) into an older version of JavaScript that is widely supported by browsers.

CHAPTER 6   THE ROLE OF TRANSPILERS AND POLYFILLS

- **How Transpilers Work**:
  - Developers write code using modern JavaScript features (e.g., ES6+).
  - The transpiler rewrites this code into equivalent, older syntax (e.g., ES5).
  - The transformed code can run in environments that do not support the original features.
- **Popular Transpilers**:
  - **Babel**: Converts modern JavaScript into ES5, widely used in modern web projects. Babel uses **plugins** and **presets** (like @babel/preset-env) to determine which transformations are applied based on target environments. This allows developers to tailor the transpilation process according to the specific JavaScript features supported by the environments they want to support.
  - **TypeScript Compiler**: Converts TypeScript (a superset of JavaScript) into plain JavaScript.

Benefits of Transpilers:

- **Future-Proofing**: Developers can use the latest features without waiting for browser adoption.
- **Consistency**: Ensures that all users, regardless of browser, experience the same functionality.

CHAPTER 6   THE ROLE OF TRANSPILERS AND POLYFILLS

Transpiler vs. Compiler

While both **transpilers** and **compilers** serve the purpose of converting code from one form to another, they differ in the following ways:

- **Transpiler**: Converts source code from one version of a language to another version of the same language. It typically focuses on source-to-source transformation (e.g., converting modern JavaScript to older JavaScript).

Example: Babel transforms ES6+ code into ES5 JavaScript, enabling compatibility with older browsers.

- **Compiler**: Converts source code written in one programming language into a completely different language, often to a lower-level language like machine code or bytecode. A compiler produces an executable file that can be run by the operating system or virtual machine.

Example: A C compiler converts C code into machine code that runs on a specific processor.

The key distinction is that a **transpiler** deals with code in the same language (but at a different level of abstraction), while a **compiler** translates between entirely different languages or machine code.

Example Arrow Functions

Suppose you write this ES6 arrow function:

```
const greet = (name) => `Hello, ${name}!`;
```

A transpiler like Babel would convert it into equivalent ES5 code.

Example:

```
var greet = function(name) {
  return "Hello, " + name + "!";
};
```

Let's dive into another interesting example of how a transpiler works, focusing on **JavaScript class syntax**, which was introduced in ECMAScript 6 (ES6), but was not natively supported in older browsers. This example will show how a transpiler like Babel can transform ES6 class syntax into an older, function-based prototype syntax for backward compatibility.

Transpiler Example: ES6 Classes to ES5

The ES6 Class Syntax

In ES6, JavaScript introduced classes as a more elegant way to create object-oriented code. Here's an example of how a class might look in ES6:

```
class Person {
    constructor(name, age) {
        this.name = name;
        this.age = age;
    }

    greet() {
        console.log(`Hello, my name is ${this.name} and I am
        ${this.age} years old.`);
    }
}

// Instantiate the class
const person1 = new Person("John", 30);
person1.greet();
// Output: Hello, my name is John and I am 30 years old.
```

CHAPTER 6   THE ROLE OF TRANSPILERS AND POLYFILLS

Transpiling the Class Syntax

Older environments, like Internet Explorer, do not support ES6 class syntax. A transpiler like **Babel** can convert this ES6 class-based code into ES5-compatible code that uses constructor functions and prototype methods.

Here's how Babel might transpile the above ES6 code:

```
// Transpiled ES5 version of the class-based code
function Person(name, age) {
    this.name = name;
    this.age = age;
}

Person.prototype.greet = function() {
    console.log("Hello, my name is " + this.name + " and I am "
    + this.age + " years old.");
};

// Instantiate the "class"
var person1 = new Person("John", 30);
person1.greet();
// Output: Hello, my name is John and I am 30 years old.
```

How the Transpiler Works:

1. **Class to Function**:
   - The class keyword is replaced with a function declaration. This is how classes work in ES5 via functions and new.

2. **Constructor**:
   - The constructor method inside the class is replaced with the regular function body.

117

3. **Methods to Prototype**:
   - The methods defined inside the class (like greet) are moved to the prototype of the constructor function to simulate the behavior of classes.

4. **New Instance**:
   - The instantiation process (new Person(...)) remains the same, but the underlying mechanism is now using the function constructor rather than the class syntax.

Why This Is Important:

- **Modern Syntax**: Developers can write cleaner, more readable code using the class syntax.
- **Backward Compatibility**: Transpilers allow developers to use modern JavaScript features without breaking compatibility with older browsers.
- **Easier Maintenance**: Transpilers help maintain a consistent developer experience across various environments.

Real-World Usage of Transpilers with Classes

In many modern JavaScript applications, classes are used extensively for defining components, especially in frameworks like **React** and **Angular**. Since ES6 class syntax is not supported in older browsers (like Internet Explorer), using a transpiler like **Babel** ensures that your app can still run in those environments.

For instance, React's component syntax has evolved to use ES6 classes (and later functional components with hooks), but if you wanted to support legacy browsers, you would need to transpile this modern code into something older browsers can understand.

CHAPTER 6   THE ROLE OF TRANSPILERS AND POLYFILLS

Example React Component Transpiled for ES5

If you're writing a React component in ES6, it might look like this:

```
// ES6 Class Component
class MyComponent extends React.Component {
    constructor(props) {
        super(props);
        this.state = { count: 0 };
    }

    increment = () => {
        this.setState({ count: this.state.count + 1 });
    }

    render() {
        return (
            <div>
                <p>Count: {this.state.count}</p>
                <button onClick={this.increment}>Increment
                </button>
            </div>
        );
    }
}
```

But Babel would transpile this into an ES5-compatible version that might look like this:

```
// Transpiled ES5 Component (using React.createClass or
function component)
var MyComponent = React.createClass({
    getInitialState: function() {
        return { count: 0 };
    },
```

119

```
        increment: function() {
            this.setState({ count: this.state.count + 1 });
        },
        render: function() {
            return (
                React.createElement("div", null,
                    React.createElement("p", null, "Count: ",
                    this.state.count),
                    React.createElement("button", { onClick:
                    this.increment }, "Increment")
                )
            );
        }
    });
```

This ES5 version uses `React.createClass` and `React.createElement` to handle components in a way that's compatible with older browsers.

Conclusion

Transpilers like Babel play a crucial role in modern web development. They allow developers to write code using modern JavaScript features such as classes while ensuring that the code will run in older environments. This not only makes the development process more efficient but also ensures that your application can reach a wider audience, including users with older browsers.

Pollyfills

A **polyfill** is a piece of code that replicates modern JavaScript functionality in environments that do not natively support it. Unlike transpilers, which rewrite syntax, polyfills provide implementations of new APIs.

CHAPTER 6   THE ROLE OF TRANSPILERS AND POLYFILLS

How the Polyfill Works

Polyfills do not convert JavaScript syntax like transpilers; instead, they mimic missing APIs. For example, if a browser doesn't support the filter() method on arrays, a polyfill can be used to implement it, allowing older browsers to use this method as if they had native support.

1. **Validation**:
   - Ensures this is not null or undefined.
   - Confirms that the callback is a function.
2. **Core Logic**:
   - Iterates over the array and applies the callback function to each element.
   - If the callback returns true, the element is pushed to the result array.
3. **Compatibility**:
   - Mimics native behavior to ensure consistent functionality.

Example:

```
if (!Array.prototype.includes) {
    Array.prototype.includes = function(value) {
        return this.indexOf(value) !== -1;
    };
}
```

1. **Promises**: ES6 introduced Promises for asynchronous programming. Before native support, libraries like Bluebird acted as polyfills.

Advantages of Polyfills:

- **Backward Compatibility**: Bridges the gap between new APIs and old browsers
- **Incremental Upgrades**: Allows developers to adopt modern features without waiting for users to upgrade browsers

Full Example – Polyfill for Array.prototype.filter:

The Array.prototype.filter method, introduced in ECMAScript 5, allows developers to create a new array containing only the elements that pass a given test. Older environments without support for this method can implement it via a polyfill:

```
if (!Array.prototype.filter) {
    Array.prototype.filter = function(callback, thisArg) {
        if (this == null) {
            throw new TypeError("Array.prototype.filter called
            on null or undefined");
        }
        if (typeof callback !== "function") {
            throw new TypeError(callback + " is not a
            function");
        }
        var result = [];
        var array = Object(this); // Convert `this` to
        an object
        var length = array.length >>> 0; // Ensure it's a
        valid length
```

CHAPTER 6   THE ROLE OF TRANSPILERS AND POLYFILLS

```
        for (var i = 0; i < length; i++) {
            if (i in array) {
                var element = array[i];
                if (callback.call(thisArg, element, i, array)) {
                    result.push(element);
                }
            }
        }
        return result;
    };
}
```

Using the Polyfill:

Once the polyfill is added, developers can use `filter` even in environments where it is not natively supported:

```
var numbers = [1, 2, 3, 4, 5];
// Use the filter method to find numbers greater than 3
var filteredNumbers = numbers.filter(function(number) {
    return number > 3;
});
console.log(filteredNumbers); // Output: [4, 5]
```

Common Use Cases for Polyfills:

1. **Array Methods**:

    - Methods like `filter`, `map`, and `reduce` are frequently polyfilled for older browsers.

2. **Promises**:

    - ES6 Promises are often polyfilled using libraries like Bluebird.

3. **Fetch API**:

   - Libraries such as whatwg-fetch provide a polyfill for modern HTTP requests.

Advantages of Polyfills:

- **Backward Compatibility**: Bridges the gap between new APIs and old browsers
- **Incremental Upgrades**: Allows developers to adopt modern features without waiting for users to upgrade browsers

Transpilers vs. Polyfills

While both tools aim to improve compatibility, their approaches differ fundamentally:

Feature	Transpilers	Polyfills
Purpose	Convert modern JavaScript into an older syntax.	Replicate new APIs or features in older environments.
Main use	Syntax transformations (e.g., converting ES6 to ES5).	Implement missing features, like fetch() or Promise.
Scope	Affects the entire codebase, transforming syntax.	Affects specific missing APIs or functions.
Example	Arrow functions converted to function.	Adding fetch for old browsers.
Usage	Required during development.	Added as runtime scripts.
Tools	Babel, TypeScript compiler.	Pollyfill.io, custom polyfills.
Environment impact	Allows new syntax in environments that don't support it.	Adds missing functionality for specific features (e.g., Promise, fetch).

CHAPTER 6 THE ROLE OF TRANSPILERS AND POLYFILLS

When to Use Transpilers vs. Polyfills

- **Transpilers**: Use a transpiler when you want to leverage modern JavaScript syntax (like ES6+) in environments that don't support it. This is especially useful when you're using features like **arrow functions**, **template literals**, or **let/const** declarations that older environments don't understand. Transpilers rewrite the syntax to something older JavaScript engines can execute, allowing your code to work across different environments.

- **When to Use**:

    - You're using newer language features like ES6/ES7 syntax.

    - You need compatibility with older browsers (e.g., Internet Explorer 11).

    - You want to ensure your code is future-proof and can take advantage of newer JavaScript features.

- **Polyfills**: Use polyfills when you need to add missing functionality for specific APIs or features that are not available in older environments. Polyfills mimic the behavior of newer web APIs (like Promise, fetch, Array.prototype.includes) in environments that don't natively support them. Unlike transpilers, polyfills don't change syntax; they add functionality.

When to Use:

- You're using new APIs that are not supported by certain browsers (like fetch or Promise).
- You want to ensure a specific feature is available in older browsers without rewriting entire syntax.
- You're dealing with missing functionality in environments that support the syntax but lack specific API support.

Why Use Transpilers and Polyfills Together?

Modern development often requires both tools:

- Transpilers handle **syntax** changes (e.g., arrow functions, classes).
- Polyfills handle **runtime** features (e.g., fetch, Map).

By combining these tools, developers ensure

- They can write modern, maintainable code.
- Users on older browsers experience the same functionality.

Challenges and Best Practices

While transpilers and polyfills offer significant benefits, they come with considerations:

1. **Performance**:
    - Transpiled code may be less efficient than native implementations.

- Overuse of polyfills can increase script size and execution time.

2. **Browser Targets**:

    - Tools like Babel allow developers to specify "browser targets," ensuring the code is only transpiled as much as necessary.

    Example:

    ```
    // Example Babel configuration
    {
      "presets": [
        ["@babel/preset-env", { "targets": "> 0.25%,
        not dead" }]
      ]
    }
    ```

3. **Maintenance**:

    - Developers need to update polyfills and transpiler configurations as standards evolve.

Best Practices

- Use **Babel preset-env** to target specific browsers dynamically.
- Include only essential polyfills to minimize script bloat.
- Test thoroughly in different environments to ensure functionality.

Future of Transpilers and Polyfills

With the increasing adoption of modern browsers, the reliance on transpilers and polyfills is gradually diminishing. However, these tools remain indispensable for

- Supporting legacy systems
- Enabling teams to adopt emerging JavaScript features confidently

Summary

Transpilers and polyfills empower developers to write cutting-edge JavaScript while ensuring backward compatibility. Transpilers like Babel rewrite modern syntax into older formats, while polyfills implement missing APIs for runtime compatibility. Together, these tools bridge the gap between innovation and practicality, enabling developers to craft experiences accessible to a broad user base. By adopting best practices and keeping an eye on evolving standards, developers can future-proof their applications and deliver robust, maintainable solutions.

CHAPTER 7

Debugging JavaScript in the Browser

Objective

Debugging is an essential skill in programming, and JavaScript is no exception. This chapter will explore various debugging techniques in JavaScript, focusing on browser-based debugging tools. We will look at how to use the browser's developer tools (DevTools) for debugging, inspect variables, trace errors, and use various debugging methods to streamline development. We will also touch on modern debugging practices that help you write cleaner and more efficient code. By the end of this chapter, you should feel confident debugging JavaScript in the browser and using these tools to solve common issues.

Introduction to Browser Developer Tools (DevTools)

Most modern web browsers, including **Google Chrome**, **Mozilla Firefox**, **Microsoft Edge**, and **Safari**, come with built-in developer tools. These tools allow you to inspect HTML, CSS, and JavaScript in real time, set breakpoints, track network requests, and analyze performance.

- **Opening DevTools:**

  - In **Google Chrome**: Press `Ctrl + Shift + I` (Windows/Linux) or `Cmd + Option + I` (Mac), or right-click a web page and select **Inspect**.

  - In **Mozilla Firefox**: Press `F12` or `Ctrl + Shift + I`, or right-click and choose **Inspect**.

  - In **Microsoft Edge**: Press `F12` or `Ctrl + Shift + I`.

  - In **Safari**: First, enable the Develop menu in Safari's Preferences (`Preferences ➤ Advanced ➤ Show Develop menu in menu bar`). Then press `Cmd + Option + I` or go to **Develop ➤ Show Web Inspector**.

Key Features of DevTools

- **Elements Panel**: Inspect and edit the HTML and CSS of your page.

- **Console Panel**: Log information, errors, and warnings. Run JavaScript code directly.

- **Sources Panel**: View and debug your JavaScript files. Set breakpoints and step through your code.

- **Network Panel**: Monitor network activity, including HTTP requests and responses.

- **Performance Panel**: Analyze your website's performance, CPU usage, and memory usage.

- **Application Panel**: Inspect data stored on the client side, such as cookies, localStorage, and indexedDB.

Console Logging: The Most Basic Debugging Tool

One of the simplest ways to debug JavaScript is by using the `console.log()` method. It allows you to print out values, messages, or objects to the browser's console for real-time inspection.

```
function add(a, b) {
    console.log("Adding", a, b);  // Logs the values of a and b
    return a + b;
}

console.log(add(3, 5));  // Logs the result of the addition
```

Best Practices for `console.log`

- Use `console.log()` to track the flow of your program.
- Log important variables, parameters, or intermediate results to confirm their values.
- For debugging complex objects, consider using `console.table()` to print them in a table format.

  ```
  const students = [
      { name: "John", grade: "A" },
      { name: "Jane", grade: "B" },
      { name: "Jack", grade: "C" }
  ];

  console.table(students);  // Displays the array in a
                                 table format
  ```

131

Other Useful Console Methods

- **console.error()**: Used to log errors
- **console.warn()**: Used to log warnings
- **console.info()**: Used for informational messages
- **console.assert()**: Logs an error message if the condition is false

Setting Breakpoints in the Sources Panel

Breakpoints are a fundamental feature of browser developer tools. They allow you to pause JavaScript execution at a specific line of code and inspect the current state of your program (variables, call stack, etc.).

How to Set Breakpoints

1. Open the **Sources panel** in DevTools.
2. Locate the JavaScript file you want to debug (on the left panel).
3. Click the line number where you want to pause the code.

Once you've set a breakpoint, the execution of your code will stop at that line, allowing you to inspect the current state of variables, step through code line by line, and understand where things are going wrong.

Types of Breakpoints

- **Line Breakpoints**: Pauses at a specific line in the code

- **Conditional Breakpoints**: Pauses only if a specific condition is met (right-click the line number and set a condition)

- **XHR/Fetch Breakpoints**: Pauses when an XMLHttpRequest or fetch request is made

- **DOM Breakpoints**: Pauses when a DOM element is modified

- **Event Listener Breakpoints**: Pauses when a specific event, like a `click` or `keydown`, is triggered

Stepping Through Code

When your code is paused at a breakpoint, you can step through it in various ways:

- **Step Over**: Executes the current line of code, but if it contains a function call, it doesn't step into that function. Use F10 (in Chrome).

- **Step Into**: If the current line contains a function call, stepping into it will take you inside the function. Use F11 (in Chrome).

- **Step Out**: Completes the current function execution and moves back to the caller. Use Shift + F11 (in Chrome).

- **Resume**: Resumes the execution of the code until the next breakpoint is hit. Use F8 (in Chrome).

Example: Setting Breakpoints in Action

Now that you know how to set breakpoints, let's go through a practical example where you can follow the process step by step. This will help you understand how to inspect variables and control the flow of your program using breakpoints.

```
// Let's simulate a simple scenario where we will use
breakpoints

// Step 1: Initialize variables
let user = { name: "Alice", age: 30 };

// Step 2: Create a function to modify user information
function updateUserInfo(user, newName, newAge) {
  // Set a breakpoint here to inspect the values of user,
  newName, and newAge
  user.name = newName; // Update name
  user.age = newAge;   // Update age
  console.log("Updated User:", user); // Log the updated
                                         user info
}

// Step 3: Call the function to update user information
updateUserInfo(user, "Bob", 25);

// Step 4: Let's simulate some calculations with conditions
function calculateDiscount(price) {
  // Set a breakpoint here to inspect price before calculation
  let discount = 0;
  if (price > 100) {
    discount = price * 0.2; // Apply a 20% discount for prices
    greater than 100
  }
```

```
    console.log("Discount:", discount); // Log the calculated
                                        discount
    return price - discount; // Return the final price after
                             discount
}

// Step 5: Call the calculateDiscount function with a price
let finalPrice = calculateDiscount(120);

// Step 6: Call the calculateDiscount function with a
different price
finalPrice = calculateDiscount(80);

// Step 7: Finish by logging the final price
console.log("Final Price after Discount:", finalPrice);
```

Guide for Setting Breakpoints in This Code

1. **Open DevTools and Locate the Code**
   Open your browser's developer tools by right-clicking and selecting **Inspect** or pressing Ctrl + Shift + I (or Cmd + Option + I on macOS). Go to the **Sources** tab where you'll see the JavaScript files.

2. **Set Breakpoint 1**
   In the code above, set a breakpoint on the line inside the updateUserInfo function where user.name = newName; is written. This will allow you to inspect the user, newName, and newAge variables before updating them.

3. **Run the Code**
   Reload the page or run the script, and the execution will pause at the line with the breakpoint you set. Now you can inspect the values of the variables.

4. **Set Breakpoint 2**
   Set another breakpoint inside the calculateDiscount function at let discount = 0;. This will allow you to inspect the price variable before any logic is applied.

5. **Step Through the Code**
   Once the breakpoint is hit, you can step through the code using the **Step Over**, **Step Into**, or **Step Out** buttons in DevTools. This will allow you to watch the execution flow and inspect how the variables change.

6. **Remove Breakpoints**
   After inspecting the necessary variables and the code execution, you can remove the breakpoints by clicking the blue markers next to the line numbers.

Using the Call Stack to Trace Execution

The **call stack** is a critical tool in debugging. It displays the sequence of function calls that led to the current point of execution, allowing you to trace the execution flow backward. When execution is paused (e.g., at a breakpoint), the call stack shows all active function calls in a **last-in, first-out (LIFO)** order.

You can click any function in the call stack to view the exact line of code where it was called.

This is particularly useful for debugging issues related to **nested function calls**, **recursion**, and **asynchronous operations** (like callbacks and promises).

Example: Understanding the Call Stack in Action

Consider the following JavaScript code with nested function calls:

```
function firstFunction() {
  console.log("Entering firstFunction");
  secondFunction();
  console.log("Exiting firstFunction");
}

function secondFunction() {
  console.log("Entering secondFunction");
  thirdFunction();
  console.log("Exiting secondFunction");
}

function thirdFunction() {
  console.log("Entering thirdFunction");
  debugger; // Pause execution here to inspect the call stack
  console.log("Exiting thirdFunction");
}

// Start execution
firstFunction();
```

Step-by-Step Debugging Guide

1. **Open DevTools and Navigate to the Sources Panel**
   Open developer tools (F12 or Ctrl + Shift + I on Windows, Cmd + Option + I on macOS), and then go to the **Sources** tab.

2. **Set a Breakpoint or Use debugger**

    a. You can set a breakpoint inside thirdFunction() at console.log("Entering thirdFunction");.

    b. Alternatively, the debugger; statement in the code will automatically pause execution.

3. **Inspect the Call Stack**

    a. When execution pauses, look at the **Call Stack** section in DevTools.

    b. You will see a stack like this:

    ```
    thirdFunction (script.js:14)
    secondFunction (script.js:9)
    firstFunction (script.js:4)
    (anonymous) (script.js:18)
    ```

    c. This shows that thirdFunction() was called by secondFunction(), which was called by firstFunction(), which was executed in the global context.

4. **Click Each Function in the Call Stack**

    a. Clicking a function in the **Call Stack** panel highlights the line where it was called.

    b. This helps trace the flow of execution backward.

5. **Resume Execution**

    a. Step through the code using **Step Over (F10)** or **Step Into (F11)** to watch how execution flows as functions return.

CHAPTER 7   DEBUGGING JAVASCRIPT IN THE BROWSER

Call Stack Execution Flow Diagram

Here's a visualization of how the call stack grows and shrinks as functions execute:

```
Step 1: Call firstFunction()
  [ firstFunction() ]   <-- Call Stack

Step 2: Call secondFunction()
  [ secondFunction() ]
  [ firstFunction() ]

Step 3: Call thirdFunction()
  [ thirdFunction() ]
  [ secondFunction() ]
  [ firstFunction() ]   <-- Execution pauses here

Step 4: thirdFunction() completes
  [ secondFunction() ]
  [ firstFunction() ]

Step 5: secondFunction() completes
  [ firstFunction() ]

Step 6: firstFunction() completes
  [ ]   <-- Stack is empty
```

Call Stack

		thirdFunction()			
	secondFunction()	secondFunction()	secondFunction()		
firstFunction()	firstFunction()	firstFunction()	firstFunction()	firstFunction()	firstFunction()
1	2	3	4	5	6

Why This Is Useful

- Helps track function execution order
- Identifies unintended function calls
- Debugs infinite recursion or deeply nested calls
- Useful for understanding event loop behavior in asynchronous code

Debugging Asynchronous JavaScript

Asynchronous JavaScript (callbacks, promises, async/await) can be tricky to debug, as it doesn't run in the same synchronous manner as regular JavaScript. Here are some tips to debug async code effectively.

Using `console.log()` with Asynchronous Code

When working with promises or async functions, `console.log()` can help track the flow.

Example:

```
function fetchData() {
    console.log('Fetching data...');
    fetch('https://api.example.com/data')
        .then(response => response.json())
        .then(data => {
            console.log('Data received:', data);
        })
```

```
        .catch(error => {
            console.error('Error fetching data:', error);
        });
}
fetchData();
```

Using Breakpoints with Asynchronous Code

Set breakpoints inside promise handlers, `async/await` functions, or callback functions to inspect the code's state at these points.

- In **async functions**, the breakpoint will stop at the `await` keyword, allowing you to inspect the promise before it resolves.

- Use **event listener breakpoints** to pause execution when a particular event (like a `click` or `load`) triggers the asynchronous code.

Debugging with debugger Statement

In addition to breakpoints, you can programmatically pause the execution of your code using the debugger statement:

```
function add(a, b) {
    debugger;  // Code execution will pause here if DevTools
               are open
    return a + b;
}
add(2, 3);
```

The debugger statement acts as an inline breakpoint. When DevTools are open, it will stop the execution at that point, allowing you to inspect the current state of variables and the call stack.

Performance and Memory Debugging

Sometimes, debugging involves identifying performance issues, memory leaks, or bottlenecks. Browser DevTools offer several tools for this:

- **Performance Panel**: Record your app's runtime performance and inspect issues like **JavaScript execution time** and **repaints**.
- **Memory Panel**: Track memory usage, identify memory leaks, and visualize the allocation of memory for objects in your app.
- **Lighthouse**: Run a performance audit to get suggestions on improving performance, accessibility, and SEO.

Debugging Tools in Popular Frameworks

Frameworks like **React** and **Angular** also have their own debugging tools that integrate with the browser's DevTools.

- **React Developer Tools**: A Chrome extension that adds React-specific debugging features. You can inspect the component hierarchy and view component state and props.

- **Redux DevTools**: For debugging applications using Redux. It allows you to inspect actions, state changes, and even time travel debugging.

- **Angular DevTools**: Provides insights into Angular's change detection, component tree, and performance issues.

Summary

In this chapter, we learned how to leverage browser developer tools (DevTools) to debug JavaScript code effectively. We explored how to set breakpoints, use the console for logging, step through code, and trace asynchronous JavaScript with breakpoints and the debugger statement. We also covered tools for performance and memory debugging. Mastering these tools is essential for identifying and fixing bugs quickly, improving code efficiency, and ensuring your applications run smoothly.

CHAPTER 8

Building Blocks of JavaScript

Objective

This chapter aims to introduce the foundational elements of JavaScript syntax, including variables, data types, and basic expressions. By the end of this chapter, you will have a strong grasp of the essential building blocks that form the basis of JavaScript code, enabling you to start writing meaningful expressions and building simple programs.

Variables: var, let, and const

In JavaScript, **variables** are used to store data that can be referenced and manipulated in code. They allow developers to save values, which can then be retrieved or updated later on. JavaScript provides three primary ways to declare variables: var, let, and const. Understanding the differences between these is key to writing clear, reliable code.

Declaring Variables with `var`

Before 2015, `var` was the only way to declare variables in JavaScript. However, `var` has certain characteristics that make it less ideal in modern programming.

- **Scope**: Variables declared with `var` are function-scoped. This means they are accessible only within the function they are declared in or globally if declared outside any function.
- **Hoisting**: JavaScript "hoists" `var` declarations to the top of their scope, meaning they are accessible even before the line where they are declared. This can lead to unintended behaviors. More on hoisting later.

```
var name = "John";
console.log(name); // Output: John
```

Declaring Variables with `let`

Introduced in ES6 (ECMAScript 2015), `let` provides a more predictable way to declare variables:

- **Scope**: `let` is block-scoped, meaning it is only accessible within the block (like an if statement or loop) where it was declared.
- **No Hoisting**: Unlike `var`, `let` does not hoist in the same way, making it less prone to accidental bugs from early references.

```
let age = 25;
if (age >= 18) {
    let isAdult = true;
```

CHAPTER 8   BUILDING BLOCKS OF JAVASCRIPT

```
        console.log(isAdult); // Output: true
}
console.log(isAdult); // Error: isAdult is not defined
```

Declaring Constants with `const`

Also introduced in ES6, `const` is used for declaring constants, which are variables with a fixed value that cannot be reassigned:

- **Immutability**: Variables declared with `const` cannot be reassigned once given an initial value.
- **Scope**: Like `let`, `const` is also block-scoped.

    ```
    const birthYear = 1990;
    console.log(birthYear); // Output: 1990
    birthYear = 2000; // Error: Assignment to constant
                        variable
    ```

`const` with Objects

While const prevents reassignment of the variable itself, **it does not make objects immutable**. The object's properties can still be modified:

```
const user = { name: "Alice" };
user.name = "Bob"; // ✓ Allowed: Modifying object properties
console.log(user.name); // Bob

user = { name: "Charlie" }; // ✗ Error: Assignment to constant
                              variable
```

CHAPTER 8   BUILDING BLOCKS OF JAVASCRIPT

> **EXERCISE 1: UNDERSTANDING VARIABLE DECLARATIONS**
>
> **Task**: Declare three variables using var, let, and const. Modify their values in different scopes and observe the behavior.
>
> **Hint**: Use a function to test var and a block (e.g., if statement) to test let and const.
>
> **Code for Reference**:
>
> ```
> var globalVar = "I am global";
> let blockLet = "I am block scoped";
> const blockConst = "I am also block scoped";
>
> // Try reassigning these variables within different scopes.
> ```

Problems with var in JavaScript

Function Scope vs. Block Scope

One of the most significant issues with var is that it is **function-scoped** rather than **block-scoped**. In other words, var variables are only scoped to the function they are defined in, not the individual blocks within that function (like if statements, loops, or try-catch blocks). This behavior can lead to unexpected issues, especially within loops. In contrast, let and const are **block-scoped**, meaning they only exist within the block {} they are declared in.

Example 1 – Scope Issue with var in a Loop:

```
for (var i = 0; i < 3; i++) {
    setTimeout(function() {
        console.log(i);
    }, 1000);
}
```

CHAPTER 8   BUILDING BLOCKS OF JAVASCRIPT

```
// Expected Output: 0, 1, 2
// Actual Output after 1 second: 3, 3, 3
```

Since var is function-scoped, the same i is shared across all loop iterations. By the time the setTimeout executes, i has already incremented to 3.

Fix – Use let for Block Scope:

```
for (let i = 0; i < 3; i++) {
    setTimeout(function () {
        console.log(i);
    }, 1000);
}
// Output after 1 second: 0, 1, 2 (Correct behavior)
```

With let, a new i is created for each loop iteration, keeping the expected value inside the callback function.

Example 2 – Function Scope Issue with var:

```
function testVar() {
    if (true) {
        var x = 10;
    }
    console.log(x); // ✓ 10 (x is accessible outside the
                    if block)
}
testVar();
```

However, using let instead of var makes the variable block-scoped:

```
function testLet() {
    if (true) {
        let y = 20;
    }
```

149

```
        console.log(y); // ✗ ReferenceError: y is not defined
}
testLet();
```

Example 3 – var Hoisting Within a Function:

```
function hoistingExample() {
    console.log(a); // ✓ Undefined (var is hoisted but not
                    initialized)
    var a = 5;
    console.log(a); // ✓ 5
}
hoistingExample();
```

With let:

```
function hoistingError() {
    console.log(b); // ✗ ReferenceError: Cannot access 'b'
                    before initialization
    let b = 10;
}
hoistingError();
```

With var, the declaration is hoisted to the top, but not its assignment. With let, the variable remains in a "temporal dead zone" until it's assigned a value.

Hoisting and Accidental Use of Undefined Variables

JavaScript **hoists** var declarations, meaning it moves the declaration of variables to the top of their scope, but not their initialization. This behavior can lead to variables being accessible before they are actually assigned a value, which often results in unexpected undefined values.

Example of Hoisting Issue with var:

```
console.log(name); // Output: undefined
var name = "Alice";
console.log(name); // Output: Alice
```

In this example, the first `console.log(name)` statement does not throw an error, even though name has not yet been assigned a value. Because var declarations are hoisted, the code behaves as if the `var name;` statement was at the top of its scope, resulting in `undefined` instead of an error.

This can lead to confusing bugs, as developers may not realize why `undefined` is appearing instead of throwing a reference error.

Avoiding the Issue with let or const:

```
console.log(name); // ReferenceError: Cannot access 'name'
                   before initialization
let name = "Alice";
console.log(name); // Output: Alice
```

With `let` (and `const`), hoisting still occurs, but JavaScript throws an error if you try to access the variable before its initialization.

Redeclaration and Accidental Overwrites

Since `var` allows redeclaration within the same scope, it is possible to accidentally overwrite variables, which can cause hard-to-track bugs in complex code.

Example of Accidental Redeclaration with var:

```
var message = "Hello";
var message = "Goodbye";
console.log(message); // Output: Goodbye
```

In this example, the var message variable is redeclared without any issues, which can sometimes cause unexpected values to appear. This can be especially problematic if the variable is overwritten in large codebases where multiple developers are working on the same code.

With let and const, redeclaring a variable within the same scope throws an error, making it safer and easier to track variable declarations.

Using let or const for Safety:

```
let message = "Hello";
let message = "Goodbye"; // Error: Identifier 'message' has
                         already been declared
```

By preventing redeclarations, let and const help avoid potential errors and ensure that each variable is defined only once in its scope.

EXERCISE 2: SPOTTING ISSUES WITH VAR

Task: Write a loop using var and print the variable inside a setTimeout to see how scope behaves. Write the same loop using let and see what happens. Without using let, try fixing the issue using a closure.

Hint: Pay attention to whether the value of var changes as expected.

Code for Reference:

```
for ( /* write your code here */ ) {
   setTimeout(() => console.log(i), 1000);
}
```

Global Variables and the Window Object

When you declare a variable with var at the global scope (outside any function), it becomes a property of the window object in the browser. This behavior can lead to unintentional side effects, as properties on window can be accessed or modified by other scripts.

CHAPTER 8   BUILDING BLOCKS OF JAVASCRIPT

Example of var Polluting the Global Scope:

```
var user = "Alice";
console.log(window.user); // Output: Alice
```

In this example, the user variable is now a property of the window object, potentially conflicting with other scripts or causing bugs if other scripts are also trying to use window.user.

Because let and const are block-scoped, they do not add the variable to window, making them safer choices for global code.

How to Get the Same Behavior Without var

If you need a global variable that's accessible through window while still using let or const, you can explicitly attach it:

```
window.myGlobal = "Accessible via window";
console.log(window.myGlobal); // "Accessible via window"
```

Alternatively, you can use Object.defineProperty to create a non-reassignable global constant:

```
Object.defineProperty(window, "MY_CONSTANT", {
  value: "I am global and immutable",
  writable: false,
  configurable: false
});
console.log(window.MY_CONSTANT); // "I am global and immutable"
window.MY_CONSTANT = "Trying to change";
console.log(window.MY_CONSTANT); // Still "I am global and
                                              immutable"
```

This ensures that your global variable behaves as expected while keeping the advantages of let and const.

CHAPTER 8   BUILDING BLOCKS OF JAVASCRIPT

Comments and Code Readability

Comments are lines in your code that are ignored by the JavaScript engine. They are used to explain code logic, making it easier for you and others to understand.

Single-Line Comments

Single-line comments are created by using // at the start of a line.

```
// This is a single-line comment
let userName = "Alice";
```

Multi-line Comments

Multi-line comments are enclosed between /* and */.

```
/*
This is a multi-line comment.
It can span multiple lines.
*/
let userAge = 30;
```

> **EXERCISE 3: WRITING READABLE CODE**
>
> **Task**: Rewrite a given code snippet by adding meaningful comments to improve its readability.
>
> **Hint**: Focus on explaining what each function and block of code does.
>
> **Code for Reference:**
>
> ```
> // Original code without comments
> function greet(name) {
> ```

```
  if (!name) {
    return "Hello, Stranger!";
  }
  return `Hello, ${name}!`;
}
```

// Add comments to explain each part of the function.

Using Operators: Arithmetic, Assignment, Comparisons and Operator Precedence

Operators are symbols that perform operations on values. JavaScript provides various operators, each with specific uses.

Arithmetic Operators

Arithmetic operators are used to perform mathematical calculations:

- \+ (**Addition**): Adds two values
- \- (**Subtraction**): Subtracts one value from another
- * (**Multiplication**): Multiplies two values
- / (**Division**): Divides one value by another
- % (**Modulus**): Returns the remainder of a division

```
let sum = 10 + 5;         // 15
let difference = 10 - 5;  // 5
let product = 10 * 5;     // 50
let quotient = 10 / 5;    // 2
let remainder = 10 % 3;   // 1
```

Assignment Operators

Assignment operators assign values to variables. The most common assignment operator is =. JavaScript also provides compound assignment operators, such as += and -=.

```
let x = 10;
x += 5; // x = x + 5; x is now 15
```

Comparison Operators

Comparison operators compare two values and return a boolean result (true or false):

- ==: Equal to
- !=: Not equal to
- ===: Strictly equal to (checks both value and type)
- !==: Strictly not equal to
- <, >, <=, >=: Less than, greater than, less than or equal to, greater than or equal to

    ```
    let a = 10;
    let b = 5;

    console.log(a > b);   // Output: true
    console.log(a === b); // Output: false
    ```

Operator Precedence

Operator precedence determines the order in which operators are evaluated in an expression. When multiple operators are used in an expression, the ones with higher precedence are evaluated first. If operators have the same precedence, the order of evaluation is determined by their associativity (whether they are evaluated left to right or right to left), for example:

```
let result = 5 + 3 * 2;   // 11, not 16
```

In this expression, the multiplication (*) has higher precedence than addition (+), so 3 * 2 is evaluated first, and then 5 + 6 is evaluated, resulting in 11.

Common Operator Precedence

Here are some common operators and their precedence from highest to lowest:

- **Parentheses ()**: Expressions inside parentheses are evaluated first.
- **Exponentiation ****: Used for powers, e.g., 2 ** 3.
- **Multiplication *, Division /, and Modulus %**: Evaluated left to right.
- **Addition + and Subtraction -**: Also evaluated left to right.
- **Comparison Operators (==, !=, >, <)**: These have lower precedence than arithmetic operations.
- **Logical Operators (&&, ||)**: Logical AND (&&) has higher precedence than logical OR (||).

Parentheses for Clarity

Using parentheses can help clarify operator precedence in complex expressions, ensuring they are evaluated in the desired order:

```
let result = (5 + 3) * 2;  // 16, ensures addition
                           happens first
```

Associativity

- **Left-to-Right Associativity**: Most operators like addition, subtraction, multiplication, etc. are evaluated from left to right.

- **Right-to-Left Associativity**: The exponentiation operator (**) and assignment operators (=, +=, etc.) evaluate from right to left.

By understanding and using operator precedence, you can write more predictable and efficient expressions, ensuring your code behaves as expected.

Constants and Immutability in JavaScript

In JavaScript, the concept of constants and immutability is essential for writing predictable and maintainable code. Let's dive into how constants work and how immutability plays a crucial role in ensuring that variables behave as expected.

1. Understanding `const` and Immutability

In JavaScript, the `const` keyword is used to declare a variable whose reference cannot be reassigned. This means that once a variable is declared with `const`, its value cannot be changed to point to a different object or primitive value.

However, **immutability** here is a bit nuanced. While the **reference** to the value is fixed, the **content** of the object or array itself can still be modified. This distinction is important when working with complex data structures like objects or arrays.

Examples of `const` Behavior:

```
const number = 42;
number = 50;  // Error: Assignment to constant variable

const person = { name: "John", age: 30 };
person.age = 31; // Allowed: Mutating properties is fine
person = { name: "Jane", age: 28 };  // Error: Cannot reassign
                                        a constant object
```

In the example above

- The variable `number` is declared using `const`, and attempting to reassign it results in an error.

- The `person` object is also declared with `const`, but we can still modify its properties (`person.age = 31` is valid).

- However, reassigning the `person` object itself to a new object will throw an error.

2. Why Use `const`?

There are several reasons to prefer `const` when declaring variables in JavaScript:

- **Prevents Reassignments**: It prevents accidental reassignments, ensuring that once a value is assigned to a variable, it remains the same throughout the code, leading to fewer bugs.
- **Improves Code Readability**: By using `const`, you're signaling that the value is not meant to change. This helps make the code more predictable and easier to understand.
- **Optimized for Performance**: Some JavaScript engines can optimize `const` variables for better performance since they know the variable won't be reassigned.

3. Immutability with Primitive Types

For **primitive types** (like numbers, strings, and booleans), `const` guarantees full immutability. Once assigned, their values cannot be changed.

```
const pi = 3.14159;
pi = 3.14;  // Error: Cannot reassign a constant variable
```

This ensures that values such as numbers or strings, once assigned, cannot be altered.

4. Immutability with Objects and Arrays

As mentioned earlier, while `const` prevents reassigning the reference to an object or array, it does **not** prevent modification of the object's or array's properties or elements. This distinction is important when considering how to handle data in your applications.

Examples with Arrays:

```
const numbers = [1, 2, 3];
numbers.push(4);   // Allowed: Mutating the array content
console.log(numbers);  // [1, 2, 3, 4]

numbers = [5, 6];  // Error: Cannot reassign the array itself
```

Examples with Objects:

```
const car = { make: "Toyota", model: "Corolla" };
car.model = "Camry";   // Allowed: Modifying properties of the object
console.log(car);  // { make: "Toyota", model: "Camry" }

car = { make: "Honda", model: "Civic" };  // Error: Cannot reassign the object
```

5. Achieving Immutability: Object.freeze()

If you want to ensure **true immutability** for objects or arrays, you can use `Object.freeze()`. This method prevents modifications to the object by making it immutable at the shallow level.

Example of Object.freeze():

```
const car = Object.freeze({ make: "Toyota", model: "Corolla" });
car.model = "Camry";   // Error: Cannot modify frozen object
console.log(car);  // { make: "Toyota", model: "Corolla" }
```

However, note that `Object.freeze()` only performs a **shallow freeze**, meaning nested objects or arrays inside the object can still be modified unless they are also frozen.

Deep Immutability:

To achieve deep immutability (where nested objects and arrays are also immutable), you'll need to use libraries or implement custom solutions, like recursively freezing objects.

6. When to Use `const`

- **Immutable References**: When you want to ensure that the reference to a value or object doesn't change, use `const`. This is particularly useful when working with **data integrity**.

- **Avoid Accidental Reassignments**: Use `const` when declaring variables whose values should remain constant throughout the scope.

- **Ensuring Predictability**: If you want to make it clear that a variable shouldn't be changed, `const` makes your intentions clear to other developers (or to your future self).

7. Practical Use Cases for const

- **Configuration Values**: For settings or configurations that should not change, such as API keys, URLs, or constant values.

- **Function Expressions**: When you assign a function to a variable, declare it as `const` to avoid reassignment.

CHAPTER 8   BUILDING BLOCKS OF JAVASCRIPT

```
const fetchData = async () => {
  // code to fetch data
};
```

This ensures that `fetchData` remains a constant function and cannot be accidentally overwritten.

Conclusion

Understanding `const` and the concept of immutability in JavaScript is crucial for writing clean and predictable code. By using `const`, you safeguard against accidental variable reassignments and communicate your intentions clearly to anyone reading your code. Additionally, while `const` doesn't make the content of objects and arrays immutable, methods like `Object.freeze()` can help achieve deeper immutability when needed.

EXERCISE 4: MODIFYING IMMUTABLE VARIABLES

Task: Declare a constant object and try modifying its properties. Observe what happens.

Hint: Use `Object.freeze()` to enforce immutability and test its behavior.

Code for Reference:

```
const user = { name: "John", age: 30 };
// Try modifying user properties here

// Use Object.freeze() and test again
Object.freeze(user);
```

Performance Implications of `const`

Using `const` to declare variables can have minor performance implications, but it's usually not because of the keyword itself but rather how it interacts with JavaScript's engine optimizations.

1. **Reduced Scope for Optimizations**
   Modern JavaScript engines like V8 optimize code execution based on the predictability of variables. When you declare a variable with `const`, the engine knows it won't be reassigned, which can simplify internal optimizations like variable hoisting and inlining. This is beneficial because

   - It eliminates potential runtime checks for reassignment.
   - It ensures the variable has a single memory reference throughout its lifecycle.

2. However, the actual performance improvement is minimal and typically negligible for most applications.

3. **Better Developer Intent**
   While not a direct performance factor, using `const` can improve code maintainability and reduce bugs, indirectly affecting performance by minimizing unintended side effects or costly debugging.

Immutability and Performance

Immutability itself has more pronounced implications for performance, depending on how it is implemented.

CHAPTER 8   BUILDING BLOCKS OF JAVASCRIPT

1. Copying Data Structures

Immutability often involves creating new data structures rather than modifying existing ones. This can introduce overhead:

- **Memory Usage**: Every new copy consumes additional memory, which can be significant for large or deeply nested objects.
- **Processing Time**: Copying data structures (e.g., deep copies) can be computationally expensive, especially in large-scale applications.

Example:

```
const originalArray = [1, 2, 3];
const newArray = [...originalArray, 4];
```

Here, spreading the array creates a new copy, which incurs some performance overhead compared with simply pushing to the original array.

2. Garbage Collection

Creating new objects for every state change increases the number of objects the JavaScript engine needs to manage. This can lead to

- More frequent garbage collection cycles
- Increased memory fragmentation

165

3. Benefits for Functional Programming

Despite potential costs, immutability is a cornerstone of functional programming, which offers advantages like

- Easier debugging and testing due to predictable state changes
- Better parallelism since immutable data structures avoid race conditions

These benefits can outweigh the performance costs in scenarios like complex UIs or distributed systems.

Optimization Techniques for Immutability

If you need to maintain immutability without excessive performance hits, consider these approaches:

1. **Use Libraries for Structural Sharing:** Libraries like Immer and Immutable.js optimize immutable operations by sharing unchanged parts of data structures. This can significantly reduce memory and processing overhead.

   ```
   import { produce } from "immer";
   const nextState = produce(currentState, draft => {
       draft.property = "newValue";
   });
   ```

2. **Shallow Copies vs. Deep Copies:** Use shallow copies wherever possible. Deep copying is significantly slower and should only be used when necessary.

3. **Memoization:** When working with immutable data, memoization can help reuse computations and avoid redundant processing.

   ```
   const expensiveComputation = memoize((data) => {
       // Perform computation
   });
   ```

When to Choose Mutability Over Immutability

In performance-critical applications, such as games, real-time data processing, or high-frequency trading systems, mutability may sometimes be preferable for

- Reducing memory allocations
- Avoiding the overhead of creating new objects

In these cases, immutability may still be simulated logically (e.g., using private state management or developer discipline) rather than strictly enforced.

Summary

In this chapter, we explored the essential building blocks of JavaScript. You learned how to declare and manage variables using var, let, and const and understood their scope and behavior. We examined JavaScript's core data types, strings, numbers, and booleans, and emphasized the importance of writing readable code with comments.

We also discussed operators, including arithmetic, assignment, and comparison, which form the basis of logic and computation in JavaScript. Diving deeper, we highlighted the significance of constants and immutability, their role in maintaining predictable code, and the potential performance implications.

With these fundamentals, you're now equipped to confidently handle JavaScript's basic constructs and move on to more complex topics in the upcoming chapters.

Full Solutions

SOLUTION TO EXERCISE 1: UNDERSTANDING VARIABLE DECLARATIONS

```
var globalVar = "I am global";
let blockLet = "I am block scoped";
const blockConst = "I am also block scoped";

function testVar() {
  var innerVar = "I am function scoped";
  console.log(innerVar);
}
testVar();

// Reassign values
globalVar = "Changed value"; // Works
blockLet = "Changed block scoped value"; // Works
// blockConst = "New value"; // Error: Assignment to constant
                             variable
```

SOLUTION TO EXERCISE 2: SPOTTING ISSUES WITH VAR

```
for (var i = 0; i < 3; i++) {
  setTimeout(() => console.log(i), 1000); // Prints: 3, 3, 3
}
```

```
for (let j = 0; j < 3; j++) {
  setTimeout(() => console.log(j), 1000); // Prints: 0, 1, 2
}
```

SOLUTION TO EXERCISE 3: WRITING READABLE CODE

```
// Function to greet a user
// If no name is provided, it defaults to "Stranger"
function greet(name) {
  // Check if name is falsy (null, undefined, empty
  string, etc.)
  if (!name) {
    return "Hello, Stranger!";
  }
  // Return a personalized greeting
  return `Hello, ${name}!`;
}
```

SOLUTION TO EXERCISE 4: MODIFYING IMMUTABLE VARIABLES

```
const user = { name: "John", age: 30 };

// Modifying properties (allowed because the object is mutable)
user.name = "Jane"; // Works
user.age = 25; // Works

// Enforcing immutability with Object.freeze()
Object.freeze(user);
user.name = "Alice"; // Fails silently (or throws an error in
                    strict mode)
console.log(user); // Outputs: { name: "Jane", age: 25 }
```

CHAPTER 9

Working with Strings and Numbers

Objective

In this chapter, we'll explore JavaScript's fundamental data types, including strings, numbers, and booleans, and learn how to work with them effectively. A key focus will be on understanding JavaScript's unique type system, covering topics such as string literals and operations, number precision and its issues, type coercion, equality quirks, and common pitfalls. By recognizing these type quirks early on, you'll gain insight into how JavaScript interprets data in different contexts and avoid common errors that can arise from implicit type conversion and unexpected behavior. This foundation will prepare you to write more predictable and reliable JavaScript code.

String Literals and Template Strings

In JavaScript, **strings** are used to represent text. Strings are sequences of characters and are one of the most widely used data types in web development, essential for everything from storing user input to displaying dynamic content.

CHAPTER 9   WORKING WITH STRINGS AND NUMBERS

String Literals

String literals are simply a series of characters enclosed in quotes. JavaScript offers single (' '), double (" "), and backticks (` `) for string declarations.

Example:

```
let singleQuote = 'Hello, World!';
let doubleQuote = "Hello, World!";
let templateString = `Hello, World!`; // Introduced in ES6
```

While single and double quotes are functionally the same, backticks are part of **template literals** in JavaScript, which allow for more flexibility in creating dynamic strings.

Template Strings

Template literals, introduced in ES6, offer several advantages over traditional string concatenation.

EXERCISE 1: USING TEMPLATE LITERALS

Task: Create a greeting message using template literals that includes a user's name and the current date.

Hint: Use new Date() to get the current date.

Code for Reference:

```
const name = "Alice";
const date = new Date().toDateString();
```

Multi-line Example:

```
const message = `This is a
multi-line string.`;
```

CHAPTER 9   WORKING WITH STRINGS AND NUMBERS

Embedded Expressions:

```
const name = 'Alice';
const greeting = `Hello, ${name}!`;
```

EXERCISE 2: MULTI-LINE STRINGS

Task: Write a function that returns a string with three lines of text using template literals.

Hint: Use backticks (`) to create the string.

Code for Reference:

```
function multilineString() {
  return `This is line 1`
}
```

Tagged Template Literals

Tags allow you to transform template literals into custom output.

```
function sanitize(strings, ...values) {
  return strings.reduce((result, str, i) => result + str + (values[i] || '').replace(/</g, '&lt;'), '');
}
const unsafe = '<script>alert("Hacked!")</script>';
const safeMessage = sanitize`Safe content: ${unsafe}`;
console.log(safeMessage); // "Safe content: &lt;script&gt;alert("Hacked!")&lt;/script&gt;"
```

173

When to Use Which?

- **Use single or double quotes** when you have simple strings and don't need string interpolation or multi-line support. They are often used when the string does not require dynamic expressions or formatting.

- **Use template literals** when you need to embed expressions within the string or when you have a multi-line string. Template literals improve readability, especially when dealing with HTML, JSON, or complex strings.

Example: Choosing Between Single and Double Quotes

When your string contains quotes inside it, using one type of quote can help you avoid the need for escaping:

```
let sentence1 = "He said, 'Hello!'"; // No escaping needed for single quotes inside double quotes
let sentence2 = 'He said, "Hello!"'; // No escaping needed for double quotes inside single quotes
```

Template literals are useful when you need to interpolate variables or expressions:

```
let age = 30;
let message = `I am ${age} years old.`; // String interpolation
```

In short, **use template literals** when you need dynamic content or multi-line strings, and stick to single or double quotes for simpler cases.

CHAPTER 9   WORKING WITH STRINGS AND NUMBERS

String Methods, Manipulation, and Comparison

JavaScript includes a variety of **string methods** that let you manipulate text in ways that enhance readability and functionality.

Common String Methods

1. length

    - Returns the number of characters in a string.

        ```
        let text = "JavaScript";
        console.log(text.length); // Output: 10
        ```

2. **toUpperCase()** and **toLowerCase()**

    - Converts a string to uppercase or lowercase.

        ```
        console.log("hello".toUpperCase());
         // Output: HELLO
        ```

3. **trim()**

    - Removes whitespace from both sides of a string.

        ```
        let padded = "   hello world   ";
        console.log(padded.trim()); // Output: "hello world"
        ```

4. **indexOf() and includes()**

    - Finds the position of a substring within a string (indexOf) or checks if a substring exists (includes).

```
let sentence = "JavaScript is fun";
console.log(sentence.indexOf("fun")); // Output: 14
console.log(sentence.includes("Java"));
// Output: true
```

5. **slice() and substring()**

   - Extracts parts of a string and returns a new string. Both methods are similar, but substring does not accept negative indices.

   - Using a single input, will extract the length of the characters from the start.

   ```
   let phrase = "JavaScript";
   console.log(phrase.slice(0, 4)); // Output: "Java"
   ```

String Comparisons

In JavaScript, comparing strings is a common operation, and it's important to understand the behavior of string comparisons, especially with respect to case sensitivity, locale, and special characters.

Basic String Comparison (Lexical Comparison)

JavaScript compares strings lexicographically (i.e., based on their Unicode values). The comparison uses the == (loose equality) or === (strict equality) operators.

- **Loose Equality (==)**: Checks if the two strings are equal after type coercion.

- **Strict Equality (===)**: Checks if the two strings are equal without type coercion. This is the more reliable method for comparison in most cases.

```
let str1 = "apple";
let str2 = "apple";
let str3 = "banana";

console.log(str1 === str2); // true: exact match
console.log(str1 === str3); // false: different strings
```

Case Sensitivity in Comparisons

String comparisons in JavaScript are **case-sensitive**. This means that uppercase and lowercase letters are treated as distinct characters.

```
let str1 = "hello";
let str2 = "Hello";

console.log(str1 === str2); // false: different case
```

If you want to perform a case-insensitive comparison, you can convert both strings to the same case using .toLowerCase() or .toUpperCase().

```
let str1 = "hello";
let str2 = "HELLO";

console.log(str1.toLowerCase() === str2.toLowerCase());
 // true: case-insensitive comparison
```

String Comparison with Special Characters

JavaScript also compares strings with special characters based on their Unicode values. For example, an exclamation mark (!) has a lower Unicode value than an uppercase letter (A).

```
let str1 = "A";
let str2 = "!";

console.log(str1 > str2); // true: 'A' comes after '!'
```

Locale-Sensitive Comparisons

To handle string comparisons that respect different languages and alphabets, JavaScript provides the `.localeCompare()` method. This method compares two strings based on the current locale and returns

- 0 if the strings are equal
- -1 if the first string is lexicographically less than the second
- 1 if the first string is lexicographically greater than the second

```
let str1 = "apple";
let str2 = "banana";

console.log(str1.localeCompare(str2));
// -1: 'apple' comes before 'banana'
```

You can also pass additional parameters to `.localeCompare()` to tailor the comparison for specific locales or sensitivity types (e.g., accent-sensitive comparisons).

Using `includes()`, `startsWith()`, and `endsWith()` for Substring Comparisons

While not direct equality checks, these string methods allow you to compare substrings within strings:

- **`includes()`**: Checks if a string contains a certain substring
- **`startsWith()`**: Checks if a string starts with a given substring
- **`endsWith()`**: Checks if a string ends with a given substring

CHAPTER 9   WORKING WITH STRINGS AND NUMBERS

```
let str = "JavaScript is awesome";

console.log(str.includes("Java")); // true: 'Java' is
in 'JavaScript'
console.log(str.startsWith("JavaScript")); // true:
starts with 'JavaScript'
console.log(str.endsWith("awesome")); // true: ends
with 'awesome'
```

These methods are the foundation for any text manipulation in JavaScript. Practice combining them to achieve more complex results.

EXERCISE 3: STRING MANIPULATION

Task: Write a function `truncate` that shortens a string to a specified length and appends "..." if it exceeds that length.

Hint: Use a combination of the above methods to accomplish this.

Code for Reference:

```
const str = "JavaScript is amazing";
```

EXERCISE 4: CAPITALIZING THE FIRST LETTER

Task: Write a function `capitalizeFirstLetter` that takes a string and returns it with the first character capitalized.

Hint: Use `charAt()` and `slice()` methods to manipulate the string.

Code for Reference:

```
const str = "hello";
```

CHAPTER 9   WORKING WITH STRINGS AND NUMBERS

Working with Numbers: Math Operations and Methods

Numbers in JavaScript are primarily used for calculations, measurements, and other numerical tasks. JavaScript has a single Number type (there's no need to specify int or float), which simplifies arithmetic operations but has some quirks due to its use of **floating-point** arithmetic.

Basic Math Operations

JavaScript provides operators for standard arithmetic operations:

- **Addition (+)**

  ```
  let sum = 5 + 10; // 15
  ```

- **Subtraction (-)**

  ```
  let difference = 20 - 10; // 10
  ```

- **Multiplication (*)**

  ```
  let product = 3 * 4; // 12
  ```

- **Division (/)**

  ```
  let quotient = 20 / 4; // 5
  ```

- **Modulus (%):** Returns the remainder of division

  ```
  let remainder = 10 % 3; // 1
  ```

CHAPTER 9   WORKING WITH STRINGS AND NUMBERS

Math Methods and Rounding

The Math object in JavaScript offers several helpful methods for working with numbers.

1. **Math.round()**

    - Rounds a number to the nearest integer.

    ```
    console.log(Math.round(4.7)); // Output: 5
    ```

2. **Math.ceil() and Math.floor()**

    - Rounds up (ceil) or down (floor) to the nearest integer.

    ```
    console.log(Math.ceil(4.3)); // Output: 5
    console.log(Math.floor(4.7)); // Output: 4
    ```

3. **Math.random()**

    - Generates a random number between 0 and 1.

    ```
    console.log(Math.random()); // Output: (random number, e.g., 0.2345)
    ```

4. **Math.max() and Math.min()**

    - Returns the maximum or minimum value in a set of numbers.

    ```
    console.log(Math.max(10, 20, 30)); // Output: 30
    ```

5. **toFixed()** and **toPrecision()**

   - These methods allow for control over the number of decimal places.

     ```
     let pi = 3.14159;
     console.log(pi.toFixed(2)); // Output: 3.14

     let num1 = 123.456789;
     let num2 = 0.000123456;

     console.log(num1.toPrecision(5)); // "123.46"
     console.log(num2.toPrecision(4)); // "0.0001235"
     ```

These methods make calculations and number formatting much easier, especially when working with complex or user-facing numeric data.

EXERCISE 5: FINDING THE MAXIMUM VALUE

Task: Write a function `findMax` that returns the largest number in an array.

Hint: Use `Math.max()` with the spread operator.

Code for Reference:

```
const arr = [1, 2, 3, 4, 5];
```

Type Coercion and Equality

Type coercion in JavaScript is the automatic or implicit conversion of values from one data type to another. While convenient in some scenarios, it can also lead to unexpected behavior if not properly understood. This section explores why type coercion is important, the difference between loose (==) and strict (===) equality, and common pitfalls with real-world examples.

CHAPTER 9   WORKING WITH STRINGS AND NUMBERS

What Is Type Coercion?

Type coercion occurs when JavaScript automatically converts a value into another type to perform an operation or comparison.

Example:

```
console.log('5' - 2); // 3 ('5' is coerced into a number)
console.log('5' + 2); // "52" (2 is coerced into a string)
```

Here, JavaScript guesses the intended operation based on the operator. Subtraction expects numbers, so it converts '5' into 5. Addition involves strings, so it concatenates.

Equality in JavaScript

JavaScript provides two types of equality operators:

1. **Loose Equality (==)**

   Converts operands to the same type before comparison.

   Example:

   ```
   console.log(5 == '5');  // true
   console.log(false == 0); // true
   console.log(null == undefined); // true
   ```

2. **Strict Equality (===)**

   Does not perform type conversion. Values must be of the same type to evaluate to true.

   Example:

   ```
   console.log(5 === '5');  // false
   console.log(false === 0); // false
   console.log(null === undefined); // false
   ```

CHAPTER 9   WORKING WITH STRINGS AND NUMBERS

Why Does This Matter?

Misunderstanding coercion can lead to subtle bugs, especially in comparisons and conditionals. Let's explore a few real-world examples.

Example 1 – User Input Validation:

Suppose you're validating user input on a form where the field age is expected to be a number:

```
function validateAge(age) {
  if (age == 18) {
    console.log("Access granted!");
  } else {
    console.log("Access denied!");
  }
}
validateAge('18'); // "Access granted!"
```

Here, the loose equality (==) operator coerces the string '18' into a number. This may seem fine, but it opens the door to unintended behavior. For example, an input of '18.0' would also pass validation. Using strict equality ensures no coercion occurs.

Example:

```
if (age === 18) {
  console.log("Access granted!");
}
```

Example 2 – Object Comparisons:

Coercion can result in false positives during object comparisons, for instance:

```
console.log([] == false);  // true
console.log({} == false);  // false
```

CHAPTER 9   WORKING WITH STRINGS AND NUMBERS

Here:

- An empty array (`[]`) is coerced into an empty string (`''`) and then into 0, making it equal to `false`.
- An empty object (`{}`) remains an object, so the comparison fails.

This behavior can cause unintended issues in conditions like

```
if (userInput == false) {
  console.log("No input provided!");
}
```

If `userInput` is `[]`, this condition evaluates as true, even though an empty array is technically a valid input.

Example 3 – Sorting Data:

Consider sorting a list of mixed data types:

```
const values = [10, '2', 8];
values.sort();
console.log(values); // ["10", "2", 8]
```

The `sort()` method coerces the values into strings, leading to unexpected order. To fix this, use a custom comparator:

```
values.sort((a, b) => Number(a) - Number(b));
console.log(values); // [2, 8, 10]
```

Pitfall: Truthy and Falsy in Conditionals

Type coercion affects truthy and falsy values in conditionals. Common falsy values include

- `false`
- `0`
- `""` (empty string)

CHAPTER 9   WORKING WITH STRINGS AND NUMBERS

- null
- undefined
- NaN

Example:

```
if ('0') {
  console.log("Truthy!");
}
```

Here, '0' is a non-empty string, so it evaluates as truthy despite looking like the number zero.

Best Practices to Avoid Coercion Issues

1. **Use Strict Equality (===) by Default**

   Strict equality avoids unintended conversions:

   ```
   if (userInput === '') {
     console.log("Input is empty");
   }
   ```

2. **Explicitly Convert Data Types**

   Instead of relying on implicit coercion, explicitly convert values:

   ```
   const userInput = "5";
   const numberInput = Number(userInput);
   if (numberInput === 5) {
     console.log("Valid number");
   }
   ```

3. **Be Cautious with Falsy Checks**

   Avoid general truthy/falsy conditions when precise checks are required:

   ```
   if (userInput === null || userInput === '') {
     console.log("Invalid input");
   }
   ```

4. **Use Type-Safe Comparisons in Arrays and Objects**

   Ensure you handle arrays and objects appropriately:

   ```
   if (Array.isArray(data) && data.length === 0) {
     console.log("Empty array!");
   }
   ```

When == Makes Sense

Despite the general recommendation to use ===, there are situations where the == operator is useful. One of the most common cases where using == is acceptable is when checking for both null and undefined at the same time. This is because, in JavaScript, null and undefined are considered loosely equal:

- null == undefined is true.
- null === undefined is false.

Therefore, when you want to check if a variable is either null or undefined, using == is both concise and reliable.

Example – Checking for Null or Undefined:

Instead of checking for both null and undefined separately

```
if (value === null || value === undefined) {
    // handle null or undefined case
}
```

you can simplify the condition by using ==:

```
if (value == null) {
    // handle null or undefined case
}
```

Here's why this works:

- value == null will return true for both null and undefined. This is because the == operator, when comparing null with undefined, does not perform any type conversion and treats them as equal.

Why Is This Useful?

- **Conciseness**: The value == null check is shorter and more concise than checking for value === null || value === undefined.

- **Clarity**: It communicates the intent clearly – you want to know if value is "empty" in a way that encompasses both null and undefined.

- **No Type Coercion Pitfalls**: This use of == is safe because it's specifically checking for null and undefined, and JavaScript's loose equality operator is designed to treat these two values as equal. This is a rare case where == is *not* performing unintended type coercion.

Example Code – Handling Optional Parameters:

Another use case where == can be beneficial is when working with optional function parameters, where null and undefined both signify the absence of a value:

```
function greet(name) {
    if (name == null) {
        console.log("Hello, Guest!");
    } else {
        console.log(`Hello, ${name}!`);
    }
}

greet();          // Hello, Guest!
greet(null);      // Hello, Guest!
greet("Alice");   // Hello, Alice!
```

In this example, both `undefined` and `null` are treated the same when calling the greet function, allowing for a cleaner, more concise way of checking for the absence of a value.

Conclusion

Understanding type coercion is crucial for writing reliable JavaScript code. While JavaScript's dynamic typing allows flexibility, it also introduces risks when types are implicitly converted. By being deliberate with your use of equality operators, explicit conversions, and type checks, you can prevent bugs and ensure your code behaves as expected in all scenarios.

- `===` is the preferred operator in JavaScript because it avoids the dangers of type coercion and provides predictable behavior.
- However, `==` can be useful in specific cases where the comparison is meant to treat `null` and `undefined` as equivalent. Using == in this context makes the code shorter and easier to understand without introducing unexpected behavior.

CHAPTER 9 WORKING WITH STRINGS AND NUMBERS

- The most common scenario where == is useful is when checking for both null and undefined at once, such as in the condition value == null.

In most other cases, it's best to stick with === to ensure that both value and type are being compared properly. By following these practices, you can write clearer, more robust code that handles all types of values safely.

EXERCISE 6: COMPARING EQUALITY

Task: Demonstrate the difference between loose (==) and strict (===) equality by comparing values of different types.

Hint: Log the results to the console.

Code for Reference:

```
console.log(5 == "5");
```

Implicit String and Number Conversion

JavaScript can sometimes surprise you by converting values unexpectedly when dealing with numbers and strings, especially when using the + operator, which is both for addition and string concatenation.

Example:

```
console.log(5 + '5');   // "55" - the number 5 is coerced into
                        a string
console.log('5' - 3);   // 2 - the string "5" is coerced into
                        a number
console.log(5 + +'5');  // 10 - using the unary +, which coerces
                        "5" to a number
```

CHAPTER 9 WORKING WITH STRINGS AND NUMBERS

The + operator will favor string concatenation if at least one operand is a string. The -, *, and / operators, however, do not concatenate and instead coerce both operands into numbers.

EXERCISE 7: IMPLICIT CONVERSION

Task: Write a function `convertAndAdd` that takes a string and a number, converts the string to a number implicitly, and returns their sum.

Hint: Use the + operator for implicit conversion.

Code for Reference:

```
const str = "10";
const num = 5;
```

Precision Limitations with Floating-Point Numbers

JavaScript uses **64-bit floating-point arithmetic** (based on the IEEE 754 standard), which means it can represent numbers very precisely, but with certain limits. Small inaccuracies can appear when working with decimals, especially in calculations.

Example:

```
console.log(0.1 + 0.2); // 0.30000000000000004 - not
                           exactly 0.3
console.log(0.1 + 0.2 === 0.3); // false
```

These rounding errors stem from how floating-point numbers are stored, a common issue in programming. In situations where precision is crucial (like financial calculations), JavaScript libraries such as **Big.js** or **Decimal.js** are useful for managing floating-point precision.

EXERCISE 8: HANDLING FLOATING-POINT PRECISION

Task: Write a function `compareFloats` that compares two floating-point numbers for equality up to two decimal places.

Hint: Use `toFixed()` to round numbers.

Code for Reference:

```
const num1 = 0.1 + 0.2;
const num2 = 0.3;
```

The NaN Type and Its Unusual Properties

JavaScript has a special numeric value, NaN (Not-a-Number), which represents an invalid number result. One of the strangest quirks of NaN is that it's the only value in JavaScript that **is not equal to itself**.

Example:

```
console.log(NaN === NaN); // false
console.log(isNaN(NaN));  // true - the only reliable way to
                          check for NaN
```

To check if a value is NaN, use the `isNaN()` function or `Number.isNaN()`, as comparing NaN directly will always result in `false`.

EXERCISE 9: CHECKING FOR NAN

Task: Write a function `isReallyNaN` that demonstrates the difference between `isNaN()` and `Number.isNaN()`.

Hint: Test the function with various inputs like `"hello"` and `NaN`.

Code for Reference:

```
const value = NaN;
```

Falsy and Truthy Values

JavaScript has a set of values that are considered **falsy** in conditional statements. These are values that evaluate to `false` when converted to a boolean. The falsy values include

- `false`
- `0`
- `''` (empty string)
- `null`
- `undefined`
- `NaN`

Truthy values, on the other hand, include everything else values that are not falsy. This includes non-empty strings, numbers other than 0, arrays, objects, and more.

Why Falsy and Truthy Matter

Understanding falsy and truthy values allows developers to write concise and readable code for conditional checks. However, they can also lead to subtle bugs if you're not careful with type coercion.

Example:

```
const input = null;

if (input) {
  console.log("This won't run because `null` is falsy.");
}
const username = "Alice";
```

```
if (username) {
  console.log("This will run because 'Alice' is truthy.");
}
```

Understanding falsy and truthy values is especially useful for concise conditional checks but can be a source of confusion if types are not explicitly handled.

Pitfalls to Watch Out For

Using falsy and truthy values without explicit type-checking can lead to unexpected behavior. Consider the following example:

```
const value = 0;

if (value) {
  console.log("This won't run because 0 is falsy.");
} else {
  console.log("This will run, even though 0 is a valid number.");
}
```

Here, 0 is a valid number, but it's treated as falsy in the condition. To avoid such issues, it's often better to explicitly check types.

Example:

```
if (value === 0) {
  console.log("Value is explicitly checked as 0.");
}
```

Falsy and Truthy in Common Use Cases

1. **Default Values Using Logical OR (||)**
   The || operator can be used to provide default values when a variable is falsy.

CHAPTER 9   WORKING WITH STRINGS AND NUMBERS

Example:

```
let name;
const displayName = name || "Guest";
console.log(displayName); // Output: "Guest"
```

2. **Short-Circuit Evaluation with Logical AND (&&)**

   The && operator stops evaluating as soon as it encounters a falsy value.

   Example:

   ```
   const isLoggedIn = true;
   const user = isLoggedIn && { name: "Alice" };
   // Returns the object only if `isLoggedIn` is truthy
   console.log(user); // Output: { name: "Alice" }
   ```

3. **Filtering Arrays**

   Falsy values can be removed from an array using the filter method and the Boolean function.

   Example:

   ```
   const mixedArray = [0, 1, false, "", "hello",
   undefined, null, true];
   const truthyValues = mixedArray.filter(Boolean);
   console.log(truthyValues); // Output: [1, "hello",
                                           true]
   ```

4. **Optional Chaining (?.)**

   Optional chaining is useful for avoiding errors when accessing properties of undefined or null.

195

CHAPTER 9   WORKING WITH STRINGS AND NUMBERS

Example:

```
const user = { profile: { name: "Alice" } };
console.log(user.profile?.name); // Output: "Alice"
console.log(user.details?.age); // Output: undefined
                                 (no error thrown)
```

Common Interview Question

"How do you distinguish between null and undefined?"
While both are falsy, they have different meanings:

- null: Represents an intentional absence of a value
- undefined: Represents a variable that has been declared but not assigned a value

Example:

```
let a = null;
let b;

console.log(a == b);  // true (loose equality)
console.log(a === b); // false (strict equality)
```

Additional Examples for Falsy and Truthy

1. **Combining Logical Operators**
   You can combine logical operators to handle more complex conditions.

   Example:

   ```
   const user = { name: "Alice", isActive: true };
   if (user && user.isActive) {
     console.log(`${user.name} is active.`);
   }
   ```

2. **Falsy Behavior in Arrays and Objects**

   Empty arrays [ ] and objects { } are considered truthy, which might seem counterintuitive.

   Example:

   ```
   if ([]) {
     console.log("An empty array is truthy!");
   }
   if ({}) {
     console.log("An empty object is truthy!");
   }
   ```

3. **Falsy in Ternary Operators**

   Using a ternary operator for concise conditional checks.

   Example:

   ```
   const age = 0;
   const message = age ? "Age is valid" : "Age is not valid";
   console.log(message); // Output: "Age is not valid"
   ```

EXERCISE 10: FILTERING FALSY VALUES

Task: Write a function `filterFalsy` that removes all falsy values from an array.

Hint: Use the `filter()` method with Boolean.

Code for Reference:

```
const arr = [0, 1, "", "hello", undefined, null, true];
```

CHAPTER 9   WORKING WITH STRINGS AND NUMBERS

EXERCISE 11: VALIDATING INPUT

Task: Write a function `isValidInput` that takes a single parameter and returns `true` if the input is truthy and `false` otherwise.

Hint: Use an `if` condition to check the truthiness of the input.

Code for Reference:

```
function isValidInput(input) {
  // Add your logic here
}
console.log(isValidInput("hello")); // Should return true
console.log(isValidInput(""));      // Should return false
```

EXERCISE 12: ASSIGNING DEFAULT VALUES

Task: Create a function `getUser` that takes a user object. If the user's name or role is falsy, assign them default values (`"Guest"` for name and `"Viewer"` for role). Return the updated object.

Hint: Use the || operator to assign defaults.

Code for Reference:

```
function getUser(user) {
  // Add your logic here
}
console.log(getUser({ name: "Alice", role: "Admin" }));
// Should return { name: "Alice", role: "Admin' }

console.log(getUser({ name: "", role: "" }));
// Should return { name: "Guest", role: "Viewer" }
```

CHAPTER 9 WORKING WITH STRINGS AND NUMBERS

EXERCISE 13: FILTERING FALSY VALUES FROM AN ARRAY

Task: Write a function `removeFalsy` that accepts an array and returns a new array with all the falsy values removed.

Hint: Use `Array.prototype.filter` with the Boolean function.

Code for Reference:

```
function removeFalsy(arr) {
  // Add your logic here
}
console.log(removeFalsy([0, "hello", "", null, 42, false]));
// Should return ["hello", 42]
```

EXERCISE 14: TRUTHY PROPERTIES IN OBJECTS

Task: Write a function `countTruthy` that accepts an object and counts how many properties have truthy values.

Hint: Use `Object.values` and a loop to iterate through the values.

Code for Reference:

```
function countTruthy(obj) {
  // Add your logic here
}
console.log(countTruthy({ a: 1, b: 0, c: "hello", d: "" }));
// Should return 2
```

CHAPTER 9   WORKING WITH STRINGS AND NUMBERS

EXERCISE 15: COMPARING FALSY VALUES

Task: Create a function compareFalsy that accepts two parameters and returns a message indicating if they are the same falsy value or different.

Hint: Use strict equality (===) for the comparison.

Code for Reference:

```
function compareFalsy(value1, value2) {
  // Add your logic here
}
console.log(compareFalsy(null, undefined));
// Should return "Different falsy values"

console.log(compareFalsy(0, 0));
// Should return "Same falsy value"
```

The Strange Case of `typeof null`

The typeof operator in JavaScript returns a string indicating the type of a value, but there's a well-known quirk with null that can trip up beginners: typeof null returns "object". This is actually a historical bug in JavaScript that has remained due to backward compatibility.

Example:

```
console.log(typeof null); // "object"
```

CHAPTER 9   WORKING WITH STRINGS AND NUMBERS

EXERCISE 16: UNDERSTANDING TYPEOF NULL

Task: Write a function `detectType` that logs the type of various values, including `null`.

Hint: Use the `typeof` operator.

Code for Reference:

```
const value = null;
```

Summary

In this chapter, we explored JavaScript's fundamental data types: strings, numbers, and booleans. We examined how to define and work with these types, along with their common methods and operations. A crucial aspect of working with JavaScript is understanding its **type system**, which can sometimes behave unexpectedly due to quirks like **type coercion** and **implicit conversions**. We highlighted how JavaScript automatically converts types in certain situations, especially when using loose equality (==), and how this can lead to surprising results. We also covered the **falsy** and **truthy** values, the peculiarities of NaN, and the **floating-point precision** limitations. Understanding these quirks helps you avoid common errors and write more predictable, reliable code. By mastering these fundamental concepts, you'll be well-equipped to handle JavaScript's dynamic typing system effectively.

CHAPTER 9 WORKING WITH STRINGS AND NUMBERS

Full Solutions

SOLUTION TO EXERCISE 1: USING TEMPLATE LITERALS

```
function createGreeting(name) {
  const date = new Date();
  return `Hello, ${name}! Today's date is ${date.
toDateString()}.`;
}

console.log(createGreeting("Alice"));
```

SOLUTION TO EXERCISE 2: MULTI-LINE STRINGS

```
function multilineString() {
  return `This is line 1
This is line 2
This is line 3`;
}

console.log(multilineString());
```

SOLUTION TO EXERCISE 3: STRING MANIPULATION

```
function truncate(str, maxLength) {
  return str.length > maxLength ? str.slice(0, maxLength) +
"..." : str;
}

console.log(truncate("JavaScript is amazing", 10));
 // Output: "JavaScript..."
```

CHAPTER 9 WORKING WITH STRINGS AND NUMBERS

SOLUTION TO EXERCISE 4: CAPITALIZING THE FIRST LETTER

```
function capitalizeFirstLetter(str) {
  return str.charAt(0).toUpperCase() + str.slice(1);
}

console.log(capitalizeFirstLetter("hello"));
// Output: "Hello"
```

SOLUTION TO EXERCISE 5: FINDING THE MAXIMUM VALUE

```
function findMax(arr) {
  return Math.max(...arr);
}

console.log(findMax([1, 2, 3, 4, 5])); // Output: 5
```

SOLUTION TO EXERCISE 6: COMPARING EQUALITY

```
console.log(5 == "5");   // Output: true (loose equality, type conversion happens)

console.log(5 === "5"); // Output: false (strict equality, no type conversion)
```

CHAPTER 9   WORKING WITH STRINGS AND NUMBERS

SOLUTION TO EXERCISE 7: IMPLICIT CONVERSION

```
function convertAndAdd(str, num) {
  return +str + num; // The + operator converts the string to a number
}

console.log(convertAndAdd("10", 5)); // Output: 15
```

SOLUTION TO EXERCISE 8: HANDLING FLOATING-POINT PRECISION

```
function compareFloats(num1, num2) {
  return num1.toFixed(2) === num2.toFixed(2);
}

console.log(compareFloats(0.1 + 0.2, 0.3)); // Output: true
```

SOLUTION TO EXERCISE 9: CHECKING FOR NAN

```
function isReallyNaN(value) {
  console.log(isNaN(value));        // Returns true for non-numeric strings, e.g., "hello"
  console.log(Number.isNaN(value)); // Returns true only for NaN
}

isReallyNaN(NaN);        // isNaN: true, Number.isNaN: true
isReallyNaN("hello");    // isNaN: true, Number.isNaN: false
```

CHAPTER 9   WORKING WITH STRINGS AND NUMBERS

SOLUTION TO EXERCISE 10: FILTERING FALSY VALUES

```
function filterFalsy(arr) {
  return arr.filter(Boolean);
}

console.log(filterFalsy([0, 1, "", "hello", undefined, null, true]));
// Output: [1, "hello", true]
```

SOLUTION TO EXERCISE 11: VALIDATING INPUT

```
function isValidInput(input) {
  return !!input; // Use double negation to convert to a boolean
}

console.log(isValidInput("hello")); // true
console.log(isValidInput(""));      // false
console.log(isValidInput(0));       // false
console.log(isValidInput(123));     // true
console.log(isValidInput(null));    // false
```

SOLUTION TO EXERCISE 12: ASSIGNING DEFAULT VALUES

```
function getUser(user) {
  return {
    name: user.name || "Guest",
    role: user.role || "Viewer",
  };
}
```

205

CHAPTER 9 WORKING WITH STRINGS AND NUMBERS

```
console.log(getUser({ name: "Alice", role: "Admin" }));
// { name: "Alice", role: "Admin" }

console.log(getUser({ name: "", role: "" }));
// { name: "Guest", role: "Viewer" }

console.log(getUser({ name: null, role: "Editor" }));
// { name: "Guest", role: "Editor" }
```

SOLUTION TO EXERCISE 13: FILTERING FALSY VALUES FROM AN ARRAY

```
function removeFalsy(arr) {
  return arr.filter(Boolean); // The Boolean function
  removes falsy values
}

console.log(removeFalsy([0, "hello", "", null, 42, false]));
// ["hello", 42]

console.log(removeFalsy([undefined, NaN, 1, "world",
{}, []]));
// [1, "world", {}, []]
```

SOLUTION TO EXERCISE 14: TRUTHY PROPERTIES IN OBJECTS

```
function countTruthy(obj) {
  return Object.values(obj).filter(Boolean).length;
 // Filter truthy values and count
}

console.log(countTruthy({ a: 1, b: 0, c: "hello", d: "" }));
// 2
```

CHAPTER 9   WORKING WITH STRINGS AND NUMBERS

```
console.log(countTruthy({ x: undefined, y: null, z:
"truthy", w: 5 }));
// 2
```

SOLUTION TO EXERCISE 15: COMPARING FALSY VALUES

```
function compareFalsy(value1, value2) {
  if (!value1 && !value2) {
    return value1 === value2
      ? "Same falsy value"
      : "Different falsy values";
  }
  return "One or both values are truthy";
}

console.log(compareFalsy(null, undefined));
// "Different falsy values"

console.log(compareFalsy(0, 0));
// "Same falsy value"

console.log(compareFalsy(false, ""));
// "Different falsy values"

console.log(compareFalsy("truthy", 0));
// "One or both values are truthy"
```

SOLUTION TO EXERCISE 16: UNDERSTANDING TYPEOF NULL

```
function detectType(value) {
  console.log(`Value: ${value}, Type: ${typeof value}`);
}

detectType(null); // Output: Value: null, Type: object
```

CHAPTER 10

Control Flow in JavaScript

Objective

In this chapter, you will learn about control flow structures in JavaScript, which allow you to create flexible and dynamic programs. These structures help you manage the flow of execution in your code based on different conditions and looping needs. Specifically, we'll cover conditional logic with `if...else` and `switch` statements; looping with `for`, `while`, and `do...while`; and the shorthand options of the ternary and nullish coalescing operators. By the end, you will be able to write JavaScript code that makes decisions and performs repetitive tasks effectively.

if and else Statements

One of the most foundational aspects of control flow in JavaScript is the ability to make decisions using `if` and `else` statements. These statements evaluate conditions and execute different blocks of code based on whether the conditions are true or false. Think of them as the decision-makers in your code, allowing you to define logic that responds dynamically to different scenarios.

Syntax:

```
if (condition) {
  // code to be executed if condition is true
}
```

When JavaScript encounters an if statement, it checks the condition inside the parentheses. If this condition evaluates to true, it runs the code inside the curly braces. If the condition is false, it simply skips that block and moves on. This structure ensures your program behaves differently based on varying inputs or states.

For example, imagine you're writing an application where users log in. You can use an if statement to display a welcome message only if the user is successfully logged in.

Example:

```
let isLoggedIn = true;

if (isLoggedIn) {
  console.log("Welcome back!");
}
```

In this example, the condition isLoggedIn determines whether the message "Welcome back!" is displayed. If isLoggedIn were false, the console.log would never run.

EXERCISE 1: MAKING DECISIONS WITH IF STATEMENTS

Task: Write an if statement that checks whether a number is positive, negative, or zero and prints a corresponding message to the console.

Hint: Use conditional checks like if (number > 0).

Code for Reference:

```
let number = 5;
// Add your if statement here.
```

CHAPTER 10   CONTROL FLOW IN JAVASCRIPT

Using else with if

Syntax:

```
if (condition) {
  // code to be executed if condition is true
} else {
  // code to be executed if condition is false
}
```

Sometimes, you want to handle both cases: what happens when the condition is true and what happens when it's false. This is where the else block comes in. It's like saying, "If this happens, do this; otherwise, do that."

Syntax:

```
let isLoggedIn = false;

if (isLoggedIn) {
  console.log("Welcome back!");
} else {
  console.log("Please log in.");
}
```

EXERCISE 2: HANDLING DEFAULTS WITH ELSE

Task: Create an if...else statement that checks whether a user is logged in. If they are logged in, print their username; otherwise, print a "Please log in" message.

Hint: Simulate the logged-in state with a boolean variable.

Code for Reference:

```
let isLoggedIn = false;
// Write your if...else statement here.
```

else if and Multiple Conditions

Sometimes, you need to evaluate more than two possibilities. In such cases, you can use the `else if` statement to check additional conditions. This is like setting up a sequence of checks: if the first condition is true, execute its block; if not, move on to the next condition, and so on.

Syntax:

```
if (condition1) {
  // code to be executed if condition1 is true
} else if (condition2) {
  // code to be executed if condition2 is true
} else {
  // code to be executed if neither condition1 nor condition2 is true
}
```

Think of `else if` as a middle ground between `if` and `else`. It lets you create branching logic where multiple paths can be evaluated, and the first condition that matches will execute its block.

Example:

```
let score = 85;

if (score >= 90) {
  console.log("Grade: A");
} else if (score >= 80) {
  console.log("Grade: B");
} else if (score >= 70) {
  console.log("Grade: C");
} else {
  console.log("Grade: F");
}
```

Here's how the program flows:

- If the score is 90 or above, it assigns an "A."
- If it's between 80 and 89, it assigns a "B."
- If it's between 70 and 79, it assigns a "C."
- Anything below 70 results in an "F."

Key Points to Note

- JavaScript evaluates conditions in the order they appear. Once a true condition is found, the remaining `else if` and `else` blocks are skipped.
- The `else` block is optional but serves as a fallback to handle cases where none of the conditions are met.

Handling Multiple Conditions in a Single Check

You can also evaluate multiple conditions simultaneously using logical operators like && (AND) and || (OR).

Example:

```
let age = 25;
if (age >= 18 && age <= 35) {
  console.log("You are in the target age group.");
} else {
  console.log("You are outside the target age group.");
}
```

Here, the condition age >= 18 && age <= 35 ensures that both conditions are true for the message to be logged. If either one is false, the `else` block runs instead.

CHAPTER 10   CONTROL FLOW IN JAVASCRIPT

By combining if, else if, and else with logical operators, you can build robust decision-making structures that handle even complex scenarios effectively.

Ternary Operator

The **ternary operator** is a shorthand for if...else statements. It's a compact and concise expression that evaluates a condition and returns one value if the condition is true and another if it's false.

Syntax:

condition ? expressionIfTrue : expressionIfFalse;

The ? and : act as separators:

- The ? divides the condition from the value to return if it's true.
- The : divides the true value from the false value.

Example:
Let's revisit the login example using the ternary operator:

```
let isLoggedIn = true;

let message = isLoggedIn ? "Welcome back!" : "Please log in.";
console.log(message);
```

Here's what happens:

- If isLoggedIn is true, the expression evaluates to "Welcome back!".
- If isLoggedIn is false, it evaluates to "Please log in.".

The ternary operator allows you to condense the logic into a single line, making it easier to read for straightforward conditions.

Why Use the Ternary Operator?

The primary advantage of the ternary operator is its brevity. It's perfect for situations where you want to assign a value or take a quick action based on a condition, without the need for multiple lines of code.

Nesting Ternary Operators

While it's possible to nest ternary operators for more complex conditions, doing so can make your code harder to read.

Example:

```
let score = 85;
let grade = score >= 90
  ? "A"
  : score >= 80
  ? "B"
  : score >= 70
  ? "C"
  : "F";
console.log(`Grade: ${grade}`);
```

This works similarly to `if-else if-else`, but it's all packed into one line. However, it's generally better to use regular `if-else` statements for more readability when dealing with complex conditions.

When to Use the Ternary Operator

The ternary operator is great for simple conditions, especially when you need to assign a value based on a condition.

> **EXERCISE 3: SIMPLIFYING CONDITIONAL LOGIC**
>
> **Task:** Rewrite an `if...else` statement as a ternary expression. Use it to assign a value to a variable based on whether a number is even or odd.
>
> **Hint:** Use `condition ? valueIfTrue : valueIfFalse`
>
> **Code for Reference:**
>
> ```
> let number = 7;
> // Convert an if...else statement to a ternary expression.
> ```

Why It Matters

Understanding and using control flow structures like `if`, `else if`, and the ternary operator is essential for writing effective JavaScript code. These constructs enable your application to respond dynamically to different conditions, making it flexible, interactive, and capable of handling real-world scenarios.

Decision-Making in Action

Control flow is the backbone of logic in programming. Whether you're building a user login system, calculating grades, or handling form inputs, decisions need to be made based on data. These tools allow you to guide your application's behavior based on the current state or user interactions.

Readability and Maintainability

Each of these constructs serves a purpose:

- **if and else:** These form the foundation of decision-making, making your code easy to understand and follow. They're best suited for straightforward conditions.

- **`else if`:** This helps you handle multiple scenarios without duplicating logic, keeping your code DRY (Don't Repeat Yourself).

- **Ternary Operator:** While it's compact, it encourages concise code for simple decisions, improving readability in the right context.

Knowing when to use each ensures your code remains maintainable and accessible to other developers (and your future self!).

Writing Better Code

Good control flow design directly impacts performance, user experience, and bug prevention. For example

- A poorly implemented `if-else` structure might lead to unintended behaviors or skipped logic.

- Overusing nested ternary operators can make debugging a nightmare.

  By thoughtfully applying these constructs, you can avoid such pitfalls and ensure your code is both functional and clean.

The Bigger Picture

Mastering these foundational tools sets you up for tackling more advanced programming concepts, such as loops, recursion, and asynchronous workflows. It also prepares you to write code that not only works but is robust, efficient, and elegant.

In short, control flow is where code starts to feel like it's "thinking." It empowers your applications to adapt, making them smarter and more user-friendly. Whether you're solving small tasks or building complex systems, these tools are your allies in crafting meaningful logic.

CHAPTER 10   CONTROL FLOW IN JAVASCRIPT

Switch Statements

A **switch statement** is another way to handle multiple conditional branches. It is useful when you have many conditions that depend on the same value. The switch statement is a cleaner alternative to using multiple if...else conditions.

Syntax:

```
switch (expression) {
  case value1:
    // code to be executed if expression === value1
    break;
  case value2:
    // code to be executed if expression === value2
    break;
  default:
    // code to be executed if expression doesn't match any case
}
```

The switch statement evaluates an expression and compares it to the values in the case blocks. When a match is found, the corresponding block is executed. The break statement ensures the program exits the switch after the matched case. If no match is found, the default block is executed (if provided).

Example:

```
let fruit = "apple";
switch (fruit) {
  case "banana":
    console.log("Bananas are yellow.");
    break;
  case "apple":
    console.log("Apples are red or green.");
    break;
  case "orange":
```

```
    console.log("Oranges are orange.");
    break;
  default:
    console.log("Unknown fruit.");
}
```

Here, the `fruit` variable is compared to each `case`, and when it matches `"apple"`, the corresponding message is logged.

Why Use a Switch Statement?

While `if...else` can handle multiple conditions, a `switch` statement is often more readable when all the conditions are based on a single expression or value. It organizes the logic into distinct cases, making it easier to manage and less prone to errors.

Fall-Through Behavior

A key feature of switch statements is the "fall-through" behavior. If you forget to use `break` after a `case`, the code will continue executing subsequent cases, even if they don't match.

Example:

```
let color = "red";
switch (color) {
  case "red":
    console.log("Red color");
  case "green":
    console.log("Green color");
    break;
  default:
    console.log("Unknown color");
}
```

In this case, both "Red color" and "Green color" will be printed because the break statement is missing in the first case.

Intentional Fall-Through

Sometimes, you might want to use fall-through intentionally to group multiple cases together.

Example:

```
let fruit = "apple";

switch (fruit) {
  case "apple":
  case "pear":
    console.log("This is a common fruit.");
    break;
  case "mango":
  case "pineapple":
    console.log("This is a tropical fruit.");
    break;
  default:
    console.log("Unknown fruit.");
}
```

Here, both "apple" and "pear" execute the same code block because of the intentional fall-through.

Switch vs. if...else

- Use a switch statement when you need to compare a single expression against multiple discrete values. It's ideal for enums, user inputs, or menu selections.

- Use if...else when dealing with conditions that involve ranges, logical operators, or more complex evaluations.

By understanding the power of switch statements and their fall-through behavior, you can choose the right control structure for cleaner and more efficient code.

EXERCISE 4: USING SWITCH FOR MULTIPLE CASES

Task: Write a switch statement that categorizes a movie rating (e.g., "G", "PG", "R") into a suitable description. Print the description for each rating, and add a default case for unknown ratings.

Hint: Use case to match specific ratings.

Code for Reference:

```
let rating = "PG";
// Add your switch statement here.
```

Loops in JavaScript

Loops are a fundamental programming tool that allow you to execute a block of code multiple times. They're incredibly powerful when working with repetitive tasks, such as iterating over an array, processing user inputs, or performing calculations. JavaScript offers several types of loops, each designed for specific scenarios: for, while, and do...while.

Let's start with one of the most commonly used loops: the **for loop**.

CHAPTER 10 CONTROL FLOW IN JAVASCRIPT

For Loop

A for loop is perfect when you know in advance how many times you want to repeat a block of code. It's especially useful when iterating through a sequence of numbers or items in a collection, like an array.

Syntax:

```
for (initialization; condition; increment/decrement) {
  // code to be executed
}
```

Here's what each part does:

- **Initialization:** Sets up a starting point, typically by defining a counter variable (e.g., let i = 0).
- **Condition:** A check that determines whether the loop should continue running. As long as this evaluates to true, the loop will execute.
- **Increment:** Updates the counter variable after each iteration (e.g., i++ to increment by 1).

Explaining the Flow

Let's break it down step by step with an example.

Example:

```
for (let i = 0; i < 5; i++) {
  console.log(`Iteration number: ${i}`);
}
```

1. **Initialization:** The loop starts with let i = 0. Here, i acts as our counter.

2. **Condition:** Before each iteration, the loop checks if i < 5. If true, the block of code runs.

3. **Execution:** Inside the loop, `console.log` prints the current value of i.

4. **Increment:** After each iteration, i++ increases the counter by 1.

The loop will repeat these steps until i < 5 evaluates to false. At that point, it stops. The output for this example would be as follows.

Output:

```
Iteration number: 0
Iteration number: 1
Iteration number: 2
Iteration number: 3
Iteration number: 4
```

When to Use a For Loop

A for loop is best when you can define the number of iterations ahead of time. Common use cases include

- Iterating through an array or a range of numbers
- Repeating a specific calculation or operation a set number of times
- Generating a sequence of elements, such as table rows or list items

Explaining the Example

Let's revisit the example.

Example:

```
let numbers = [10, 20, 30, 40, 50];
for (let i = 0; i < numbers.length; i++) {
  console.log(`Element at index ${i}: ${numbers[i]}`);
}
```

In this example

1. **Initialization:** We start with i = 0.
2. **Condition:** The loop runs while i < numbers.length. Since numbers has five elements, the loop runs five times.
3. **Execution:** Inside the loop, numbers[i] retrieves the element at the current index, and console.log displays it.
4. **Increment:** After each iteration, i++ ensures we move to the next index.

The output will be

```
Element at index 0: 10
Element at index 1: 20
Element at index 2: 30
Element at index 3: 40
Element at index 4: 50
```

This straightforward pattern highlights why for loops are so widely used; they're precise, predictable, and easy to read.

Why It Matters

The `for` loop is a fundamental building block in JavaScript, and its importance goes beyond just repeating tasks. Here's why mastering the `for` loop is essential:

1. **Structured Iteration:** The `for` loop provides a clear and concise way to iterate through a block of code when the number of repetitions is known beforehand. This structure makes it easy to read and maintain.

2. **Efficiency with Collections:** It's particularly useful for iterating over arrays, where you often need to access each element or perform operations on them. The loop counter gives you full control over the order and specific elements to process.

3. **Code Optimization:** When used correctly, the `for` loop allows for optimizations that can make your code faster and more efficient. By controlling every aspect of the iteration, you can reduce unnecessary computations and memory usage.

4. **Foundation for Advanced Patterns:** The `for` loop serves as a stepping stone to understanding more advanced concepts like recursion, iteration protocols, and working with modern array methods such as `map`, `filter`, and `reduce`.

5. **Real-World Use Cases:** Whether you're generating dynamic content on a web page, processing data in an array, or running simulations, the `for` loop provides the control and predictability you need to build robust solutions.

CHAPTER 10   CONTROL FLOW IN JAVASCRIPT

By understanding and effectively using the for loop, you're not just learning a syntax; you're gaining a tool that underpins countless operations in JavaScript.

While Loop

The while loop is a versatile tool that runs a block of code as long as a specified condition is true. Unlike a for loop, which is often used when the number of iterations is predetermined, a while loop is ideal for situations where you may not know beforehand how many times the loop should run.

Syntax:

```
while (condition) {
  // code to be executed
}
```

The condition is evaluated before each iteration of the loop:

- If the condition is true, the code inside the loop runs.
- If the condition is false, the loop stops.

Explaining the Flow

Let's break it down with an example.

Example:

```
let count = 0;

while (count < 3) {
  console.log(`Count is: ${count}`);
  count++;
}
```

Here's what happens step by step:

1. **Initialization:** We start with count = 0.
2. **Condition:** Before each iteration, the loop checks if count < 3.
3. **Execution:** If the condition is true, console.log runs, displaying the current value of count.
4. **Update:** After executing the loop's block, count++ increments the value of count.

This process repeats until count reaches 3, at which point the condition becomes false, and the loop exits.

The output will be

```
Count is: 0
Count is: 1
Count is: 2
```

When to Use a While Loop

A while loop shines in situations where the number of iterations depends on a dynamic condition, for example:

- Waiting for user input or an external event
- Processing data until a specific condition is met
- Continuously polling or checking a state, such as waiting for a server response

Potential Pitfall: Infinite Loops

One thing to watch out for with while loops is the possibility of creating an infinite loop. This happens when the condition never becomes false, causing the loop to run endlessly.

To prevent infinite loops

- Always ensure the condition will eventually become `false`.
- Update variables involved in the condition within the loop.

Practical Example Waiting for User Input

Here's a real-world scenario:

```
let password = "";
while (password !== "1234") {
  password = prompt("Enter the correct password:");
}
console.log("Access granted!");
```

- The loop keeps running until the user enters `"1234"`.
- Once the condition (`password !== "1234"`) becomes `false`, the loop exits, and the success message is displayed.

This example highlights the flexibility of `while` loops in handling scenarios where the stopping condition isn't known ahead of time.

Why It Matters

The `while` loop is more than just a tool for repetition; it's a key player in handling dynamic and unpredictable conditions in your code. Here's why it matters:

1. **Dynamic Conditions:** Unlike a `for` loop, a `while` loop doesn't rely on a predetermined number of iterations. This makes it perfect for situations where the stopping condition is based on real-time data, such as waiting for user input or processing live updates.

2. **Flexibility in Logic:** A `while` loop gives you complete control over the flow of your program. You can handle complex scenarios, like continuously checking a system state or retrying an operation until it succeeds, without the rigidity of fixed iteration counts.

3. **Error Handling and Recovery:** Many error-handling patterns use `while` loops to repeatedly attempt an operation until it succeeds or a maximum retry limit is reached. For instance, reconnecting to a server when the connection drops can be elegantly managed with a `while` loop.

4. **Core to Event-Driven Programming:** In event-driven programming, a `while` loop often works behind the scenes to keep your application responsive by continuously monitoring conditions or handling tasks like processing queued events.

By mastering the `while` loop, you'll gain a versatile tool that allows you to handle uncertainty and make your code more adaptive to real-world challenges.

Do...While Loop

The do...while loop is a variation of the while loop, with one key difference: the code block inside a do...while loop is always executed at least once, regardless of the condition. This makes it particularly useful when you want to ensure that a block of code runs before evaluating a condition.

Syntax:

```
do {
  // code to be executed
} while (condition);
```

Here's how it works:

1. The code inside the do block runs first, unconditionally.
2. After executing the code, the condition is evaluated.
3. If the condition is true, the loop runs again. If false, the loop stops.

Explaining the Flow with an Example

Consider this example:

```
let num = 0;

do {
  console.log(`Number is: ${num}`);
  num++;
} while (num < 3);
```

Let's walk through what happens step by step:

1. **Initial Execution:** The code inside the do block runs immediately, printing Number is: 0, and increments num to 1.

CHAPTER 10   CONTROL FLOW IN JAVASCRIPT

2. **Condition Check:** The loop checks the condition num < 3. Since it's true, the loop executes again.

3. **Repeat Until the Condition Is False:** This continues until num reaches 3. At that point, the condition becomes false, and the loop exits.

The output will be

```
Number is: 0
Number is: 1
Number is: 2
```

When to Use a Do...While Loop

The do...while loop is a good choice when you need to guarantee at least one execution of the loop, regardless of the condition, for example:

- Prompting a user for input until they provide valid data
- Initializing or setting up a resource before checking conditions

Practical Example User Input Validation

Here's a real-world scenario:

```
let password;

do {
  password = prompt("Enter your password:");
} while (password !== "securePassword");

console.log("Access granted!");
```

In this case, the do block runs at least once to prompt the user for a password.

If the condition (password !== "securePassword") is still true, the loop prompts the user again until they enter the correct password.

Why It Matters

The do...while loop's guarantee of at least one execution gives it a unique place in your toolkit. Here's why it's important:

1. **Ensuring First Execution:** Sometimes, you need to execute a block of code unconditionally before deciding whether to repeat it. The do...while loop simplifies this logic.

2. **Error Prevention:** It can help prevent edge cases where a while loop might inadvertently skip execution if the initial condition is false.

3. **Real-World Flexibility:** Many real-world scenarios, like user input validation or setup operations, benefit from the predictable behavior of the do...while loop.

By understanding when and how to use the do...while loop, you can write more robust and flexible code for situations where first-time execution is non-negotiable.

forEach Loop

The forEach loop is a modern, elegant way to iterate over arrays in JavaScript. Unlike traditional loops, which require manual handling of loop counters and conditions, the forEach loop focuses purely on executing a provided function for each element in the array. This makes it especially useful for writing cleaner, more readable code.

CHAPTER 10   CONTROL FLOW IN JAVASCRIPT

Syntax:

```
array.forEach(function(element, index, array) {
  // Code to execute for each element
});
```

Here

- element is the current element being processed.
- index (optional) is the index of the current element.
- array (optional) is the array that forEach is being called on.

Explaining the Flow with an Example

Here's an example to clarify how the forEach loop works:

```
const fruits = ["apple", "banana", "cherry"];

fruits.forEach((fruit, index) => {
  console.log(`Fruit ${index + 1}: ${fruit}`);
});
// Output:
// Fruit 1: apple
// Fruit 2: banana
// Fruit 3: cherry
```

Let's break it down:

1. The forEach method is called on the fruits array.
2. For each element in the array, the callback function is executed with the current fruit and its index as arguments.

3. The loop automatically moves to the next element after each iteration, without the need to manually increment a counter.

Output:

```
Fruit 1: apple
Fruit 2: banana
Fruit 3: cherry
```

Why Use forEach?

The `forEach` loop shines when you want to perform an action for each item in an array without needing to explicitly manage iteration details, for example:

- Printing items from a shopping list
- Modifying DOM elements for every data point
- Logging or debugging items in an array

Benefits of `forEach`

- **Readability:** `forEach` is often more readable for simple operations on each array element, as it abstracts away loop control variables (`i` in a `for` loop).
- **Function Context:** Each iteration is executed as a function, which makes `forEach` highly compatible with JavaScript's functional programming style.

Limitations of forEach

- **No Breaking or Continuing:** Unlike for and while loops, forEach does not support break or continue statements. If you need to exit early, a traditional for loop or the some/every array methods might be more suitable.

- **Asynchronous Operations:** forEach is not inherently asynchronous, and using it with await requires careful handling. When using await, a for...of loop is often preferred.

Practical Example Processing Data

Consider this scenario where you want to calculate the total cost of items in a shopping cart:

```
const cart = [
  { item: "Laptop", price: 1000 },
  { item: "Phone", price: 500 },
  { item: "Tablet", price: 300 },
];

let total = 0;

cart.forEach(function(product) {
  total += product.price;
});

console.log(`Total cost: $${total}`);
```

This code

1. Iterates over each object in the `cart` array
2. Adds the `price` of each item to the `total` variable
3. Outputs the total cost after all iterations

Why It Matters

The `forEach` loop isn't just a convenient alternative; it's a step toward writing more expressive and maintainable JavaScript. Here's why it matters:

1. **Improved Readability:** By abstracting away counters and conditions, the `forEach` loop allows you to focus on the logic rather than the mechanics of iteration.
2. **Cleaner Code:** With fewer variables and manual increments, `forEach` produces concise and less error-prone code.
3. **Functional Programming Approach:** It encourages a functional style of programming, which is increasingly favored in modern JavaScript for its simplicity and composability.
4. **Real-World Relevance:** Most data-processing tasks whether it's rendering UI components, calculating totals, or transforming arrays benefit from the simplicity of `forEach`.

By mastering `forEach`, you're taking a significant step toward writing cleaner, more expressive code that aligns with modern JavaScript practices.

for...of Loop

The for...of loop is a modern JavaScript construct designed specifically for iterating over iterable objects like arrays, strings, maps, sets, and more. Unlike the traditional for loop or forEach, the for...of loop gives you direct access to the values of an iterable without dealing with counters or indices.

Syntax:

```
for (const value of iterable) {
  // Code to execute for each value
}
```

Here

- value represents the current value in the iterable object.
- iterable is the collection or object being iterated over (e.g., an array, string, or set).

Explaining the Flow with an Example

Here's an example with an array:

```
const colors = ["red", "blue", "green"];

for (const color of colors) {
  console.log(color);
}
```

Step-by-step Breakdown:

1. The for...of loop begins by accessing the first element of the colors array ("red").

2. Inside the loop, the color variable takes the value "red", which is then logged.
3. The loop proceeds to the next element ("blue") and repeats the process.
4. This continues until all elements of the array have been iterated over.

Output:

red
blue
green

Why Use for...of?

The for...of loop excels in scenarios where you care about the values themselves rather than their indices, for instance

- Iterating through the characters of a string
- Traversing elements in a Set or values in a Map
- Working with arrays when indices are unnecessary

Practical Example Summing Numbers in an Array

Here's a common use case:

Example:

```
const numbers = [10, 20, 30];
let sum = 0;

for (const num of numbers) {
  sum += num;
}
```

CHAPTER 10 CONTROL FLOW IN JAVASCRIPT

```
console.log(`Total sum: ${sum}`);
```

- The `for...of` loop accesses each number in the numbers array.
- Each value is added to the sum variable.
- The total sum, 60, is displayed.

Advanced Example Iterating Through a String

You can also use `for...of` to iterate through the characters of a string.
Example:

```
const word = "hello";
for (const char of word) {
  console.log(char);
}
```

Output:

```
h
e
l
l
o
```

Why It Matters

The `for...of` loop stands out for its simplicity and power, especially in handling modern JavaScript structures. Here's why it's a must-know:

1. **Direct Access to Values:** Unlike traditional loops that rely on indices, `for...of` directly gives you the values, making the code cleaner and easier to understand.

239

2. **Versatile Iteration:** Beyond arrays, `for...of` works with strings, maps, sets, and other iterables, making it highly versatile.

3. **Error Reduction:** By abstracting away index management, `for...of` reduces the likelihood of off-by-one errors or incorrect bounds checks.

4. **Modern JavaScript Paradigm:** It aligns with ES6+ practices, promoting modern and efficient coding techniques.

In short, mastering the `for...of` loop empowers you to handle a wide range of iteration tasks with clarity and precision, making your code more elegant and less error-prone.

Where to Use `for...of` vs. `forEach`

- Use `for...of` when you need more control over loop flow or are working with non-array iterables (like strings or maps).

- Use `forEach` when you only need to apply a function to each item in an array without altering the loop flow.

EXERCISE 5: ITERATING WITH FOR LOOPS

Task: Use a `for` loop to print the numbers from 1 to 10. Add a conditional statement inside the loop to highlight even numbers.

Hint: Use the % operator to check for even numbers.

Code for Reference:

```
// Write a for loop to print numbers from 1 to 10.
```

CHAPTER 10   CONTROL FLOW IN JAVASCRIPT

Using Break and Continue Statements

In JavaScript, the break and continue statements allow you to modify the default flow of loops, making your code more flexible and adaptive to complex scenarios. While break stops the loop entirely, continue skips the current iteration and proceeds to the next one.

These tools are particularly useful for handling edge cases, filtering data, or managing early exits when certain conditions are met.

Break Statement

The break statement immediately terminates the loop when encountered. This is helpful when you've found what you're looking for or no longer need to continue iterating.

Example with break:

```
const numbers = [1, 2, 3, 4, 5];
for (const num of numbers) {
  if (num === 3) {
    console.log("Found 3, stopping the loop.");
    break;
  }
  console.log(num);
}
```

What Happens Here:

1. The loop starts iterating over the numbers array.
2. When the value 3 is encountered, the break statement is executed.
3. The loop stops completely, and the remaining numbers are not processed.

Output:

```
1
2
Found 3, stopping the loop.
```

Continue Statement

The continue statement skips the current iteration and moves on to the next one. It's ideal for cases where you want to exclude specific values or handle them differently without breaking the loop.

Example with continue:

```
const numbers = [1, 2, 3, 4, 5];
for (const num of numbers) {
  if (num % 2 === 0) {
    continue; // Skip even numbers
  }
  console.log(num);
}
```

What Happens Here:

1. The loop starts iterating over the numbers array.
2. For each even number (2 and 4 in this case), the continue statement is executed, skipping the console.log for that iteration.
3. Odd numbers are logged as usual.

Output:

```
1
3
5
```

Why Use Break and Continue?

These statements give you greater control over how loops behave, allowing you to

1. **Optimize Loops:** Stop processing early when you've found what you need.
2. **Handle Special Cases:** Skip over unwanted elements or manage exceptions without cluttering your loop logic.
3. **Improve Readability:** By reducing the need for deeply nested conditionals, break and continue make your loops cleaner and easier to follow.

Practical Example Searching for a Value:

```
const items = ["apple", "banana", "cherry", "date"];
for (const item of items) {
  if (item === "cherry") {
    console.log("Found cherry! Exiting the loop.");
    break;
  }
  console.log(`Checked: ${item}`);
}
```

Output:

```
Checked: apple
Checked: banana
Found cherry! Exiting the loop.
```

This approach prevents unnecessary iterations after finding the desired value, making the code efficient.

When to Use Break and Continue

- Use break when you need to **terminate the loop** early, such as when finding a specific value or reaching a stopping condition.
- Use continue when you want to **skip over certain iterations** without halting the loop entirely, such as filtering out unwanted data.

By mastering these statements, you can write loops that are both efficient and expressive, tailored to your specific requirements.

> **EXERCISE 6: CONTROLLING LOOP EXECUTION**

Task: Write a loop that prints numbers from 1 to 10 but skips numbers divisible by 3. Exit the loop entirely when the number reaches 7.

Hint: Use continue to skip and break to exit.

Code for Reference:

```
// Add a loop with break and continue statements.
```

Why Loops Matter

Loops are an essential concept in JavaScript and in programming in general because they give you the power to automate repetitive tasks. Instead of writing the same block of code multiple times, loops allow you to iterate through collections, process data, and efficiently manage operations.

Key Benefits of Loops

1. **Efficiency:** Loops reduce the need for repetitive code. Whether you're processing large arrays, transforming data, or iterating over strings, loops make the process more efficient.

2. **Automation:** When dealing with multiple similar tasks, like updating items in a list or searching for specific values, loops help you automate the process instead of handling each item manually.

3. **Clean Code:** Without loops, your code would be cluttered with repetitive statements. Loops help reduce boilerplate and make your code more concise and easier to maintain.

4. **Dynamic Flexibility:** Depending on the loop you choose (`for`, `while`, `do...while`, `for...of`), you have dynamic control over how many times the loop runs, the conditions to stop, and how data is accessed, making them highly flexible tools for various scenarios.

5. **Control Flow:** When combined with `break` and `continue`, loops allow you to manage your flow precisely. You can exit early when a condition is met (`break`) or skip specific iterations (`continue`), giving you full control over your logic.

Real-World Use Cases

1. **Processing Arrays:** Whether you're performing calculations or transforming elements, loops let you iterate over arrays and modify data without manually handling each element.

2. **Data Fetching and Display:** When you need to display dynamic content on a web page, such as displaying a list of items retrieved from an API, loops are essential for rendering each item dynamically.

3. **Games and Animations:** Loops are vital in gaming engines and animations, where you need to continuously check game states, update positions, and handle interactions.

In summary, loops are fundamental to programming because they allow you to automate repetitive tasks, improve the efficiency of your code, and keep it neat and readable. By using loops effectively, you can solve problems faster and more cleanly, which is why every JavaScript developer needs to master them.

Nullish Coalescing Operator (??)

In JavaScript, there are a few ways to check for missing or undefined values, but the nullish coalescing operator (??) brings a more targeted approach. It allows you to provide a fallback value only when the left-hand side is null or undefined. This is particularly helpful when you're dealing with variables that could be falsy but are still valid, like 0 or an empty string.

How It Works

The nullish coalescing operator checks if the value on the left is `null` or `undefined`. If it is, it returns the value on the right-hand side. Otherwise, it returns the value on the left. This behavior is different from the logical OR (||), which checks for any falsy value, including 0, `false`, or an empty string.

Syntax:

```
let result = value1 ?? value2;
```

- If `value1` is `null` or `undefined`, `result` will be assigned `value2`.
- Otherwise, `result` will take the value of `value1`.

Example:

```
let username = null;
let defaultName = "Guest";

let user = username ?? defaultName;
console.log(user);   // Output: Guest
```

What Happens Here:

- The `username` is `null`, so the nullish coalescing operator falls back to the `defaultName`, which is "Guest".
- If `username` were an empty string or 0, the value would have stayed as "" or 0, respectively, because those values are **not** considered nullish (`null` or `undefined`).

Why Is This Useful?

You might be wondering, "Why not just use ||?" The key difference is that || will treat **any falsy value** like 0, false, NaN, or an empty string as a reason to apply the fallback. But in many cases, those falsy values are perfectly valid. That's where ?? comes in handy. It only applies the fallback when the value is truly absent, i.e., null or undefined.

For example, imagine a scenario where you're expecting a number or an empty string, and you don't want to overwrite it just because it's falsy:

```
let age = 0;
let defaultAge = 18;

let finalAge = age ?? defaultAge;
console.log(finalAge);  // Output: 0
```

In this case, age is 0, but the ?? operator leaves it unchanged, whereas || would have applied the fallback 18, assuming 0 is falsy.

Real-World Use Case

The nullish coalescing operator is especially useful in situations where you might be fetching data from an external source or handling user input, and you want to ensure that you're only using a fallback when a value is truly missing, not when it's falsy but valid, for example, when working with default settings or optional configuration options in a function:

```
function greet(name) {
  let displayName = name ?? "Anonymous";
  console.log(`Hello, ${displayName}!`);
}

greet();  // Output: Hello, Anonymous!
greet("Alice");  // Output: Hello, Alice!
```

Why It Matters

The nullish coalescing operator (??) simplifies your code by offering a precise way to handle null or undefined values. It's particularly useful when working with default values without accidentally overwriting legitimate falsy values like 0 or "".

By using ??, you can make your code more predictable, avoid unintended overwrites, and improve its readability by clearly defining when you want a fallback.

Logical Nullish Assignment (??=)

The logical nullish assignment (??=) operator is a shorthand way of assigning a value to a variable only if that variable is null or undefined. This can save you from having to write out more verbose checks when you want to ensure that a variable has a default value if it hasn't been set yet.

How It Works

The ??= operator checks if the variable on the left is null or undefined. If it is, it assigns the value on the right to that variable. If the variable already has a valid value (i.e., not null or undefined), it keeps its original value.

Syntax:

variable ??= value;

- If variable is null or undefined, variable will be assigned value.
- Otherwise, variable will keep its current value.

Example:

```
let userPreference = null;
let defaultPreference = "dark mode";

userPreference ??= defaultPreference;
console.log(userPreference);  // Output: dark mode
```

What Happens Here:

- Since `userPreference` is `null`, the `??=` operator assigns `defaultPreference` to `userPreference`.
- If `userPreference` had been something like `"light mode"`, the `??=` operator would have left it unchanged.

Why Is This Useful?

The `??=` operator is useful when you want to set a default value only if a variable hasn't already been initialized. This prevents overwriting valid values like 0, `false`, or an empty string, which are not considered "nullish."

For example, let's consider a scenario where you're initializing a variable to a default value, but you want to keep any valid, existing value:

```
let count = 0;  // Initial count value is 0
let defaultCount = 10;

count ??= defaultCount;
console.log(count);  // Output: 0 (unchanged)
```

Here, even though `count` is falsy (0), the `??=` operator doesn't change it because 0 is a valid value. It only updates `count` if it's `null` or `undefined`.

Real-World Use Case

This operator is especially helpful when dealing with optional values or settings. For example, imagine you're working with a user settings object where some properties might not be set yet. The logical nullish assignment allows you to set defaults without accidentally overwriting valid falsy values like false or 0.

Example:

```
let settings = { theme: null, notifications: false };

settings.theme ??= "light";
// Only updates if null or undefined
settings.notifications ??= true;
// Only updates if null or undefined

console.log(settings);
// Output: { theme: "light", notifications: false }
```

In this case, theme is updated to "light", but notifications remains false because it's a valid value.

Comparison to ||=

While similar, ||= is broader, applying to any "falsy" value. Consider the following:

```
let count = 0;
count ||= 10;
console.log(count); // Output: 10 (because 0 is falsy)

count = 0;
count ??= 10;
console.log(count); // Output: 0 (because 0 is not null or undefined)
```

Using ??= here ensures that values like 0 are preserved, while ||= would replace 0 with 10.

Why It Matters

The logical nullish assignment (??=) operator is a convenient, concise way to handle default values without overwriting already set or valid values. By using ??=, you can simplify your code, reduce verbosity, and make your intention clearer when dealing with potentially missing or uninitialized variables.

Summary of the ??= Operator

The ??= operator helps

- Set default values for variables that are null or undefined without impacting other falsy values.
- Keep code concise when handling optional or missing data, reducing the need for conditional statements.

EXERCISE 7: ASSIGNING DEFAULT VALUES WITH NULLISH COALESCING

Task: Create an object with a settings property. Use the ??= operator to assign default values to the settings only if they are null or undefined.

Hint: You can initialize the object as { settings: null }.

Code for Reference:

```
let config = { settings: null };
// Use ??= to assign a default value to settings.
```

CHAPTER 10 CONTROL FLOW IN JAVASCRIPT

Comparing Control Flow Mechanisms

At this point, we've covered several key control flow mechanisms in JavaScript, each with its own use cases and characteristics. To help solidify your understanding, let's compare these mechanisms side by side. The table below summarizes the key points, allowing you to easily reference when to use each structure in your code:

Control Flow	Description	Use Case	Example
if/else statements	Conditional statements used to evaluate expressions and execute code based on whether the condition is true or false.	When you need to evaluate one or more conditions and take different actions.	if (x > 5) { /* code */ } else { /* code */ }
Switch statements	A clean way to handle multiple conditions based on a single value. It has fall-through behavior, which requires careful handling.	Use when you need to handle several possible conditions based on a single value.	switch(x) { case 1: /* code */ break; default: /* code */ }
For loop	Used when you know how many times you need to iterate through the code block.	When you need a fixed number of iterations.	for (let i = 0; i < 5; i++) { /* code */ }
While loop	Continues to run as long as the condition is true. The number of iterations is not known ahead of time.	When you don't know how many times you need to repeat a block of code.	while (condition) { /* code */ }

(continued)

253

CHAPTER 10   CONTROL FLOW IN JAVASCRIPT

Control Flow	Description	Use Case	Example
do...while loop	Similar to while, but guarantees at least one iteration before checking the condition.	When you want the code block to run at least once before checking the condition.	do { /* code */ } while (condition);
forEach	An array-specific method for iterating through the elements in an array.	For array manipulation or iteration.	array.forEach(item => { /* code */ });
for...of loop	Iterates over iterable objects (arrays, strings, maps, etc.), providing a simpler alternative to a for loop.	When you need to iterate over arrays, strings, or any iterable objects.	for (let item of array) { /* code */ }
Break statement	Immediately exits the loop, stopping further iterations.	Use to exit a loop early based on a condition.	for (let i = 0; i < 5; i++) { if (i === 3) break; }
Continue statement	Skips the current iteration and moves to the next one.	When you need to skip an iteration based on a condition.	for (let i = 0; i < 5; i++) { if (i === 3) continue; }
Nullish coalescing operator (??)	Returns the right-hand operand when the left-hand operand is null or undefined.	To provide a fallback value when dealing with null or undefined.	let result = value ?? 'default';
Logical nullish assignment (??=)	Assigns a value only if the variable is null or undefined.	To assign a default value to a variable only when it is null or undefined.	x ??= 10;

254

This comparison should help you choose the right control flow mechanism depending on your specific coding scenario.

Summary

In this chapter, we've covered the fundamental concepts that allow you to control the flow of your code in JavaScript. These control flow structures are essential for creating dynamic and flexible applications. Here's a recap of the key points:

1. **if/else Statements**:

    We started with the basic decision-making structures in JavaScript, `if` and `else`. These statements evaluate a condition and execute a block of code based on whether the condition is true or false. The `else if` clause allows handling multiple conditions, and we also introduced the ternary operator (`? :`) for shorter conditional expressions.

2. **Switch Statements**:

    Next, we explored `switch` statements, which are ideal when you need to handle multiple possible conditions based on a single value. Switch statements are cleaner alternatives to long chains of `if/else` conditions and come with the notable feature of fall-through behavior, something you need to manage carefully to avoid unintended code execution.

3. **Loops**:

   Loops are a cornerstone of repetition in JavaScript. We looked at different types of loops:

   - **For Loop**: Used when you know exactly how many times to repeat a block of code
   - **While Loop**: Ideal for situations where you want the loop to run as long as a condition is true, without knowing in advance how many iterations you'll need
   - **do...while Loop**: Similar to the `while` loop, but guarantees at least one execution of the code block before checking the condition
   - **forEach**: A method specific to arrays that allows iteration over elements in a clean and functional way
   - **for...of Loop**: A newer loop type that iterates over iterable objects like arrays, strings, and maps, providing a simpler and more readable alternative to `for` loops when working with collections

4. **Break and Continue Statements**:

   We also discussed the `break` and `continue` statements, which are used to modify the default flow of loops. The `break` statement immediately exits the loop, while `continue` skips to the next iteration, both providing greater control over how loops are executed.

5. **Nullish Coalescing Operator (??)**:

    The nullish coalescing operator allows you to handle cases where a value might be null or undefined by providing a fallback value, without mistakenly overriding valid falsy values like 0 or an empty string. This operator makes your code more predictable and avoids unintended overwrites.

6. **Logical Nullish Assignment (??=)**:

    Finally, the logical nullish assignment operator is a shorthand for assigning a default value to a variable only if it's null or undefined. This provides a concise and safe way to ensure variables are initialized without affecting valid falsy values.

These control flow mechanisms empower you to write more dynamic, efficient, and readable JavaScript code. Whether you're making decisions, repeating tasks, or managing default values, understanding these concepts is crucial for writing effective JavaScript applications.

Full Solutions

SOLUTION TO EXERCISE 1: MAKING DECISIONS WITH IF STATEMENTS

```
let number = 5;
if (number > 0) {
   console.log("The number is positive.");
} else if (number < 0) {
   console.log("The number is negative.");
} else {
   console.log("The number is zero.");
}
```

CHAPTER 10　CONTROL FLOW IN JAVASCRIPT

SOLUTION TO EXERCISE 2: HANDLING DEFAULTS WITH ELSE

```
let isLoggedIn = false;
if (isLoggedIn) {
  console.log("Welcome, user123!");
} else {
  console.log("Please log in.");
}
```

SOLUTION TO EXERCISE 3: SIMPLIFYING CONDITIONAL LOGIC

```
let number = 7;
let result = number % 2 === 0 ? "Even" : "Odd";
console.log(result);
```

SOLUTION TO EXERCISE 4: USING SWITCH FOR MULTIPLE CASES

```
let rating = "PG";
switch (rating) {
  case "G":
    console.log("General Audience");
    break;
  case "PG":
    console.log("Parental Guidance Suggested");
    break;
  case "R":
    console.log("Restricted");
    break;
  default:
    console.log("Unknown Rating");
}
```

SOLUTION TO EXERCISE 5: ITERATING WITH FOR LOOPS

```
for (let i = 1; i <= 10; i++) {
  if (i % 2 === 0) {
    console.log(`${i} is even`);
  } else {
    console.log(i);
  }
}
```

SOLUTION TO EXERCISE 6: CONTROLLING LOOP EXECUTION

```
for (let i = 1; i <= 10; i++) {
  if (i % 3 === 0) continue;
  if (i === 7) break;
  console.log(i);
}
```

SOLUTION TO EXERCISE 7: ASSIGNING DEFAULT VALUES WITH NULLISH COALESCING

```
let config = { settings: null };
config.settings ??= "Default Settings";
console.log(config.settings);
```

SOLUTION TO EXERCISE 5: ITERATING WITH FOR LOOPS

```
for (let i = 1; i <= 10; i++) {
  if (i % 2 === 0) {
    console.log(`${i} is even`);
  } else {
    console.log(i);
  }
}
```

SOLUTION TO EXERCISE 6: CONTROLLING LOOP EXECUTION

```
for (let i = 1; i <= 10; i++) {
  if (i % 3 === 0) continue;
  if (i === 7) break;
  console.log(i);
}
```

SOLUTION TO EXERCISE 7: ASSIGNING DEFAULT VALUES WITH NULLISH COALESCING

```
let config = { settings: null };
config.settings ??= "Default Settings";
console.log(config.settings);
```

CHAPTER 11

Functions and Scope

Objective

In this chapter, we will cover the basics of defining and invoking functions in JavaScript, discuss function parameters and return values, and explore the key differences between function expressions and function declarations. We will also explore the power of **arrow functions** in JavaScript and introduce **currying** as an advanced technique for cleaner and more reusable functions. Additionally, we'll dive into how JavaScript handles **scope** to determine the accessibility of variables.

Defining Functions: function Keyword

Functions in JavaScript are one of the fundamental building blocks of the language. A function is a block of code designed to perform a particular task. Functions allow us to group code together, execute it multiple times, and return values.

Function Declaration

The most common way to define a function in JavaScript is using the `function` keyword. Here's a basic example of a function declaration.

Example:

```
function greet(name) {
  console.log(`Hello, ${name}!`);
}

greet("Alice");  // Output: Hello, Alice!
```

In this example

- The function keyword is followed by the function name (greet).
- The function takes one parameter, name, and prints a greeting message.
- The function is invoked with the argument "Alice", which results in the output "Hello, Alice!".

Function Expressions

In addition to declarations, JavaScript also supports **function expressions**, which define functions inside expressions. These can be anonymous or named.

Example:

```
const greet = function(name) {
  console.log(`Hello, ${name}!`);
};

greet("Bob");  // Output: Hello, Bob!
```

The primary difference between a function declaration and a function expression is that **function expressions are not hoisted**, whereas function declarations are. This means that function expressions must be defined before they are called.

Function Hoisting

With function declarations, the entire function is hoisted to the top of its scope, meaning you can call the function before it's defined.

Example:

```
greet("Charlie");  // Output: Hello, Charlie!

function greet(name) {
  console.log(`Hello, ${name}!`);
}
```

However, **function expressions are not hoisted**:

```
greet("Charlie");  // Error: greet is not a function

const greet = function(name) {
  console.log(`Hello, ${name}!`);
};
```

Function Parameters and Return Values

Functions can accept parameters and return values, allowing them to be more dynamic and flexible. They behave like local variables and cannot be changed or accessed outside the function.

Function Parameters

Parameters are the values you pass to a function when calling it. These values are used inside the function. In JavaScript, function parameters are **optional**, and if you don't pass an argument for a parameter, the parameter gets a value of undefined.

CHAPTER 11   FUNCTIONS AND SCOPE

Example:

```
function add(a, b) {
  return a + b;
}

console.log(add(5, 3));  // Output: 8
console.log(add(5));     // Output: NaN
console.log(add());      // Output: NaN
```

EXERCISE 1: UNDERSTANDING VARIABLE DECLARATIONS

Task: Declare three variables in a function using var, let, and const. Modify their values in different scopes and observe the behavior.

Hint: Use a function to test var and a block (e.g., an if statement) to test let and const.

Code for Reference:

```
function testScope() {
  var a = 10;
  let b = 20;
  const c = 30;
  // Add code to test variable re-declarations and scope.
}
```

CHAPTER 11　FUNCTIONS AND SCOPE

Default Parameters

You can assign default values to parameters in case they are not passed in the function call. Default values only apply when no parameters are provided or when the provided value is undefined.

Example:

```
function greet(name = "Stranger") {
  console.log(`Hello, ${name}!`);
}

greet("Alice");   // Output: Hello, Alice!
greet();          // Output: Hello, Stranger!
```

> **EXERCISE 2: EXPLORING DEFAULT PARAMETERS**

Task: Create a function that calculates the area of a rectangle. The function should accept two parameters: `length` and `width`. If no value is provided for `width`, it should default to 10.

Hint: Test the function by providing one, both, or no arguments.

Code for Reference:

```
function calculateArea(length, width) {
  // Your code here.
}
```

Rest Parameters

If you need to pass a variable number of arguments, you can use the **rest parameter** syntax. This allows you to collect all remaining arguments into an array.

265

CHAPTER 11   FUNCTIONS AND SCOPE

Example:

```
function sum(...numbers) {
  return numbers.reduce((acc, num) => acc + num, 0);
}
console.log(sum(1, 2, 3, 4));  // Output: 10
```

In this example, numbers will be an array containing all the passed arguments to the function.

Key Benefits

1. **Array-Like Structure**: Unlike the arguments object, which is available in traditional functions but lacks array methods, rest parameters are real arrays. This means you can use array methods like .map(), .reduce(), .forEach(), and others directly on the args array.

   ```
   function sum(...numbers) {
       return numbers.reduce((acc, num) => acc + num, 0);
   }
   console.log(sum(1, 2, 3, 4)); // Output: 10
   ```

   In the above example, numbers is a real array, so we can use the .reduce() method to calculate the sum of all the arguments passed.

2. **Improved Readability and Flexibility**: Rest parameters provide a more readable and flexible way to work with multiple arguments than the arguments object, as they directly return an array. Additionally, they are always the last parameter in the function definition.

3. **Combining with Other Parameters**: Rest parameters can be used in combination with other named parameters, but they must be placed at the end of the parameter list.

   ```
   function greet(greeting, ...names) {
       console.log(greeting + ' ' + names.join(', '));
   }
   
   greet('Hello', 'John', 'Jane', 'Jim');
   // Output: Hello John, Jane, Jim
   ```

   In this example, the first argument is assigned to greeting, while the remaining arguments are captured by the rest parameter names.

Key Differences from arguments Object

- **Real Array**: Unlike the arguments object, which is an array-like object but lacks array methods (such as .map() or .reduce()), rest parameters are actual arrays, making them more flexible and easier to work with.

- **No Need for Indexing**: The arguments object requires manual indexing to access individual arguments, whereas rest parameters provide direct access to an array.

EXERCISE 3: FINDING THE MAXIMUM NUMBERS WITH REST PARAMETERS

Task: Write a function that accepts any number of arguments using rest parameters and returns the maximum value among them.

CHAPTER 11   FUNCTIONS AND SCOPE

Hint: Use the Math.max method with the spread operator to find the maximum value.

Code for Reference:

```
function findMax(...numbers) {
  // Your code here.
}
```

Destructured Parameters

Destructured parameters simplify working with objects or arrays directly in function signatures, making the code cleaner and more readable. To highlight the value of destructuring, let's first look at how similar examples would appear without destructuring.

Example 1: Without Destructuring (Objects)

Let's first look at a function that doesn't use destructuring. Imagine you have a function displayUser that takes a user object as a parameter. Inside the function, you manually extract the name, age, and city properties from the user object.

```
function displayUser(user) {
  const name = user.name;
  const age = user.age;
  const city = user.city;

  console.log(`Name: ${name}, Age: ${age}, City: ${city}`);
}
const user = { name: 'Alice', age: 30, city: 'Toronto' };
displayUser(user);
```

Output:

Name: Alice, Age: 30, City: Toronto

How It Works: The `displayUser` function accepts a user object. Inside the function, we manually access each property (`user.name`, `user.age`, `user.city`) and assign it to a local variable. While this approach works, it can get repetitive and cumbersome, especially when dealing with objects that have many properties.

With Destructuring

Destructuring simplifies this by allowing you to extract properties directly in the function's parameter list. This reduces the need for extra lines of code and makes it more readable.

```javascript
function displayUser({ name, age, city }) {
  console.log(`Name: ${name}, Age: ${age}, City: ${city}`);
}
const user = { name: 'Alice', age: 30, city: 'Toronto' };
displayUser(user);
```

Output:

Name: Alice, Age: 30, City: Toronto

Explanation:

- In the `displayUser` function, instead of passing the entire user object and then accessing its properties inside the function, we directly destructure the object in the function's parameter list.

- `{ name, age, city }` is a shorthand for extracting the properties from the user object and assigning them to variables with the same name.

CHAPTER 11   FUNCTIONS AND SCOPE

- The function body becomes cleaner because you no longer need to reference user.name, user.age, and user.city; you can directly use the variables name, age, and city.

Advantages of Destructuring:

1. **Cleaner Code:** Reduces the need for extra lines to access object properties.
2. **Improved Readability:** It's immediately clear which properties are expected from the object.
3. **Easier Maintenance:** If you change the object's properties, only the parameter list needs to be updated.

This technique is particularly helpful in cases where you're passing complex objects (like configuration settings or response data) to functions and only need certain properties.

Example 2: Without Destructuring (Arrays)

Just like with objects, destructuring can also be used to simplify extracting values from arrays. Without destructuring, we would typically access array elements by their index, but destructuring lets us do this in a more concise and readable way.

Without Destructuring

In the following example, we have a function calculate that takes an array numbers. Without destructuring, you would manually access each element of the array by its index to extract values:

```
function calculate(numbers) {
  const a = numbers[0];
```

```
  const b = numbers[1];
  return a + b;
}
console.log(calculate([3, 5]));
```

Output:

8

Explanation:

- The function `calculate` takes an array `numbers` as an argument. Inside the function, we explicitly index into the array using `numbers[0]` and `numbers[1]` to assign the first and second elements to variables a and b.

- While this works, it can feel verbose, especially if the array has many elements or you only need a few of them.

With Destructuring

Destructuring makes this process much cleaner and more readable. Here, we can extract the first two elements of the array directly in the function's parameter list:

```
function calculate([a, b]) {
  return a + b;
}
console.log(calculate([3, 5])); // Output: 8
```

Output:

8

Explanation:

- In this version of the `calculate` function, we use destructuring in the parameter list to directly unpack the first two values from the array `[a, b]`.

- The syntax `[a, b]` extracts the first element and assigns it to a and the second element to b.

- The result is that the function is much cleaner and easier to read since there is no need to manually reference the array indices.

Why Destructuring Arrays Is Useful:

1. **Concise Code:** The array elements are extracted and assigned to variables in one step, eliminating the need for multiple indexing operations.

2. **Improved Readability:** It's immediately clear that you're working with the first two elements of the array, making the function's purpose clearer.

3. **Less Error-Prone:** With destructuring, you're less likely to make mistakes like referencing the wrong index, especially when dealing with larger arrays.

Destructuring is a powerful feature that helps to simplify and streamline the process of working with arrays, especially when only a few elements are needed from a larger collection.

Example 3: Real-World Use Case – API Responses

When dealing with data returned from APIs, it's common to receive large objects, but often you only need a small subset of the properties. Destructuring is especially useful in these scenarios, as it allows you to extract only the properties you need, making your code cleaner and easier to maintain.

CHAPTER 11   FUNCTIONS AND SCOPE

Without Destructuring

In this example, we have a function `fetchUserData` that takes a `user` object and extracts the `id` and `email` properties from it. Without destructuring, we manually assign these values to variables inside the function.

```
function fetchUserData(user) {
  const id = user.id;
  const email = user.email;

  console.log(`User ID: ${id}, Email: ${email}`);
}
const apiResponse = { id: 101, email: 'user@example.com', role: 'admin' };
fetchUserData(apiResponse);
```

Output:

```
User ID: 101, Email: user@example.com
```

Explanation:

- The `fetchUserData` function accepts the entire user object, and then we manually extract `id` and `email` from the object using `user.id` and `user.email`.

- This works, but as the object structure grows (e.g., adding more properties), the code becomes more cumbersome. You would need to continue referencing each property, which can become error-prone and harder to maintain.

With Destructuring

By using destructuring, we can simplify the function's parameter list, directly extracting the properties we need from the user object.

```
function fetchUserData({ id, email }) {
  console.log(`User ID: ${id}, Email: ${email}`);
}
const apiResponse = { id: 101, email: 'user@example.com', role: 'admin' };
fetchUserData(apiResponse);
```

Output:

User ID: 101, Email: user@example.com

Explanation:

- In this version, the fetchUserData function directly destructures the id and email properties from the user object in the parameter list.
- The destructuring syntax { id, email } makes it clear that the function is only concerned with these two properties, reducing unnecessary lines of code and improving the clarity of the function signature.

Key Benefits of Destructuring in Function Parameters

1. **Improved Readability:**
    - Destructuring simplifies the function signature, making it clear which properties from the object are needed. This helps other developers (or your future self) quickly understand what the function does without diving into the function body.

2. **Reduced Boilerplate Code:**

   - Destructuring eliminates the need for multiple variable assignments (`const id = user.id; const email = user.email;`). This keeps your code concise, especially when you only need a few properties from an object.

3. **Minimized Errors:**

   - When you manually access properties from an object multiple times, there's a higher chance of making a typo (e.g., `user.emial` instead of `user.email`). Destructuring reduces this risk by clearly defining the properties you're interested in up front.

4. **Better Maintenance:**

   - As your project evolves and new properties are added to objects, destructuring ensures that changes are localized to the function signature. If the structure of the object changes, you only need to adjust the destructured properties in the parameter list rather than modifying multiple lines inside the function body.

Real-World Use Case

This approach is especially common in modern JavaScript applications, where APIs often return complex objects. Destructuring helps streamline the process of extracting only the data you need and can significantly enhance the maintainability and clarity of your code. Whether you're handling user data, configuration objects, or API responses, destructuring is an invaluable tool for writing clean and efficient JavaScript.

CHAPTER 11   FUNCTIONS AND SCOPE

Returning Values from Functions

In JavaScript, functions can return values, which are sent back to the caller using the `return` statement. This is an essential feature of functions, as it allows them to produce and send results for further use.

Returning Single Values

Let's start with a basic example where a function returns a single value. In this case, the function `multiply` takes two numbers as parameters and returns their product.

Example:

```
function multiply(a, b) {
  return a * b;
}
let result = multiply(4, 5);
console.log(result);   // Output: 20
```

Explanation:

- The `multiply` function takes two arguments, a and b, and returns their product using the `return` statement.

- The function is called with the arguments 4 and 5, and the result of 4 * 5, which is 20, is returned and logged to the console.

- If a function does not explicitly return a value, JavaScript will return `undefined` by default.

Returning Multiple Values

JavaScript also allows functions to return multiple values, making it easier to work with complex data. This can be done using arrays or objects. Let's explore both options.

Example 1 – Returning Multiple Values Using an Object:
In this example, the getStats function calculates the sum and average of an array of numbers. It returns these values as an object with two properties: sum and average.

```
function getStats(numbers) {
  const sum = numbers.reduce((a, b) => a + b, 0);
  const average = sum / numbers.length;
  return { sum, average };
}
const stats = getStats([10, 20, 30]);
console.log(stats); // Output: { sum: 60, average: 20 }
```

Explanation:

- The function getStats takes an array of numbers as input.
- It uses the reduce method to calculate the sum of the numbers and then calculates the average by dividing the sum by the number of elements in the array.
- These two values (sum and average) are returned in an object, making it easy to access and use them in one step.
- The output logs the object { sum: 60, average: 20 }, showing the sum and average of the numbers.

CHAPTER 11   FUNCTIONS AND SCOPE

Benefits of Returning Multiple Values with Objects:

- **Descriptive:** Using object keys like sum and average makes it clear what the values represent, improving readability and making the code self-documenting.
- **Scalable:** If you need to return additional statistics, you can easily add new properties to the object without changing the function's interface too much.

Example 2 – Returning Values Using Arrays:

Another common approach to returning multiple values is using arrays. In this example, the getMinMax function returns the minimum and maximum values from an array.

```
function getMinMax(numbers) {
  return [Math.min(...numbers), Math.max(...numbers)];
}
const [min, max] = getMinMax([5, 10, 15]);
console.log(`Min: ${min}, Max: ${max}`); // Output: Min: 5, Max: 15
```

Explanation:

- The getMinMax function uses the Math.min and Math.max functions to find the smallest and largest numbers in the array numbers.
- It returns the minimum and maximum values in an array.
- The array is destructured into two variables min and max when the function is called, making it easy to access both values.
- The output logs Min: 5, Max: 15, showing the smallest and largest values from the array.

Benefits of Returning Multiple Values with Arrays:

- **Simplicity:** Returning values in an array is straightforward and works well when the order of values is clear and fixed (e.g., min first, max second).

- **Convenience:** Array destructuring allows easy assignment of the returned values to separate variables in one step.

Conclusion:

- **Returning a Single Value:** Functions can return a single value, which is useful for simple calculations or when only one result is needed.

- **Returning Multiple Values:** You can return multiple values from a function using arrays or objects. Arrays work well when the order of the returned values is important, while objects are ideal for returning multiple related values with descriptive keys.

- **Destructuring:** With destructuring, you can directly extract the values returned in an array or object, making the code cleaner and easier to understand.

This flexibility in returning values allows you to write more powerful and flexible functions, which can handle a variety of data types and structures efficiently.

Validating Function Arguments

Validating function arguments is a crucial part of writing reliable JavaScript functions. Proper validation ensures that your functions behave predictably and prevents runtime errors that can be hard to debug.

CHAPTER 11   FUNCTIONS AND SCOPE

Let's explore three common methods of argument validation: manual validation, using default values, and employing early returns for complex validation.

Example 1 – Manual Validation:

In this example, we will manually validate the arguments passed to the `divide` function to ensure they are numbers and that the denominator is not zero.

```
function divide(a, b) {
  if (typeof a !== 'number' || typeof b !== 'number') {
    throw new Error('Arguments must be numbers');
  }
  if (b === 0) {
    throw new Error('Division by zero is not allowed');
  }
  return a / b;
}
try {
  console.log(divide(6, 3)); // Output: 2
  console.log(divide(6, 0)); // Error: Division by zero is
                                not allowed
} catch (error) {
  console.error(error.message);
}
```

Explanation:

- The `divide` function first checks whether both arguments a and b are of type number. If either is not a number, an error is thrown with the message `'Arguments must be numbers'`.

- Next, it checks if b is zero, throwing an error `'Division by zero is not allowed'` to prevent a runtime error from dividing by zero.

- The `try...catch` block is used to handle these errors and log them to the console when an invalid argument is passed.

- The output demonstrates both valid and invalid function calls: one that returns 2 (valid) and another that throws an error for division by zero.

Key Takeaway: Manual validation allows you to catch specific errors like type mismatches or invalid values before the function proceeds with its logic.

Example 2 – Using Default Values:

```
function greet(name = 'Guest') {
  console.log(`Hello, ${name}!`);
}

greet('Alice'); // Output: Hello, Alice!
greet();        // Output: Hello, Guest!
```

Explanation:

- The greet function accepts a parameter name. If no value is provided for name, it defaults to `'Guest'`.

- The first call to greet(`'Alice'`) outputs Hello, Alice! because `'Alice'` is passed as an argument.

- The second call to greet() outputs Hello, Guest! because no argument is passed, and the default value `'Guest'` is used.

Key Takeaway: Default values make functions more flexible and ensure that a valid value is always available, even if the caller omits an argument.

Example 3 – Early Returns for Complex Validation:

In some cases, validation requires checking multiple conditions before proceeding. Early returns allow you to exit the function as soon as an invalid condition is met, reducing the need for nested `if` statements.

```
function processOrder(order) {
  if (!order || !order.items || order.items.length === 0) {
    console.log('Invalid order');
    return;
  }
  console.log(`Processing ${order.items.length} items.`);
}
processOrder({ items: ['apple', 'banana'] });
// Output: Processing 2 items.
processOrder(); // Output: Invalid order
```

Explanation:

- The `processOrder` function checks if the `order` object is valid. It ensures that `order` exists, that `order.items` is defined, and that `order.items` contains at least one item.

- If any of these conditions are not met, the function logs `'Invalid order'` and immediately returns, skipping the processing logic.

- The first call to `processOrder` is valid, so it processes the order and logs `Processing 2 items`.

- The second call, which passes no argument, fails the validation, logging `'Invalid order'`.

CHAPTER 11   FUNCTIONS AND SCOPE

Key Takeaway: Early returns help reduce nesting and make the code more readable by handling invalid cases up front. This technique is particularly useful for functions with complex validation logic.

Summary of Techniques

1. **Manual Validation:** Check the types and values of function arguments before performing any operations. This ensures the function operates as expected and prevents errors.

2. **Default Values:** Set default values for parameters to ensure a function always has valid input, even when arguments are omitted.

3. **Early Returns:** Quickly return from the function if any validation conditions fail, reducing the need for deep nesting and improving readability.

By incorporating these validation techniques, you can write more robust and predictable functions, ultimately improving the reliability of your JavaScript code.

Arrow Functions

Arrow functions, introduced in ES6 (ECMAScript 2015), offer a more concise and readable syntax for defining functions. They are commonly used for inline functions, and they simplify function expressions by eliminating the need for the `function` keyword, curly braces, and the `return` statement in certain cases. Arrow functions are particularly useful in array methods such as .map(), .filter(), and .reduce(), where they make the code more concise and readable.

Let's dive into the syntax and examples.

Basic Syntax:

The basic syntax for an arrow function involves the following structure:

```
const functionName = (parameter1, parameter2) => expression;
```

In the example below, the add function adds two numbers. The syntax uses the arrow (=>) to define the function, and because it is a simple expression, the result is implicitly returned without needing the return keyword:

```
const add = (a, b) => a + b;
console.log(add(3, 4));  // Output: 7
```

Explanation:

- The add function takes two parameters, a and b.
- The function body contains the expression a + b, which is implicitly returned, so no need for a return statement.
- The output of calling add(3, 4) is 7.

Key Takeaway: Arrow functions provide a compact syntax that makes your code cleaner and more concise, especially for simple operations.

Single Parameter

If the function has only one parameter, you can omit the parentheses around the parameter. This is another feature that reduces the verbosity of arrow functions.

Example:

```
const square = x => x * x;
console.log(square(5));  // Output: 25
```

CHAPTER 11 FUNCTIONS AND SCOPE

Explanation:

- The `square` function has a single parameter, x, so the parentheses around x are optional.
- The function returns the square of x without needing a `return` keyword.
- The output of calling `square(5)` is 25.

Key Takeaway: Arrow functions allow for even more concise syntax when dealing with a single parameter, improving readability.

No Parameters

If the function takes no parameters, you must use empty parentheses to define it.

Example:

```
const greet = () => console.log("Hello!");
greet();  // Output: Hello!
```

Explanation:

- The greet function does not take any parameters, so it's defined with empty parentheses ().
- The function simply logs "Hello!" to the console when called.
- The output of calling `greet()` is "Hello!".

Key Takeaway: Arrow functions with no parameters are still concise and clear. The empty parentheses indicate no arguments are needed for the function.

285

Benefits of Arrow Functions

1. **Concise Syntax:** Arrow functions are more succinct than regular function expressions, making your code more compact and readable.

2. **Implicit Return:** For single-expression bodies, arrow functions implicitly return the result of the expression, eliminating the need for an explicit return statement.

3. **No this Binding:** One of the major advantages of arrow functions is that they do not bind their own this. Instead, they inherit this from the surrounding context, which makes them particularly useful in scenarios like callbacks, where maintaining the correct this value is important.

Arrow functions are a great tool for simplifying your code, especially when working with inline functions or functions that only need to perform simple operations.

The this Keyword: Understanding Context

In JavaScript, the this keyword is one of the most important and often misunderstood aspects of the language. Understanding how this works is crucial because its behavior changes depending on where and how a function is called.

This section will explain how the this keyword behaves in different contexts, how to use it effectively, and how to control its value when necessary.

What Is `this`?

The `this` keyword refers to the **execution context** of a function. In simple terms, it's a reference to the object that is currently executing the code. The value of `this` is determined by how a function is called, not where it's defined.

Here are a few scenarios to illustrate how `this` behaves:

- **In a Method**: `this` refers to the object that owns the method.

- **In a Regular Function**: In non-strict mode, `this` refers to the global object (in browsers, it's `window`).

- **In an Arrow Function**: Arrow functions do not have their own `this` context; they inherit it from the surrounding (lexical) context.

`this` in Methods

When a function is called as a method of an object, `this` refers to the object itself. This is the most common and intuitive use of `this`.

```
const person = {
  name: "John",
  greet: function() {
    console.log(`Hello, my name is ${this.name}`);
  }
};
person.greet();  // "Hello, my name is John"
```

In this case, `this.name` refers to the `name` property of the `person` object because `greet` is called as a method of `person`.

`this` in Regular Functions

In non-strict mode, when a regular function is called in the global scope or in a standalone manner (not as a method of an object), `this` refers to the global object. In browsers, this is the `window` object.

```
function showGlobal() {
  console.log(this);  // In non-strict mode, `this` refers to
                      the `window` object
}
showGlobal();
```

However, in **strict mode**, `this` will be `undefined` when called in a global context or within a function that's not bound to an object.

```
"use strict";
function showStrict() {
  console.log(this);  // `this` will be `undefined` in
                      strict mode
}
showStrict();
```

`this` in Arrow Functions

Arrow functions have a unique behavior when it comes to `this`. Unlike regular functions, arrow functions do not have their own `this`. Instead, they **lexically bind** `this` to the surrounding (enclosing) context in which they are defined.

```
const person = {
  name: "John",
  greet: () => {
```

CHAPTER 11 FUNCTIONS AND SCOPE

```
    console.log(`Hello, my name is ${this.name}`);  // `this`
    does NOT refer to `person`
  }
};

person.greet();  // `this.name` is `undefined` because `this`
is inherited from the outer context
```

In the example above, `this` refers to the context outside the `person` object (likely the global object or `undefined` in strict mode), not to the `person` object. This behavior is one of the key distinctions between regular and arrow functions.

Binding this with .bind(), .call(), and .apply()

JavaScript provides methods to explicitly set the value of `this`. These methods are `.bind()`, `.call()`, and `.apply()`. They are useful when you want to call a function but control the `this` context.

.bind()

The `.bind()` method creates a new function that, when invoked, has its `this` value set to the provided object.

```
const person = {
  name: "John",
  greet: function() {
    console.log(`Hello, my name is ${this.name}`);
  }
};

const greetJohn = person.greet.bind(person);
greetJohn();  // "Hello, my name is John"
```

289

In this case, `.bind()` ensures that `this` inside the `greet` function always refers to the `person` object, even if `greet` is called elsewhere.

.call() and .apply()

Both `.call()` and `.apply()` immediately invoke the function with a specified `this` value, but they differ in how arguments are passed to the function:

- `.call()` accepts arguments directly after the `this` value.
- `.apply()` accepts arguments as an array.

```
const person = {
  name: "John"
};

function greet(greeting) {
  console.log(`${greeting}, my name is ${this.name}`);
}

greet.call(person, "Hello");   // "Hello, my name is John"
greet.apply(person, ["Hello"]); // "Hello, my name is John"
```

In both cases, `this` is explicitly set to the `person` object.

`this` in Constructors and Classes

In JavaScript, when using a constructor function or class to create new objects, `this` refers to the new instance that is being created.

Constructor Function:

```
function Person(name) {
  this.name = name;
}
```

```
const john = new Person("John");
console.log(john.name);  // "John"
```

Here, this.name refers to the name property of the newly created object.

this in Classes

In ES6, classes provide a more structured way to define constructor functions.

```
class Person {
  constructor(name) {
    this.name = name;
  }

  greet() {
    console.log(`Hello, my name is ${this.name}`);
  }
}

const john = new Person("John");
john.greet();  // "Hello, my name is John"
```

In both examples, this refers to the instance of the Person object being created.

this in Event Handlers

In the context of event handling, this typically refers to the element that triggered the event, unless the event handler is written as an arrow function (which inherits the this value).

```
const button = document.querySelector("button");
```

```
button.addEventListener("click", function() {
  console.log(this);  // `this` refers to the button element
});

button.addEventListener("click", () => {
  console.log(this);  // `this` refers to the outer context,
                      not the button
});
```

In the first event handler, this refers to the button element that was clicked. In the second, this refers to the surrounding lexical context due to the arrow function, which is typically the global object or undefined in strict mode.

Conclusion

The this keyword is central to JavaScript's object-oriented nature and can sometimes be a source of confusion. The value of this depends on how and where a function is invoked. It refers to the object that owns the function (in methods), the global object (in regular functions), or is lexically bound to its surrounding context (in arrow functions). Understanding how to manipulate and control this using .bind(), .call(), and .apply() is essential for managing function context and ensuring your code behaves as expected.

By mastering the intricacies of this, you can write more predictable, maintainable JavaScript and avoid common pitfalls that arise from misunderstandings about the execution context.

CHAPTER 11   FUNCTIONS AND SCOPE

> **EXERCISE 4: ARROW FUNCTIONS AND CONTEXT**

Task: Rewrite a regular function that calculates the square of a number as an arrow function. Test the behavior of `this` in both cases by placing them inside an object method.

Hint: Compare `this` when using regular functions vs. arrow functions.

Code for Reference:
```
const obj = {
  number: 5,
  regularSquare: function (n) {
    // Your code here.
  },
  arrowSquare: (n) => {
    // Your code here.
  }
};
```

Scope: Global vs. Local Variables

In JavaScript, **scope** refers to the context in which variables and functions are accessible. Understanding how scope works is crucial for managing where and how your variables can be accessed and modified. There are two main types of scope in JavaScript: **global scope** and **local scope**.

Global Scope

A variable defined outside of any function or block is said to have **global scope**. This means that the variable can be accessed and modified from anywhere in your JavaScript code, including inside functions or blocks.

Example:

```
let globalVar = "I am global";

function greet() {
  console.log(globalVar);
}

greet();  // Output: I am global
```

Explanation:

- In this example, the variable `globalVar` is defined outside the `greet()` function, so it is in the global scope.
- The `greet()` function has access to the global variable and logs its value when called.
- When `greet()` is executed, it outputs "I am global" because `globalVar` is accessible anywhere in the code.

Key Takeaway: Variables in the global scope are accessible from any part of the code, including within functions. However, overuse of global variables can lead to potential issues like accidental modifications or conflicts between variables.

Local Scope

In JavaScript, **local scope** refers to variables that are defined within a function. These variables can only be accessed inside that function and are not accessible from outside. This helps ensure that function-specific data is isolated and protected from other parts of the program.

Example:

```
function greet() {
  let localVar = "I am local";
  console.log(localVar);
}
greet();   // Output: I am local
console.log(localVar);   // Error: localVar is not defined
```

Explanation:

- The variable `localVar` is declared inside the `greet()` function, which means it has local scope.

- It is accessible only within the `greet()` function and can be logged successfully inside it.

- Trying to access `localVar` outside of the function results in an error because it is not defined in the global or outer scope.

Key Takeaway: Variables defined within a function (local variables) are confined to that function. They cannot be accessed outside the function unless explicitly returned or exposed.

Block Scope

Before ES6, JavaScript had only function scope, meaning variables declared inside functions were accessible throughout the entire function. With the introduction of `let` and `const` in ES6, JavaScript now supports **block scope**, meaning variables declared with these keywords are only accessible within the nearest enclosing block (such as a loop or conditional statement).

Example:

```
if (true) {
  let blockScopedVar = "I am block scoped";
  console.log(blockScopedVar);  // Output: I am block scoped
}
console.log(blockScopedVar);  // Error: blockSccpedVar is
                                 not defined
```

Explanation:

- The variable blockScopedVar is declared inside an if block using let. This means its scope is confined to the block.
- Inside the if block, the variable is accessible and can be logged.
- Outside the block, trying to access blockScopedVar results in an error because it only exists within the if block's scope.

Key Takeaway: Variables declared with let and const have block scope, meaning they are only accessible within the block (defined by curly braces {}). They do not leak outside the block like variables declared with var.

Lexical Scope

Lexical scope is a crucial concept in JavaScript. It means that a function's scope is determined by where the function is defined, not where it is called. This allows JavaScript to "remember" the scope in which a function was created, which is essential for understanding **closures**.

Example:

```
function outerFunction() {
  let outerVar = "I am from outer!";

  function innerFunction() {
    console.log(outerVar);  // Accessing outerVar from the
                            outer function
  }

  innerFunction();
}
outerFunction();  // Output: I am from outer!
```

Explanation:

- innerFunction() is defined inside outerFunction(), and it has access to variables in outerFunction()'s scope.

- Even though innerFunction() is called inside outerFunction(), it "remembers" the scope where it was defined and can access outerVar, which is declared in the outer function.

Key Takeaway: Lexical scoping allows functions to access variables from their enclosing scope, which is vital for closures. It means a function's scope chain is determined by where it was created, not where it is executed.

CHAPTER 11   FUNCTIONS AND SCOPE

Currying in JavaScript
What Is Currying?

Currying is a functional programming technique where a function that takes multiple arguments is transformed into a sequence of functions, each taking one argument. The main advantage of currying is that it allows partial application of a function, meaning you can create specialized functions by pre-filling some arguments. However, in performance-sensitive applications, excessive currying should be avoided as it can introduce memory overhead. Each curried function returns a new function, which could lead to increased memory consumption, especially when curried functions are created in large numbers at runtime. This could impact performance in high-volume scenarios.

Example:

```
// Basic example of currying
function multiply(a) {
  return function(b) {
    return a * b;
  };
}
const multiplyBy2 = multiply(2); // Pre-filling the first
                                    argument
console.log(multiplyBy2(5));     // Output: 10
console.log(multiplyBy2(10));    // Output: 20
```

In this example, `multiply` is a curried function. When we call `multiply(2)`, it returns a new function that takes b and multiplies it by 2. This allows us to create a specialized function, `multiplyEy2`, that always multiplies any number by 2.

CHAPTER 11   FUNCTIONS AND SCOPE

Benefits of Currying

1. **Reusability**: Currying makes it easy to create new functions from existing ones. For example, if you need to create several functions that multiply numbers by different constants (e.g., `multiplyBy2`, `multiplyBy3`, etc.), currying makes this efficient and concise.

2. **Partial Application**: Currying allows for partial application of arguments. This is especially useful when you want to pass some arguments to a function in advance, leaving the rest to be provided later.

   For example, let's say you have a function that formats a message:

   ```
   function formatMessage(greeting, name) {
     return `${greeting}, ${name}!`;
   }

   const greet = formatMessage.bind(null, "Hello");
   console.log(greet("Alice"));  // Output: Hello, Alice!
   ```

   With currying, you can achieve similar results by pre-filling one argument:

   ```
   function curriedFormatMessage(greeting) {
     return function(name) {
       return `${greeting}, ${name}!`;
     };
   }

   const greet = curriedFormatMessage("Hello");
   console.log(greet("Alice"));  // Output: Hello, Alice!
   ```

3. **Cleaner Code**: Currying can make your code more readable and concise by avoiding repeated boilerplate and allowing functions to be more declarative.

4. **Functional Composition**: Currying works well in functional programming patterns like **composing** multiple small functions into larger ones. You can create small, reusable functions and combine them into more complex behaviors.

5. **Immutability and Side Effect-Free**: Curried functions tend to be immutable and free from side effects, making them easier to reason about and test.

Popular Use Cases for Currying

Event Handlers

You can create specialized event handlers by currying. For example, instead of passing all parameters to an event listener, you can create specific functions by currying the handler.

The `logEvent` Function

Example:

```
function logEvent(eventType) {
  return function(message) {
    console.log(`${eventType}: ${message}`);
  };
}
```

CHAPTER 11   FUNCTIONS AND SCOPE

1. **The Outer Function (logEvent):**
   The logEvent function takes a parameter eventType, which will be used to determine the type of event (e.g., INFO, ERROR, etc.).

2. **The Inner Function (Returned by logEvent):**
   When logEvent is called with a specific eventType, it returns a **new function** that expects a message parameter. This inner function logs a message to the console with the event type prefixed.
   The key idea here is that the returned function can access the eventType parameter, even though it is defined in the outer function. This happens due to **closures**, where the inner function "remembers" the values of variables from its outer function.

3. **Console Logging:**
   The inner function outputs a log in the format eventType: message, where eventType is the event type provided when calling logEvent and message is the input passed to the returned function.

How the Code Works:

```
const infoLogger = logEvent("INFO");
const errorLogger = logEvent("ERROR");
```

- When you call logEvent("INFO"), it returns a new function that logs messages with the prefix INFO. This returned function is assigned to the infoLogger variable.

- Similarly, calling logEvent("ERROR") returns a function that logs messages with the prefix ERROR, which is assigned to the errorLogger variable.

301

CHAPTER 11 FUNCTIONS AND SCOPE

At this point

- `infoLogger` is a function that will log messages with the `INFO` prefix.

- `errorLogger` is a function that will log messages with the `ERROR` prefix.

  ```
  infoLogger("This is an info message");  // Output:
  INFO: This is an info message
  errorLogger("This is an error message");  // Output:
  ERROR: This is an error message
  ```

- When `infoLogger("This is an info message")` is called, it logs `INFO: This is an info message` to the console, because the `eventType` was set to `INFO` when `logEvent("INFO")` was called.

- Similarly, when `errorLogger("This is an error message")` is called, it logs `ERROR: This is an error message`, because the `eventType` was set to `ERROR` when `logEvent("ERROR")` was called.

Key Concepts Illustrated in This Example

- **Higher-Order Functions (HOFs):**
  `logEvent` is a higher-order function because it returns another function. Higher-order functions are functions that either take other functions as arguments or return functions.

- **Closures:**
  The inner function returned by `logEvent` has access to the `eventType` parameter from the outer `logEvent`

CHAPTER 11   FUNCTIONS AND SCOPE

function, even after `logEvent` has finished executing. This is an example of a closure, an inner function that "remembers" variables from its outer function.

- **Reusability:**
  By calling `logEvent` with different arguments (`"INFO"`, `"ERROR"`), we create two distinct loggers `infoLogger` and `errorLogger` that can be used independently. This makes the code reusable and adaptable for different types of events.

Why This Is Useful

This pattern is particularly useful when you need to create specialized functions based on a common behavior. In this case, instead of writing separate logging functions for each event type, you create a single `logEvent` function that can be reused for different types of events. It makes your code more modular and easier to maintain, as you can easily adjust the logging behavior for different event types without repeating code.

Functional Programming Libraries

Many functional programming libraries like **Lodash** and **Ramda** use currying to enable more flexible, readable, and chainable operations. Functions in these libraries are designed to be curried, allowing users to compose them as needed.

Pure Functions vs. Impure Functions:

- **Pure Functions**: A pure function's output is determined solely by its input values, with no observable side effects. This makes them easier to reason about, test, and compose. For example, a curried function from Ramda or Lodash that performs transformations on data without modifying any external state is considered pure.

- **Impure Functions**: In contrast, impure functions may rely on or modify external states, such as global variables or interacting with the I/O (e.g., making HTTP requests, modifying a DOM). Because of this, their behavior can change depending on factors outside the function's parameters, which can make debugging and testing harder.

Functional programming libraries generally promote **pure functions** because of their predictability and ease of composition, helping to avoid side effects and improving code maintainability. In libraries like Lodash and Ramda, curried functions are commonly pure, enabling you to compose smaller, more predictable pieces of logic together for more complex operations.

Configuration Settings

Currying can be helpful when working with configuration-based APIs. It allows you to pre-fill configuration parameters and create specialized functions with minimal code.

Example:

```
function setConfig(apiUrl) {
  return function(method) {
    return function(data) {
      // Simulate an API call
      console.log(`Making ${method} request to ${apiUrl} with data:`, data);
    };
  };
}
```

```
const apiV1 = setConfig("https://api.example.com/v1");
const postRequest = apiV1("POST");
postRequest({ name: "John Doe" });  // Output: Making POST
request to https://api.example.com/v1 with data: { name:
'John Doe' }
```

1. **The Outer Function (setConfig):**
   The `setConfig` function takes a parameter `apiUrl` that represents the base URL of an API. It returns a **curried function**, which is a function that returns another function.

   - This pattern is useful when you need to build a series of functions, each taking specific arguments. In this case, you first provide the API URL.

2. **The Inner Function (method):**
   When you call `setConfig()`, it returns another function that takes the `method` parameter. This method represents the HTTP method, such as GET, POST, PUT, etc.

3. **The Nested Inner Function (data):**
   Finally, this returned function takes a `data` argument, which represents the data to be sent in the API request (in a real-world application, this could be the request body for a POST request). It simulates an API call by logging the HTTP method, API URL, and the data to the console.

Each function in this chain has access to the variables defined in the outer functions due to JavaScript's **lexical scoping**. This is what allows the functions to "remember" the `apiUrl` and `method` even after they are executed.

CHAPTER 11 FUNCTIONS AND SCOPE

The Code Execution:

```
const apiV1 = setConfig("https://api.example.com/v1");
```

- The first line creates a new instance of the setConfig function by calling it with the API URL https://api.example.com/v1.
- The setConfig function returns the next function, which expects the HTTP method parameter.

  ```
  const postRequest = apiV1("POST");
  ```

- Now, apiV1("POST") is called with the HTTP method POST. This returns another function that expects the data parameter. So postRequest is a function waiting for data to be passed in.

  ```
  postRequest({ name: "John Doe" });
  ```

- When postRequest({ name: "John Doe" }) is called, it executes the third function and logs the following output to the console:

  ```
  Making POST request to https://api.example.com/v1 with data: { name: 'John Doe' }
  ```

Key Concepts Illustrated in This Example

- **Currying:**
  Currying is a functional programming technique where a function takes multiple arguments, but instead of receiving them all at once, it returns a series of functions that each take one argument. In this case, setConfig returns a function that expects method, and that function returns another one that expects data.

306

- **Closures:**
  Closures allow inner functions to access variables from their outer functions, even after the outer functions have finished executing. In this case, the inner functions returned by `setConfig` still have access to `apiUrl` and `method`, even after `setConfig` has finished executing.

Why This Is Useful

This pattern is powerful when you want to set up reusable logic that is partially configured (like the API URL) and then execute different actions with various methods (like POST, GET, etc.) and data. You can extend this pattern to create more complex, reusable API request functions for different endpoints and HTTP methods.

Mathematical Operations

Currying is especially useful in mathematical operations where you often deal with partially applied functions, such as when building reusable, configurable math functions.

The `curriedAdd` Function:

```
function curriedAdd(a) {
  return function(b) {
    return a + b;
  };
}
```

1. **The Outer Function (`curriedAdd`):**
   The `curriedAdd` function takes a single argument a and **returns a new function**. This returned function takes another argument b.

CHAPTER 11   FUNCTIONS AND SCOPE

2. **The Inner Function**:
   The inner function (which is returned by curriedAdd) accepts the argument b and returns the sum of a and b. The key here is that the value of a is preserved from the outer function (curriedAdd), thanks to **closures**. This allows the inner function to access a even after the outer function has finished executing.

3. **Closure**:
   The inner function "remembers" the value of a from its outer scope (when curriedAdd is first called), allowing the summation to occur later when b is provided.

How the Code Works:

```
const add5 = curriedAdd(5);
```

- Calling curriedAdd(5) returns the inner function, but now that function has access to the value 5 for a.
  - The add5 function is essentially equivalent to function(b) { return 5 + b; }.

```
console.log(add5(3));   // Output: 8
```

- When add5(3) is called, it invokes the inner function with b set to 3. Inside the inner function, a is still 5 (the value passed to curriedAdd), so the result is 5 + 3, which equals 8. This is then logged to the console.

CHAPTER 11   FUNCTIONS AND SCOPE

Key Concepts Illustrated in This Example

- **Currying**:
  The curriedAdd function is an example of currying. Instead of taking both a and b as arguments in a single function call, the function is split into two steps. First, a is passed to curriedAdd, and then the resulting function is called with b. This allows for partial application of the function; once a value is provided for a, you can continue to call the returned function with different values for b.

- **Closures**:
  The inner function in curriedAdd has access to a even after curriedAdd has finished executing, demonstrating the concept of closures.

- **Partial Application**:
  Currying can be seen as a form of partial application, where you provide a function with one argument at a time. This can be useful in cases where you have a series of operations with one common argument (like adding 5 to different numbers), and you can "pre-fill" that argument, creating specialized functions like add5.

Why This Is Useful

Currying allows for **more flexible and reusable code**. You can create specialized functions by partially applying arguments, as shown with add5. It's especially useful in functional programming or scenarios where you repeatedly use the same argument in multiple function calls. This technique can make your code more modular and reduce duplication.

CHAPTER 11   FUNCTIONS AND SCOPE

In real-world scenarios, currying can be used to create higher-order functions for things like configuration, event handling, or API calls, where certain values (like a constant or configuration) are preset and the rest of the arguments are supplied later.

Impact on Performance and Memory
Partial Application and Reuse

Currying allows you to create **specialized functions** by pre-filling some arguments, which can result in improved performance in scenarios where a function needs to be repeatedly called with similar arguments. Since the curried function only needs to receive one argument at a time, it can help avoid creating new function calls each time, potentially leading to faster execution when used in loops or with frequently called functions.

For example, consider a scenario where you're repeatedly calling a function with one fixed argument.

Example:

```
function multiply(a, b) {
  return a * b;
}

const multiplyBy2 = multiply.bind(null, 2);
console.log(multiplyBy2(5));  // Output: 10
console.log(multiplyBy2(10)); // Output: 20
```

Here, currying allows you to create the multiplyBy2 function once and then reuse it multiple times, which can be more memory-efficient than defining separate functions for each multiplication.

Memoization

Currying can be combined with **memoization**, a technique that stores the results of expensive function calls and returns the cached result when the same inputs occur again. When combined with currying, the function can cache intermediate results based on the pre-filled arguments, potentially improving performance by reducing redundant calculations.

Here's an example of currying with memoization:

```
function memoizedAdd(a) {
  const cache = {};
  return function(b) {
    if (cache[b]) {
      console.log("Fetching from cache:", b);
      return cache[b];
    } else {
      console.log("Calculating result for:", b);
      let result = a + b;
      cache[b] = result;
      return result;
    }
  };
}
const add5 = memoizedAdd(5);

console.log(add5(10)); // Output: Calculating result for: 10
console.log(add5(10)); // Output: Fetching from cache: 10
```

In this case, memoizedAdd caches the result of each computation, improving performance when the same argument (10) is provided multiple times. The currying structure allows for effective caching based on the initial a argument and any subsequent b arguments.

Memory Overhead

Memory overhead is a key consideration in performance-sensitive applications, as it impacts how much memory is consumed and can affect the overall efficiency of your code.

On the other hand, while currying can enhance **reusability** and **modularity**, it can introduce **memory overhead**. Each curried function returns a new function, which could lead to more memory consumption, particularly when functions are curried excessively. This memory overhead could be noticeable in high-volume scenarios where you have many functions being created at runtime.

While currying is useful in functional programming for creating specialized functions through partial application, it's important to balance its advantages with performance concerns. Excessive currying can lead to increased function closures, and in some cases, it may be more efficient to avoid it in favor of other techniques, especially when dealing with large-scale applications or situations with constrained memory.

For instance, the following example shows a function being curried many times.

Example:

```
function curriedMultiply(a) {
  return function(b) {
    return function(c) {
      return function(d) {
        return a * b * c * d;
      };
    };
  };
}

const multiplyBy2 = curriedMultiply(2);
const multiplyBy2And3 = multiplyBy2(3);
```

```
const result = multiplyBy2And3(4)(5);
console.log(result);   // Output: 120
```

In this case, multiple functions are created and stored in memory at each step. If currying is applied too frequently or in performance-critical situations, this can result in more memory usage than necessary.

Summary of Currying's Performance and Memory Impact

- **Performance Improvement**: Currying can help with performance indirectly by reducing redundant calculations, especially when combined with **partial application** and **memoization**.

- **Memory Considerations**: While currying allows for **cleaner, reusable code**, it can introduce additional memory overhead due to the creation of new functions at each curried stage. However, this is generally a minor concern unless currying is used excessively in memory-sensitive applications.

- **Best Use Cases**: Currying is particularly useful when creating specialized functions, improving the readability and maintainability of code, and optimizing for repetitive function calls with similar parameters.

While currying does not directly improve performance in all cases, when combined with techniques like memoization, it can be a useful tool for optimizing repetitive calculations and minimizing redundant work in more complex applications.

CHAPTER 11   FUNCTIONS AND SCOPE

Key Takeaways

- **Currying Enhances Reusability**: By breaking a function into smaller, specialized functions that can be applied incrementally, currying promotes code reuse and flexibility, particularly in functional programming paradigms.

- **Ideal for Partial Application**: Currying allows you to create specialized versions of a function by presetting some arguments. This is particularly useful when working with functions that require repeated operations with some common arguments.

- **Currying Leads to Cleaner Code**: Instead of writing multiple variations of the same function, currying enables you to write a more generic function and customize its behavior through partial application, leading to more concise and maintainable code.

- **Performance Considerations**: While currying may add an overhead due to the creation of multiple function closures, the performance impact is often negligible unless working with extremely large datasets or highly performance-sensitive tasks. Additionally, **tail call optimization (TCO)** can help mitigate some of the performance concerns in recursive functions. In languages that support TCO, functions that perform recursion in a tail position (i.e., the recursive call is the last operation) can be optimized by the engine to avoid adding new frames to the call stack. This can prevent stack overflow errors in deep recursion and improve performance. However, note that JavaScript engines, such as V8, do not currently support tail call optimization, so recursive functions may still result in stack overflow errors or memory overhead when the recursion is too deep.

- **Memory Impact**: Currying can increase memory usage slightly because each curried function creates a new closure. This overhead should be considered when dealing with functions that are invoked frequently in memory-constrained environments.

- **Currying and Memoization**: Combining currying with memoization techniques can help optimize repeated function calls, improving performance by caching results for previously encountered arguments.

- **Best Used with Caution**: Currying provides significant benefits for reusable and flexible code but should be used wisely. It is not always a performance booster in all contexts, so it's important to evaluate its impact based on the specific use case.

EXERCISE 5: CURRYING

Task: Create a curried function that adds three numbers.

Hint: The curried function should allow you to call it as add(1)(2)(3) and return the sum.

Code for Reference:

```
function add(a) {
  // Your code here.
}
```

CHAPTER 11 FUNCTIONS AND SCOPE

Immediately Invoked Function Expressions (IIFEs)

An **Immediately Invoked Function Expression (IIFE)** is a function that is defined and immediately invoked or executed. It's a common pattern used to create a local scope, especially in JavaScript where there is no block scope for variables (prior to ES6). Using IIFEs helps to avoid polluting the global scope by encapsulating variables within a function, thus keeping the global environment cleaner and preventing potential naming conflicts.

Example 1 – Basic Syntax:

```
(function () {
  console.log('This runs immediately!');
})();
```

This is the most basic form of an IIFE. Here's how it works:

1. **Function Definition**:
   The function is enclosed in parentheses (), which turns it into an expression. Normally, functions are declared using the function keyword, but wrapping the function in parentheses signals to JavaScript that the function should be treated as an expression, not a declaration.

2. **Immediate Invocation**:
   After the function is defined, the () after the closing parenthesis immediately calls the function.

3. **Execution**:
   As a result, the function is invoked right away, and the code inside it runs immediately. In this example, the message 'This runs immediately!' is logged to the console.

Why Use an IIFE?

1. **Encapsulation**:
   IIFEs are useful for encapsulating variables and logic in a function scope, so they don't pollute the global scope. This avoids potential conflicts with other parts of your code or third-party libraries. Variables declared inside an IIFE are not accessible outside of it.

2. **Avoiding Global Scope Pollution**:
   In JavaScript, variables declared outside of any function are part of the global scope, and they can accidentally overwrite other variables or functions with the same name. Using an IIFE helps to limit the scope of variables to only where they're needed.

3. **Execution Context**:
   Since IIFEs are executed immediately, they are ideal for situations where you need to perform an operation just once, like initializing a configuration or setting up an event listener.

Example 2 – Encapsulation of Variables:

This example demonstrates how **Immediately Invoked Function Expressions (IIFEs)** can be used to create private variables and methods that are encapsulated within a function. In this case, we're using an IIFE to create a **counter** object with methods that can increment the counter and reset it, while keeping the count variable private.

```
const counter = (function () {
  let count = 0;
  return {
    increment() {
```

CHAPTER 11 FUNCTIONS AND SCOPE

```
      count++;
      return count;
    },
    reset() {
      count = 0;
    }
  };
})();

console.log(counter.increment()); // Output: 1
console.log(counter.increment()); // Output: 2
counter.reset();
console.log(counter.increment()); // Output: 1
```

How It Works:

```
const counter = (function () {
  let count = 0;   // Private variable

  return {
    increment() {
      count++;   // Increment the private count variable
      return count;   // Return the current count value
    },
    reset() {
      count = 0;   // Reset the count to zero
    }
  };
})();
```

IIFE Definition and Execution:

- The function is immediately invoked, creating a local scope. Inside this scope, we define a private variable count, which is not accessible from outside the IIFE.

- The function returns an **object** that contains two methods: increment() and reset(). These methods have access to the count variable because they are defined within the same scope as count.

Private count Variable:

- The count variable is encapsulated within the IIFE, so it cannot be accessed or modified directly from outside the IIFE. This is important for data encapsulation and preventing external code from inadvertently changing the counter's value.

Methods:

- **increment()**: Increments the count by 1 and returns the new value
- **reset()**: Resets the count to 0

How to Use:

Once the IIFE has executed, it returns an object, which is stored in the counter variable. This object has two methods: increment and reset, which can be used to interact with the private count variable.

```
console.log(counter.increment());   // Output: 1
```

Here, counter.increment() increments the count from 0 to 1 and returns the updated value, which is logged to the console.

```
console.log(counter.increment());   // Output: 2
```

Calling counter.increment() again increases count to 2.

```
counter.reset();
console.log(counter.increment());   // Output: 1
```

After calling `counter.reset()`, the count is reset to 0. The next call to `counter.increment()` increments it from 0 to 1 again.

Why This Works:

- **Encapsulation:** The variable `count` is private and not accessible outside the IIFE. The methods `increment` and `reset` are returned and can access `count` because they share the same scope.
- **Stateful Object:** The returned object (`counter`) maintains the state of the `count` variable across function calls. This allows you to keep track of the state without exposing the `count` variable directly.

This pattern of using IIFEs to encapsulate private variables and exposing only specific methods to interact with the data is commonly used in JavaScript, especially when you want to create modules or keep certain data hidden from the outside world.

Real-World Use Case: Initializing Configurations

This example demonstrates how **Immediately Invoked Function Expressions (IIFEs)** can be used to initialize configurations and keep certain settings encapsulated, providing a clean, isolated environment for configuration management.

```
const config = (function () {
  const settings = {
    apiUrl: 'https://api.example.com',
    timeout: 5000
  };
  return settings;
})();

console.log(config.apiUrl); // Output: https://api.example.com
```

CHAPTER 11 FUNCTIONS AND SCOPE

How It Works:

```
const config = (function () {
  const settings = {
    apiUrl: 'https://api.example.com',
    timeout: 5000
  };
  return settings;
})();
```

IIFE Definition and Execution:

- The function is immediately invoked, creating a local scope.

- Inside the function, an object `settings` is created, containing two properties: `apiUrl` and `timeout`. These properties define configuration values like the API URL and request timeout.

- The IIFE then **returns** the `settings` object, which is assigned to the `config` variable.

Encapsulation of Configuration Data:

- The `settings` object is defined inside the IIFE and is not directly accessible from outside the function. However, the returned object (`settings`) is accessible through the `config` variable, but the internal workings of the IIFE (like the initialization process) are hidden from the outside world.

- This ensures that the configuration object is safely initialized and encapsulated, without exposing the `settings` object or any unnecessary implementation details to the global scope.

How to Use:

Once the IIFE has executed, the returned `settings` object is assigned to the `config` variable. You can access the configuration properties through `config`, but the inner details of the function (like the actual definition of `settings`) are hidden from the global scope.

```
console.log(config.apiUrl);   // Output: https://api.example.com
```

Here, `config.apiUrl` outputs the value `'https://api.example.com'`, which is part of the `settings` object returned by the IIFE.

Why This Works:

- **Encapsulation:** The `settings` object is encapsulated within the IIFE. This means that only the returned object is accessible, and you can't directly modify or access the internal variables (such as `settings`) from outside the function.

- **Safe Initialization:** The IIFE ensures that the configuration is set up and ready to use as soon as the script is executed. The `config` object holds the initialized configuration values, which can then be used throughout your code.

- **Avoid Global Namespace Pollution:** Without using an IIFE, the `settings` object would likely be declared in the global scope, which could lead to naming conflicts or accidental overwriting. By using an IIFE, we avoid polluting the global namespace and keep our code modular and clean.

This pattern is commonly used for **module creation** or for setting up configuration data that should not be tampered with, ensuring that global variables are kept to a minimum. It is especially useful in cases where the configuration needs to be initialized once and used throughout the application without risk of accidental changes.

Global Variable Pollution

Global variable pollution happens when variables are declared in the global scope. This can cause problems such as variable name conflicts and unexpected behavior due to unintended changes from different parts of the code.

Example 1 – Common Problem with Global Variables:

```
var counter = 0; // Global variable
function increment() {
  counter++;
}
increment();
console.log(counter); // Works, but pollutes global namespace
```

In this example

- The counter variable is declared globally using var. This means it can be accessed and modified from anywhere in the program.
- The increment() function increases the value of counter.
- After calling increment(), the value of counter becomes 1, which is logged to the console.

However, this approach has a **major issue**:

- **Global Scope Pollution:** By declaring counter as a global variable, it is accessible throughout the entire program. This can lead to **unintended modifications** from other parts of the code. For example, if another part of the code accidentally uses or changes the value of counter, it might break your program or cause unexpected behavior.

Best Practice: Use IIFEs or Modules

To prevent global variable pollution, you can use an **Immediately Invoked Function Expression (IIFE)** or modules to **encapsulate variables** within a local scope. This approach helps ensure that variables don't unintentionally leak into the global scope.

Here's how you can rewrite the example using an IIFE:

```
(function () {
  let counter = 0;
  function increment() {
    counter++;
    console.log(counter);
  }
  increment();
})();

console.log(typeof counter); // Output: undefined
```

In this improved example

- The IIFE is used to **encapsulate** the counter variable within a local scope.

- The counter variable is now local to the function and cannot be accessed or modified outside the IIFE.

- After running the increment() function inside the IIFE, the value of counter is printed as 1 inside the function.

- typeof counter outside the IIFE results in undefined because counter does not exist in the global scope.

Why This Is Better:

- **Encapsulation:** The counter variable is kept private within the IIFE. It can only be accessed and modified by the functions inside the IIFE, preventing any unintended changes from the outside.

- **Avoids Global Pollution:** By using the IIFE pattern, we ensure that counter does not leak into the global scope. This minimizes the risk of naming conflicts and unintended interactions between different parts of the program.

- **Clean Code:** Your global namespace remains clean and uncluttered, which makes the code more maintainable and reduces the chance of errors in large applications.

Conclusion:

To avoid global variable pollution, it's important to either

1. Use **local scope** inside functions (as in the IIFE example).

2. Use **modules** (in modern JavaScript) to scope variables to specific modules and prevent them from leaking into the global space.

By following these practices, you can ensure your code is more robust, maintainable, and less prone to bugs caused by unintended global variables.

Closures

A **closure** is a powerful concept in JavaScript where a function "remembers" the environment in which it was created, even after the outer function has finished executing. In other words, a closure allows a function to access variables from its **lexical scope** (the scope in which the function was defined) even after that scope has been exited.

Basic Closure

```
function outer() {
  let count = 0;
  return function inner() {
    count++;
    return count;
  };
}
const counter = outer();
console.log(counter()); // Output: 1
console.log(counter()); // Output: 2
```

In this example

1. **Outer Function** (outer):

    - Defines a variable count with an initial value of 0.

    - Returns an inner function (inner), which increments count and returns its value.

2. **Inner Function** (inner):

    - This function forms a closure. It has access to the count variable from the outer function, even though outer has finished executing.

3. **Closure in Action**:

    - When you invoke outer(), it returns the inner function.

    - Even though the outer function has finished executing, the inner function still has access to count because it was "closed over" by the closure.

    - Each time counter() (the inner function) is called, it increments the count variable and returns the updated value.

How It Works:

- **Lexical Scope:** When outer() is called, it creates its own local scope with the count variable. The inner() function is returned, and this function "remembers" the count variable from the outer() function's scope, even after outer() has finished executing.

- **Closure Mechanism:** Every time you call counter(), it uses the count variable from the closure. This allows count to persist between calls to counter(), maintaining its state across multiple invocations.

Output Breakdown:

1. The first time counter() is called

    - count is incremented from 0 to 1, and the value 1 is returned.

2. The second time counter() is called

    - count is incremented from 1 to 2, and the value 2 is returned.

Despite outer() having finished execution, the inner function maintains its reference to count, and the state persists between function calls.

Key Takeaways:

- **Closure** allows functions to "remember" and access variables from their outer scope, even after the outer function has returned.

- Closures are useful for creating **private variables** and maintaining state across function calls, especially in scenarios like **counters**, **event handlers**, and **callback functions**.

- **Encapsulation**: Closures help you encapsulate functionality and protect variables from being accessed or modified directly by the outside world.

Basic Account Closure

In this example, we use a closure to simulate a **bank account** with private balance variable management. The closure ensures that the balance variable remains private and can only be accessed or modified via the provided methods (deposit and withdraw).

```
function bankAccount(initialBalance) {
  let balance = initialBalance;
  return {
    deposit(amount) {
      balance += amount;
      console.log(`Deposited: ${amount}, Balance: ${balance}`);
    },
    withdraw(amount) {
```

```
      if (amount > balance) {
        console.log('Insufficient funds');
        return;
      }
      balance -= amount;
      console.log(`Withdrawn: ${amount}, Balance: ${balance}`);
    }
  };
}

const myAccount = bankAccount(100);
myAccount.deposit(50); // Output: Deposited: 50, Balance: 150
myAccount.withdraw(30); // Output: Withdrawn: 30, Balance: 120
```

Explanation:

1. **Bank Account Closure:**

    - The function bankAccount accepts an initialBalance parameter and defines a local variable balance within the function's scope.

    - The balance variable is **encapsulated** within the bankAccount function and cannot be accessed directly from outside the function.

    - Instead, the function returns an object containing two methods: deposit and withdraw.

2. **Deposit Method:**

    - The deposit method accepts an amount and adds it to the balance and then logs the updated balance.

    - This method has access to the balance variable from the outer scope (via the closure).

3. **Withdraw Method:**

    - The withdraw method accepts an amount and checks if the user has enough funds by comparing the amount with the balance.
    - If the amount is greater than the balance, it logs "Insufficient funds".
    - Otherwise, it subtracts the amount from the balance and logs the updated balance.

How It Works:

- When you create a bank account with const myAccount = bankAccount(100);, the balance is set to 100.
- The deposit and withdraw methods can be used to change the balance. These methods both form closures that have access to the balance variable.
- Each call to deposit or withdraw modifies the state of the balance within the closure, but the balance variable itself remains hidden from the outside world.

Key Closure Concept:

- The balance variable is **private** to the bankAccount function. You can't directly modify balance from outside the closure.
- The closure provides controlled access to balance through the deposit and withdraw methods, encapsulating the logic for managing the account's state.

This pattern is commonly used in JavaScript to simulate **private variables** or to **encapsulate logic** within an object.

When to Use Closures

Data Encapsulation with Closures

In this example, we're using closures to encapsulate a private variable (count) that can only be accessed and modified through the returned function.

```
function createCounter() {
  let count = 0; // private variable
  return function () {
    count++;
    return count;
  };
}
const counter = createCounter();
console.log(counter()); // Output: 1
console.log(counter()); // Output: 2
```

Explanation:

- **createCounter Function:**
    - Inside the createCounter function, we define a local variable count that is initialized to 0.
    - The createCounter function returns an anonymous function (a closure) that has access to the count variable from its lexical scope.
- **Closure:**
    - The returned function forms a closure because it "remembers" the count variable even after the createCounter function has finished executing.

- Every time the returned function is called, it increments the count and returns the updated value. The count is not accessible directly from outside, providing a form of data encapsulation.
- **Instance of the Counter:**
  - When you call createCounter(), you get a new instance of the counter with its own count variable. This instance is separate from other counters created by calling createCounter() again.
- **Output:**
  - The first time counter() is called, the output is 1 because count is incremented from 0.
  - The second time counter() is called, the output is 2, showing that the state (the value of count) is maintained across function calls, thanks to the closure.

Key Concept:

- Closures are used here to maintain a private count variable, which can only be modified through the function returned by createCounter. This technique is useful for encapsulating data and preventing unauthorized access or modification.

Maintaining State in Asynchronous Code

In this example, we use closures to preserve a variable (startTime) in an asynchronous operation. This is important for scenarios where you need to retain state after the asynchronous task completes.

```
function fetchData(url) {
  const startTime = Date.now();
  return function () {
    console.log(`Fetching from ${url} took ${Date.now() -
    startTime}ms`);
  };
}
const logTime = fetchData('https://example.com');
setTimeout(logTime, 1000); // Logs time after 1 second
```

Explanation:

- **fetchData Function:**
    - The fetchData function accepts a url and captures the current time (startTime) when the function is invoked.
    - The returned function (a closure) has access to startTime, even after fetchData finishes executing.

- **Closure:**
    - When the logTime function is called inside setTimeout, it still "remembers" the startTime variable from the original invocation of fetchData, even though fetchData has already completed.

- **Asynchronous Operation:**
    - The setTimeout function simulates an asynchronous task by calling logTime after 1 second. When logTime is executed, it calculates how much time has passed since startTime and logs the result.

- **Output:**
    - The log message will indicate how long the asynchronous operation took, showing how closures preserve the `startTime` even after the asynchronous delay.
- **Key Concept:**
    - Closures are extremely useful for managing state in asynchronous operations, where maintaining access to variables (like `startTime`) after the function has returned would otherwise be challenging.

Dynamic Function Factories

Here, closures allow us to create reusable functions that perform operations based on parameters passed at runtime.

```
function multiplier(factor) {
  return function (number) {
    return number * factor;
  };
}
const double = multiplier(2);
console.log(double(5)); // Output: 10
```

- **Explanation:**
    - **multiplier Function:**
        - The `multiplier` function takes a `factor` as an argument and returns a new function that multiplies its argument (`number`) by this `factor`.

- **Closure:**
  - The returned function is a closure because it "remembers" the `factor` value from the `multiplier` function when it was created.
  - In the case of `double`, the `factor` is 2, so the returned function multiplies any number passed to it by 2.
- **Reusable Functions:**
  - By calling `multiplier(2)`, we create a new function (`double`) that always doubles the numbers passed to it. You could create similar functions for other factors (like `multiplier(3)` for tripling numbers).
- **Output:**
  - Calling `double(5)` returns 10, as 5 is multiplied by the factor 2.

Key Concept:

- Closures enable dynamic function creation, allowing you to customize the behavior of functions based on runtime values, making your code more flexible and reusable.

Higher-Order Functions

Higher-order functions (HOFs) are functions that **accept other functions as arguments** or **return functions as results**. They are foundational to functional programming in JavaScript. They enable powerful abstractions and are widely used in JavaScript.

CHAPTER 11 FUNCTIONS AND SCOPE

Array Methods (map)

In this example, we use the map method, which is a built-in higher-order function in JavaScript. It takes a callback function as an argument and applies that function to every item in an array.

```
const numbers = [1, 2, 3, 4];
const doubled = numbers.map(num => num * 2);
console.log(doubled); // Output: [2, 4, 6, 8]
```

Explanation:

- **map Method:**
    - The map method is a higher-order function that iterates over the numbers array and applies the provided callback function (num => num * 2) to each element.
- **Callback Function:**
    - The function num => num * 2 is passed as an argument to map. It takes each number in the array and multiplies it by 2.
- **Output:**
    - The map method returns a new array, doubled, where each element of the original array is multiplied by 2. The output is [2, 4, 6, 8].

Key Concept:

- The map method is a higher-order function because it takes a function (num => num * 2) as an argument and applies it to each element in the array.

Custom Higher-Order Function

This example demonstrates creating a custom higher-order function called logger, which takes a function as an argument and logs details about the function call before invoking the function itself.

```
function logger(func) {
  return function (...args) {
    console.log(`Calling ${func.name} with arguments: ${args}`);
    return func(...args);
  };
}
const add = (a, b) => a + b;
const loggedAdd = logger(add);
console.log(loggedAdd(3, 4)); // Logs details, then outputs 7
```

Explanation:

- **logger Function:**
    - The logger function is a higher-order function that takes another function (func) as its argument and returns a new function.
    - The returned function logs the function's name and arguments before calling the original function (func) with the provided arguments (args).
- **add Function:**
    - The add function simply adds two numbers together.

- **loggedAdd Function:**
  - The loggedAdd function is the result of calling logger(add). It logs details about the call to add (its name and arguments) and then invokes the add function with the arguments passed to it.
- **Output:**
  - First, the console logs the message `Calling add with arguments: [3, 4]`, and then the add function returns 7, which is logged by `console.log(loggedAdd(3, 4))`.

Key Concept:
- The logger function is a higher-order function because it takes another function (add) as an argument and returns a new function that enhances the behavior of add by logging additional details.

When to Use Higher-Order Functions

Higher-order functions are useful in various scenarios where you want to abstract logic, build extensible systems, manage events or callbacks, and create reusable utilities. Let's explore some common use cases.

Abstracting Repeated Logic

Higher-order functions help eliminate repetitive code by abstracting common patterns like iteration or filtering.

Example Array Manipulation:

```
const numbers = [1, 2, 3, 4, 5];
const squares = numbers.map((n) => n * n); // Abstracted logic
console.log(squares); // Output: [1, 4, 9, 16, 25]
```

Explanation:

- The map method abstracts the logic of squaring each number in the array. This allows us to avoid writing a loop manually, improving code readability and reusability.

Key Concept:

- HOFs like map abstract the logic of applying a function to every element of an array, reducing boilerplate code.

Creating Middleware/Plugins

HOFs are ideal for designing extensible systems, like middleware in frameworks or plugins in libraries.

Example Middleware Chain:

```
function logger(next) {
  return function (action) {
    console.log(`Action: ${action}`);
    next(action);
  };
}
const applyMiddleware = logger((action) => console.log(`Final: ${action}`));
applyMiddleware('SAVE_DATA'); // Logs intermediate and final actions
```

Explanation:

- The logger function is a higher-order function that takes another function (next) as an argument and returns a new function that logs the action before passing it to next.

- applyMiddleware is a function created by calling logger. It logs the action ('SAVE_DATA') before passing it to the next function in the chain.

Key Concept:

- This is an example of using HOFs to create middleware, which allows you to add new functionality (like logging) to existing functions without modifying them directly.

Event Handling and Callbacks

HOFs are perfect for managing asynchronous workflows or events by passing and chaining callbacks.

Example Event Listener:

```
function addClickListener(element, callback) {
  element.addEventListener('click', callback);
}
addClickListener(button, () => console.log('Button clicked!'));
```

Explanation:

- The addClickListener function is a higher-order function that accepts an element and a callback function. It attaches the callback function to the click event of the element.

Key Concept:

- This demonstrates how HOFs can be used to manage event handling, allowing you to define custom behavior (the callback function) whenever a click event occurs.

Custom Utilities and Composition

Function composition is the process of combining multiple functions to create a new function where the output of one function becomes the input of another. It's a key concept in functional programming that enables modular and reusable code. In JavaScript, you can compose functions to create complex operations by chaining them together.

For example, if you have two functions

```
const addOne = (x) => x + 1;
const double = (x) => x * 2;
```

you can compose them into a new function where the output of addOne becomes the input to double.

Example Function Composition:

```
function compose(f, g) {
  return function (x) {
    return f(g(x));
  };
}

const addOne = (x) => x + 1;
const double = (x) => x * 2;

const addThenDouble = compose(double, addOne);
console.log(addThenDouble(5)); // Output: 12
```

In this example, the compose function takes two functions, f and g, and returns a new function that applies g first and then applies f to the result.

Benefits of Function Composition:

1. **Modularity**: Function composition allows you to break down complex operations into smaller, more manageable functions, making your code easier to read and maintain.

2. **Reusability**: Smaller, composable functions are reusable across different parts of your code, reducing duplication.

3. **Testability**: Since the composed functions are simple and focused on a single task, they are easier to test individually.

Using Function Composition with Higher-Order Functions (HOFs):

Higher-order functions (HOFs) can be used in function composition to create flexible utilities. For example, you can use HOFs to apply multiple operations to a set of data in a composed manner:

```
const addOne = (x) => x + 1;
const double = (x) => x * 2;

const addThenDouble = compose(double, addOne);
console.log(addThenDouble(5));   // Output: 12
```

Here, the compose function is used to combine addOne and double into a new function, addThenDouble, which applies both operations in sequence.

Conclusion

Higher-order functions are an essential part of JavaScript, enabling more abstract, reusable, and flexible code. They are particularly useful for abstracting repeated logic, designing extensible systems like middleware, managing event handling, and dynamically composing functions for custom behaviors.

EXERCISE 6: WORKING WITH HIGHER-ORDER FUNCTIONS

Task: Create a function that accepts another function as an argument and invokes it with a number.

Hint: Define a callback function that doubles the number and pass it as an argument.

Code for Reference:

```
function higherOrderFunction(callback) {
  let number = 5;
  // Call the callback with number.
}
function double(n) {
  return n * 2;
}
```

Summary

In this chapter, we explored the foundational concepts of **functions and scope**, diving into essential topics that shape how JavaScript handles behavior and variable visibility. We began with the basics of defining functions using `function` declarations, expressions, and the concise arrow syntax, before moving into advanced features like **function parameters** (default, rest, and destructured) and the importance of **return values** in building reusable code.

We then delved into the concept of **scope**, distinguishing between global and local variables, and explored how closures enable functions to retain access to their originating scope. Along the way, we introduced powerful patterns like **Immediately Invoked Function Expressions (IIFEs)**, which provide a mechanism for creating isolated scopes, and discussed the risks of **global variable pollution** in larger codebases.

To further deepen our understanding, we examined **higher-order functions**, which enhance code reusability and abstraction by working with functions as arguments or return values. We also discussed **validating function arguments**, ensuring robust and error-resistant code, and techniques for **returning multiple values**, such as using arrays or objects.

Finally, we emphasized practical applications, including real-world examples of **destructured parameters**, closures for data encapsulation, and the role of **this** in various contexts. These concepts equip you to write modular, maintainable, and efficient JavaScript code.

By mastering these topics, you have taken a significant step toward building sophisticated and scalable applications while adhering to best practices in function design and scope management.

Full Solutions

SOLUTION TO EXERCISE 1: UNDERSTANDING VARIABLE DECLARATIONS

```
function testScope() {
  var a = 10;
  let b = 20;
  const c = 30;

  if (true) {
    var a = 40; // Re-declared and changes globally.
    let b = 50; // Block-scoped.
    const c = 60; // Block-scoped.
    console.log("Inside block:", a, b, c); // 40, 50, 60
  }

  console.log("Outside block:", a, b, c); // 40, 20, 30
}
testScope();
```

CHAPTER 11 FUNCTIONS AND SCOPE

SOLUTION TO EXERCISE 2: EXPLORING DEFAULT PARAMETERS

```
function calculateArea(length, width = 10) {
  return length * width;
}
console.log(calculateArea(5)); // 50
console.log(calculateArea(5, 8)); // 40
console.log(calculateArea()); // NaN (length is required)
```

SOLUTION TO EXERCISE 3: FINDING THE MAXIMUM NUMBERS WITH REST PARAMETERS

```
function findMax(...numbers) {
  return Math.max(...numbers);
}
console.log(findMax(1, 5, 3, 9, 2)); // 9
console.log(findMax(-10, -3, -25)); // -3
console.log(findMax()); // -Infinity (no arguments provided)
```

SOLUTION TO EXERCISE 4: ARROW FUNCTIONS AND CONTEXT

```
const obj = {
  number: 5,
  regularSquare: function (n) {
    console.log(this.number); // 5
    return n * n;
  },
  arrowSquare: (n) => {
    console.log(this.number); // undefined
    return n * n;
```

345

CHAPTER 11 FUNCTIONS AND SCOPE

```
    }
  };
  obj.regularSquare(3);
  obj.arrowSquare(3);
```

SOLUTION TO EXERCISE 5: CURRYING

```
  function add(a) {
    return function (b) {
      return function (c) {
        return a + b + c;
      };
    };
  }
  console.log(add(1)(2)(3)); // 6
```

SOLUTION TO EXERCISE 6: WORKING WITH HIGHER-ORDER FUNCTIONS

```
function higherOrderFunction(callback) {
  let number = 5;
  console.log(callback(number));
}
function double(n) {
  return n * 2;
}
higherOrderFunction(double); // 10
```

CHAPTER 12

Objects and Arrays

Objective

This chapter will provide you with a comprehensive understanding of objects and arrays, which are essential structures in JavaScript for organizing and manipulating data. You will learn how to create and interact with objects and arrays; explore various methods to access, modify, and iterate over their contents; and become familiar with techniques for looping through these structures efficiently. Additionally, this chapter will introduce the concept of prototypes and how JavaScript uses prototypal inheritance to allow objects to share properties and methods, providing a basis for more advanced concepts and programming patterns.

Introduction to Objects and Arrays

Objects and arrays are fundamental data structures in JavaScript, allowing you to store and organize data. While arrays are collections of items arranged in an indexed order, objects are collections of properties, where each property is defined by a key–value pair. Mastering these structures will significantly enhance your ability to store and manipulate data efficiently.

CHAPTER 12   OBJECTS AND ARRAYS

What Are Objects in JavaScript?

An **object** in JavaScript is a collection of **key–value pairs** where the keys are property names (strings or symbols) and the values can be any valid JavaScript data type, including functions. Objects allow you to create structured, reusable code for real-world entities like users, products, or systems.

Why Use Objects?

- **Model Real-World Entities**: Group related properties and behaviors.
- **Organize Code**: Encapsulate functionality to avoid clutter in your programs.
- **Enable Reusability**: Share and manipulate structured data easily.

Example – Defining an Object with Properties and Methods:

```
const car = {
  make: "Tesla",
  model: "Model S",
  year: 2023,
  start() {
    console.log(`${this.make} ${this.model} is starting...`);
  },
  stop() {
    console.log(`${this.make} ${this.model} has stopped.`);
  },
};
```

```
console.log(car.make); // Output: Tesla
car.start(); // Output: Tesla Model S is starting...
car.stop(); // Output: Tesla Model S has stopped.
```

In this example, `start` and `stop` are methods, while `make`, `model`, and `year` are properties. Methods define the behavior of the object.

EXERCISE 1: UNDERSTANDING OBJECTS

Task: Create an object representing a car with properties like `make`, `model`, and `year`. Access the properties using dot notation and bracket notation.

Hint: Use both syntaxes to access the same property.

Code for Reference:

```
let car = {
  make: "Toyota",
  model: "Corolla",
  year: 2020
};

// console log the properties here
```

Methods for Creating Objects

JavaScript provides several techniques to create objects. Let's dive into each approach in detail.

Object Literals

The simplest way to create an object is through object literals, which use curly braces {} to define properties and methods.

CHAPTER 12 OBJECTS AND ARRAYS

Example – A Simple Object:

```
const user = {
  name: "Alice",
  age: 30,
  greet() {
    console.log(`Hi, I'm ${this.name}.`);
  },
};

user.greet(); // Output: Hi, I'm Alice.
```

Advantages:

- Concise syntax for static objects.
- Directly initialize properties and methods.

Use Case:

Best for defining small, standalone objects without dynamic logic.

EXERCISE 2: OBJECT LITERALS

Task: Create an object using an object literal to represent a book with `title`, `author`, and `pages`.

Hint: Use key–value pairs to define properties.

Code for Reference:

```
let book = {
  // Define properties here
};
```

CHAPTER 12   OBJECTS AND ARRAYS

Using the `Object` Constructor

The Object constructor creates a new object dynamically. Properties can then be added to the object using dot notation or square brackets.

Example – Object Constructor:

```
const person = new Object();
person.name = "John";
person.age = 25;
person.sayHello = function () {
  console.log(`Hello, I'm ${this.name}.`);
};

person.sayHello(); // Output: Hello, I'm John
```

When to Use:

Useful when you need to dynamically create an object but is less preferred compared with literals due to verbosity.

Use Cases for Objects

Objects are perfect for grouping related data, such as storing user details, configuration settings, or structured responses from an API.

Using Object.create()

The `Object.create()` method allows you to create an object with a specific prototype. This approach is beneficial for inheritance and prototype-based object creation.

Example – Prototypal Inheritance:

```
const animal = {
  speak() {
    console.log("Generic animal sound");
  },
};
```

351

```
const dog = Object.create(animal);
dog.speak(); // Output: Generic animal sound

dog.bark = function () {
  console.log("Woof!");
};

dog.bark(); // Output: Woof!
```

Benefits:

- Precise control over prototypes
- Useful for performance-critical applications where inheritance is key

Factory Functions

A **factory function** is a function that returns an object. This approach encapsulates logic, making it reusable for creating similar objects.

Factory Functions vs. Constructor Functions

Both factory functions and constructor functions are used to create objects, but they differ in syntax, usage, and flexibility. Factory functions return an object directly and allow more flexibility, while constructor functions use the new keyword to create objects and are typically associated with traditional object-oriented programming paradigms.

Feature	Factory Functions	Constructor Functions
Syntax	No new keyword. Returns an object directly.	Requires the new keyword to create an object.
Flexibility	More flexible, allows you to return different types of objects.	Less flexible, typically returns the same type of object.
Prototype	Objects do not automatically inherit from a prototype.	Objects inherit from the prototype defined by the constructor.
Inheritance	Custom inheritance must be manually set up.	Inheritance is handled via the prototype chain.
Use cases	Used for creating similar objects without the need for new.	Typically used when you want to create objects with a common prototype.
this keyword	this is not used in factory functions.	this refers to the created object.

Example – A Constructor Function for Users:

```
function User(name, age) {
this.name = name;
this.age = age;
this.isAdmin = false;

this.greet = function() {
    console.log(`Hi, I'm ${this.name}, and I am ${this.age}
    years old.`);
};
}
```

```
const user1 = new User("Alice", 30);
const user2 = new User("Bob", 25);

user1.greet(); // Output: Hi, I'm Alice, and I am 30 years old.
user2.greet(); // Output: Hi, I'm Bob, and I am 25 years old.
```

Explanation:

- The User constructor function uses the new keyword to create a new instance of the object.
- Inside the constructor, this refers to the newly created object, allowing you to set its properties and methods.
- To create a new user, you simply call new User("Alice", 30) or new User("Bob", 25).

Example – A Factory Function for Users:

```
function createUser(name, age) {
  return {
    name,
    age,
    isAdmin: false,
    greet: function () {
      console.log(`Hi, I'm ${this.name}, and I am ${this.age}
      years old.`);
    },
  };
}

const user1 = createUser("Alice", 30);
const user2 = createUser("Bob", 25);

user1.greet(); // Output: Hi, I'm Alice, and I am 30 years old.
user2.greet(); // Output: Hi, I'm Bob, and I am 25 years old.
```

CHAPTER 12   OBJECTS AND ARRAYS

Explanation:

- The createUser function is a **factory function**, meaning it returns a new object each time it is called.

- Inside the function, an object is returned with properties (name, age, isAdmin) and methods (greet).

- The key difference from a constructor function is that you don't use the new keyword. Instead, calling createUser("Alice", 30) directly returns an object.

- Each call to createUser creates a new object, so user1 and user2 are separate instances of the object.

- Unlike constructor functions, the factory function doesn't rely on the this keyword, making it more flexible in certain scenarios.

Comparison with Constructor Functions

- **Factory Function**: More flexible, no need for the new keyword, and it can return objects in various shapes. It's ideal for situations where object creation may need more logic or customization.

- **Constructor Function**: Uses the new keyword, and objects are created using the this keyword within the constructor. Ideal for simpler scenarios where you don't need extra logic during object creation.

EXERCISE 3: FACTORY FUNCTIONS

Task: Write a factory function to create a `product` object with `name`, `price`, and a method `applyDiscount` that reduces the price by a given percentage. Create two product objects and call the `applyDiscount` method on them.

Hint: Use a method inside the factory function to modify the object's state.

Code for Reference:

```
function createProduct(name, price) {
  return {
    name,
    price,
    applyDiscount(discountPercentage) {
      // Logic to reduce price
    }
  };
}
// Create product objects here
```

Constructor Functions

Constructor functions serve as blueprints for objects. Using the new keyword automatically creates a new object, binds this, and sets up inheritance from Function.prototype.

Example – Car Constructor:

```
function Car(make, model, year) {
  this.make = make;
  this.model = model;
  this.year = year;
```

CHAPTER 12   OBJECTS AND ARRAYS

```
    this.start = function () {
      console.log(`${this.make} ${this.model} is starting.`);
    };
}
const myCar = new Car("Toyota", "Camry", 2023);
myCar.start(); // Output: Toyota Camry is starting.
```

Best Practices:

- Use meaningful names for constructor functions (capitalize the name).
- Avoid defining methods directly on the object for memory efficiency; prefer `prototype`.

Classes (ES6 Syntax)

Classes provide a more structured and intuitive way to define objects and their behaviors. They act as syntactic sugar over constructor functions.

Example – Class Syntax:

```
class Person {
  constructor(name, age) {
    this.name = name;
    this.age = age;
  }

  greet() {
    console.log(`Hello, my name is ${this.name}.`);
  }
}

const person1 = new Person("Emma", 28);
person1.greet(); // Output: Hello, my name is Emma.
```

CHAPTER 12 OBJECTS AND ARRAYS

Advantages:

- Readable and consistent syntax
- Supports inheritance via extends

Adding Methods to Objects

Methods define the behavior of objects. They are functions stored as properties.

Example – Object with Methods:

```
const calculator = {
  add(a, b) {
    return a + b;
  },
  subtract(a, b) {
    return a - b;
  },
};
console.log(calculator.add(5, 3)); // Output: 8
console.log(calculator.subtract(5, 3)); // Output: 2
```

Example – Dynamic Method Assignment:

```
const operations = {};
operations.multiply = function (a, b) {
  return a * b;
};
console.log(operations.multiply(2, 3)); // Output: 6
```

Dynamic Object Properties and Computed Property Names

Dynamic Property Assignment

You can add, modify, or delete properties after an object is created.

Example – Dynamic Method Assignment:

```
const user = {};
user.name = "Alice";
user.age = 30;

console.log(user); // Output: { name: 'Alice', age: 30 }

delete user.age;

console.log(user); // Output: { name: 'Alice' }
```

Computed Property Names

Use expressions to create property names dynamically.

Example – Dynamic Property Assignment:

```
const key = "age";
const person = {
  name: "John",
  [key]: 25,
};

console.log(person); // Output: { name: 'John', age: 25 }
```

CHAPTER 12 OBJECTS AND ARRAYS

EXERCISE 4: DYNAMIC PROPERTIES

Task: Add a new property to an object dynamically using square brackets.

Hint: Use a variable to hold the property name.

Code for Reference:

```
let user = {};
let propertyName = "age";
// Add property here
```

Summary of Object Creation Methods

This section has covered the diverse ways to create objects in JavaScript, each suitable for specific scenarios:

- **Object Literals**: Quick and simple for static objects.
- **Object Constructor**: Dynamic, but verbose.
- **Object.create()**: Prototypal inheritance and flexible prototype control.
- **Factory Functions**: Encapsulate creation logic and return new objects.
- **Constructor Functions**: Define reusable blueprints for similar objects.
- **Classes (ES6)**: Modern, intuitive syntax for defining object structures and behavior.

Mastering these techniques ensures you can create and manage objects effectively in any JavaScript project.

CHAPTER 12   OBJECTS AND ARRAYS

Arrays: Creation, Accessing, and Methods

Arrays are fundamental data structures in JavaScript, allowing you to store, manage, and manipulate collections of data efficiently. They are versatile, supporting a wide range of operations and methods, and are commonly used in almost every application to handle lists, sequences, or collections of items.

This section explores creating arrays, accessing and modifying their elements, and leveraging built-in methods for various operations. By understanding arrays thoroughly, you can work more effectively with data in JavaScript.

What Are Arrays in JavaScript?

An **array** is a special type of object in JavaScript that stores ordered collections of items. Each item, or element, is identified by its index, which starts at 0. Arrays can hold elements of any data type, including other arrays, creating multidimensional arrays.

Why Use Arrays?

- **Data Storage**: Store lists or sequences of data compactly.
- **Iteration**: Process elements efficiently using loops or higher-order methods.
- **Dynamic Size**: Arrays in JavaScript are dynamic and can grow or shrink as needed.
- **Diverse Operations**: Built-in methods simplify common tasks like sorting, filtering, and mapping.

Creating an Array

JavaScript offers multiple ways to create arrays. Understanding these approaches helps you choose the right one for specific use cases.

Using Array Literals

The simplest way to create an array is using square brackets [ ]. This method initializes an array with specified elements or as an empty array.

Example – Creating Arrays with Literals:

```
const fruits = ["apple", "banana", "cherry"];
const emptyArray = [];

console.log(fruits[0]); // Output: apple
console.log(emptyArray.length); // Output: 0
```

Advantages:

- Concise syntax
- Ideal for static or predefined data

Using the Array Constructor

The Array constructor creates arrays dynamically. You can pass either a single numeric value to define the array length or multiple elements.

Access array elements by their index, starting from 0.

Example – Using the Array Constructor:

```
const numbers = new Array(5); // Creates an array with 5 undefined slots
const mixed = new Array(1, "hello", true); // Creates an array with specified elements

console.log(numbers.length); // Output: 5
console.log(mixed[1]); // Output: hello
```

CHAPTER 12 OBJECTS AND ARRAYS

When to Use:
- For dynamic array creation
- When defining arrays programmatically

Using `Array.of()`

`Array.of()` creates arrays from its arguments. Unlike the `Array` constructor, it avoids ambiguity when handling numbers.

Example – Array.of():

```
const arr = Array.of(5); // Creates an array with one element: 5
console.log(arr); // Output: [5]
```

Benefits:
- Eliminates confusion with single numeric arguments
- Useful for uniform array initialization

Using `Array.from()`

`Array.from()` creates arrays from array-like or iterable objects, such as strings, sets, or NodeLists.

Example – Converting a NodeList to an Array:

```
const divsList= document.querySelectorAll('div');
const divsListArray = Array.from(divsList);
console.log(divsListArray); // Output: List of divs
```

Example – Using a Mapping Function:

```
const doubled = Array.from([1, 2, 3], (x) => x * 2);
console.log(doubled); // Output: [2, 4, 6]
```

CHAPTER 12 OBJECTS AND ARRAYS

EXERCISE 5: CREATING ARRAYS WITH ARRAY.FROM()

Task: Create an array of numbers from 1 to 5 using `Array.from()` and a mapping function.

Hint: Use a mapping function to generate the array.

Code for Reference:

```
let numbers = Array.from({ length: 5 }, (v, i) => {
  // Map logic here
});
```

Accessing and Modifying Arrays

Accessing Elements

Access elements using their index, which starts at 0. Negative indices are not supported directly but can be emulated with helper functions.

Example – Index Access:

```
const colors = ["red", "green", "blue"];

console.log(colors[0]); // Output: red
console.log(colors[2]); // Output: blue
```

Modifying Elements

Assign a new value to an existing index to modify it.

Example – Modifying an Array:

```
const numbers = [10, 20, 30];
numbers[1] = 25;

console.log(numbers); // Output: [10, 25, 30]
```

Adding and Removing Elements

JavaScript arrays are dynamic, allowing you to add or remove elements easily.

Adding Elements

- **Using push()**: Adds elements to the end of the array
- **Using unshift()**: Adds elements to the beginning

Example – Adding Elements:

```
const animals = ["dog", "cat"];
animals.push("rabbit");
console.log(animals); // Output: ['dog', 'cat', 'rabbit']

animals.unshift("bird");
console.log(animals); // Output: ['bird', 'dog', 'cat',
                                  'rabbit']
```

Removing Elements

- **Using pop()**: Removes the last element
- **Using shift()**: Removes the first element

Example – Removing Elements:

```
const items = ["a", "b", "c"];
items.pop();
console.log(items); // Output: ['a', 'b']

items.shift();
console.log(items); // Output: ['b']
```

CHAPTER 12   OBJECTS AND ARRAYS

Iterating Over Arrays

Looping through arrays is a common task. JavaScript provides multiple techniques for iteration.

Traditional Loops

Example – for Loop:

```
const scores = [10, 20, 30];
for (let i = 0; i < scores.length; i++) {
  console.log(scores[i]);
}
```

forEach Method

The forEach method executes a provided function once for each array element.

Example – forEach Loop:

```
const cities = ["Toronto", "New York", "Berlin"];
cities.forEach((city) => console.log(city));
```

EXERCISE 6: USING FOREACH

Task: Use forEach to iterate over an array of numbers and log each number to the console.

Hint: Pass a callback function to forEach.

Code for Reference:

```
let numbers = [1, 2, 3, 4, 5];
// Iterate using forEach
```

Array Methods

Transformation Methods

- **map()**: Creates a new array with transformed elements
- **filter()**: Creates a new array with elements that pass a condition

Example – Using map and filter:

```
const numbers = [1, 2, 3, 4];
const squared = numbers.map((num) => num * num);
console.log(squared); // Output: [1, 4, 9, 16]

const even = numbers.filter((num) => num % 2 === 0);
console.log(even); // Output: [2, 4]
```

Search Methods

- **find()**: Finds the first element that matches a condition
- **includes()**: Checks if an element exists in the array

Example – Using find and includes:

```
const ages = [15, 20, 25];
const adult = ages.find((age) => age >= 18);
console.log(adult); // Output: 20

console.log(ages.includes(15)); // Output: true
```

Sorting Methods

- **sort()**: Sorts an array in place
- **reverse()**: Reverses the array order

Example – Sorting an Array:

```
const names = ["Charlie", "Alice", "Bob"];
names.sort();

console.log(names); // Output: ['Alice', 'Bob', 'Charlie']
```

Performance Considerations:

- Both sort() and reverse() modify the array **in place**, which can be inefficient if you need to keep the original array intact.

- Sorting with the default sort() method uses a lexicographic order, which can lead to performance inefficiencies when working with numbers or complex objects.

- Sorting large arrays can be an expensive operation, especially if the array is not already partially sorted. It's important to consider that sorting methods generally have a time complexity of **O(n log n)** in the average case (for algorithms like QuickSort), but the actual time taken will depend on the specific implementation and size of the array.

Alternative: Using .slice() for Non-mutating Sort

To avoid modifying the original array, you can use .slice() to create a shallow copy of the array before applying sort() or reverse().

Example Using .slice()

```
const numbers = [5, 3, 8, 1];

// Create a sorted copy of the array without modifying the
original
const sortedNumbers = numbers.slice().sort((a, b) => a - b);
console.log(sortedNumbers); // Output: [1, 3, 5, 8]
console.log(numbers); // Output: [5, 3, 8, 1] (original array
                is unchanged)

// Create a reversed copy of the array without modifying the
original
const reversedNumbers = numbers.slice().reverse();
console.log(reversedNumbers); // Output: [1, 8, 3, 5]
console.log(numbers); // Output: [5, 3, 8, 1] (original array
                is unchanged)
```

Using .slice() creates a shallow copy of the array, allowing you to sort or reverse it without affecting the original array. This approach can be especially useful when you want to maintain immutability, but keep in mind that creating a shallow copy with .slice() may introduce a slight overhead compared with mutating the array directly.

Multidimensional Arrays

Multidimensional arrays store arrays within arrays, useful for grids or matrices.

Example – A 2D Array:

```
const matrix = [
  [1, 2],
  [3, 4],
];

console.log(matrix[0][1]); // Output: 2
```

Common Operations on Multidimensional Arrays:

- Access nested elements via multiple indices.
- Iterate with nested loops.

Looping Through Arrays and Objects

Iterating Over Properties

You can loop over an object's properties using for...in. It's usually not recommended when working with arrays.

Example:

```
for (let key in person) {
  console.log(`${key}: ${person[key]}`);
}
```

Object.keys(), Object.values(), and Object.entries()

JavaScript provides methods for working with properties:

- **Object.keys(obj):** Returns an array of the object's keys
- **Object.values(obj):** Returns an array of the object's values
- **Object.entries(obj):** Returns an array of key-value pairs as arrays

Example:

```
console.log(Object.keys(person));    // Output: ["name", "age", "location"]
console.log(Object.values(person));  // Output: ["John", 31, "New York"]
console.log(Object.entries(person)); // Output: [["name", "John"], ["age", 31],[ "location", "New York"]]
```

The forEach Method

forEach is an array method that lets you iterate over elements in a clean, concise way:

```
colors.forEach(color => console.log(color));
```

In this example

- The function is defined with the arrow (=>) syntax.
- Arrow functions implicitly return the result of the expression, so there's no need to explicitly use the return keyword when the function body is a single expression.

Using for...of for Arrays

The for...of loop is ideal for iterating over arrays because it provides direct access to elements:

```
for (let color of colors) {
  console.log(color);
}
```

Working with Nested Arrays and Objects

Arrays and objects can be nested, creating structures that are common in real-world data like API responses. Access nested data by chaining array and object accessors:

```
const team = [
  { name: "Alice", role: "developer" },
  { name: "Bob", role: "designer" }
];
```

```
for (const member of team) {
  console.log(`${member.name}: ${member.role}`);
}
```

Prototypes and Prototypal Inheritance

JavaScript uses a unique inheritance model known as prototypal inheritance, where objects can inherit properties and methods from other objects. This inheritance model operates through the concept of prototypes. Every JavaScript object has an internal link to another object called its prototype. When you try to access a property that doesn't exist on the object itself, JavaScript looks up the property in the prototype chain.

Understanding Prototypes

A prototype is essentially a template object from which other objects inherit properties and methods. If an object does not have a property being accessed, JavaScript will look for that property in the object's prototype, creating a chain known as the "prototype chain."

Creating an Object with Prototypes

JavaScript functions are often used to create objects with shared properties or methods. When you create an object using a constructor function or class, JavaScript automatically assigns a prototype to it.

Example:

```
function Person(name) {
  this.name = name;
}
```

```
Person.prototype.greet = function() {
  return `Hello, my name is ${this.name}`;
};

const alice = new Person("Alice");
console.log(alice.greet()); // Output: "Hello, my name
                                          is Alice"
```

In this example

- The `Person` constructor function is used to create a new `Person` object.
- `greet` is added to `Person.prototype`, making it accessible to all instances of `Person`.

Prototype Chain and Inheritance

In JavaScript, objects can inherit properties and methods from other objects. The prototype chain is a key concept that enables this inheritance. Every object in JavaScript has a prototype property, which points to another object, and this chain continues until it reaches null. This allows objects to "inherit" the properties and methods of their prototype objects.

Understanding the Prototype Chain

When you try to access a property or method on an object, JavaScript first checks the object itself. If the property or method is not found, it looks up the prototype chain until it either finds the property or reaches the end of the chain (which is null).

Example:

```
console.log(alice.hasOwnProperty("greet")); // Output: false
console.log("greet" in alice);              // Output: true
```

CHAPTER 12 OBJECTS AND ARRAYS

Here, greet is not a direct property of alice, but JavaScript finds it in the prototype chain.

Overwriting in the Prototype Chain

While the prototype chain is a powerful feature for inheritance, **you should be careful about overwriting methods or properties in the prototype**. Overwriting methods in the prototype can lead to unexpected behavior, especially when multiple instances of an object are involved, as changes will apply to all instances that inherit from that prototype.

Example Potential Issue with Overwriting:

```
function Person(name) {
  this.name = name;
}

Person.prototype.greet = function() {
  return `Hello, my name is ${this.name}`;
};

const john = new Person('John');
const jane = new Person('Jane');

// Overwriting the method on the prototype
Person.prototype.greet = function() {
  return `Hi, I'm ${this.name}`;
};

console.log(john.greet());  // Output: Hi, I'm John
console.log(jane.greet());  // Output: Hi, I'm Jane
```

In this example, overwriting the greet method in the prototype affects both john and jane objects. This shows how changes to the prototype can impact all instances that share that prototype.

Best Practices for Using Prototypes and Inheritance

- **Avoid overwriting existing prototype methods** unless you are certain it won't cause conflicts with other parts of your code. If you need to add new functionality, consider adding new methods instead of replacing existing ones.

- **Use composition over inheritance** where possible to reduce tight coupling between objects.

- **Be mindful of method resolution order** when working with multiple prototypes or inheritance chains to ensure the correct method is called.

By carefully managing inheritance and avoiding unintended overwriting, you can harness the full power of the prototype chain while keeping your code clean and maintainable.

Using Object.create() for Prototype-Based Inheritance

You can also use `Object.create()` to create objects with a specific prototype, providing a cleaner approach to prototype-based inheritance.

Example:

```
const animal = {
  speak() {
    console.log("Animal sound");
  }
};

const dog = Object.create(animal);
dog.speak(); // Output: "Animal sound"
```

375

In this example

- dog inherits from animal, so it has access to the speak method.

Performance Implications of Object.create()

While Object.create() is useful for setting up prototype-based inheritance, **it has some performance considerations**:

1. **Prototype Chain Lookup Overhead**
   Since properties and methods are inherited via the prototype chain, accessing them requires JavaScript to traverse up the chain if they are not directly found on the object. In deep prototype chains, this lookup can introduce minor performance overhead compared with accessing properties directly on the object.

2. **Lack of Constructor Function Optimizations**
   Unlike constructor functions, which benefit from JavaScript engine optimizations like inline caching, Object.create() does not leverage the same optimizations. This can make it **slightly slower** in object creation compared with using constructor functions or ES6 classes.

3. **Instance-Specific Properties Must Be Manually Defined**
   Since Object.create() does not invoke a constructor, you must manually define instance properties. This can lead to additional memory usage if not managed correctly.

   ```
   const dog = Object.create(animal);
   dog.name = "Buddy"; // Manually defining instance property
   ```

When to Use Object.create()

- Use it when you **explicitly need to set the prototype of an object** without invoking a constructor.

- It is useful for **creating lightweight object hierarchies** when deep prototype chains are not a concern.

- Consider alternatives like **ES6 classes** or **constructor functions** if performance is a critical factor.

Why Prototypes Are Useful

Prototypes provide a way to efficiently share methods and properties among instances of objects without duplicating them. This approach is memory-efficient and encourages reusability, which is particularly valuable when dealing with a large number of objects that share similar behavior.

Classes and Their Relation to Prototypes

Why Use Classes?

While JavaScript has always been a prototype-based language, the introduction of classes in ES6 provides a way to define reusable blueprints for objects with clearer and more structured syntax. This shift in syntax makes object-oriented programming in JavaScript more accessible, especially for those familiar with other languages like Java or C#.

Because of their readability and ease of use, classes are now the preferred way to define and structure code in modern JavaScript. In fact, popular frameworks such as Angular and React rely heavily on classes, making this knowledge essential for working with these tools.

Defining a Class

A class is defined using the class keyword, and within it, we can define a constructor, properties, and methods.

Example:

```
class Person {
  constructor(name) {
    this.name = name;
  }
  greet() {
    return `Hello, my name is ${this.name}`;
  }
}
const bob = new Person("Bob");
console.log(bob.greet()); // Output: "Hello, my name is Bob"
```

In this example

- **Constructor**: The constructor method is a special function that is automatically called when creating a new instance of the class.

- **Methods**: Methods defined inside the class body (like greet) are stored on the class's prototype, making them shared across instances.

Inheritance with Classes

Classes also support inheritance, allowing one class to inherit properties and methods from another using the extends keyword.

Example:

```
class Animal {
  speak() {
    return "Some sound";
  }
}

class Dog extends Animal {
  speak() {
    return "Woof!";
  }
}

const myDog = new Dog();
console.log(myDog.speak()); // Output: "Woof!"
```

Here, `Dog` inherits from `Animal`, and we override the `speak` method to provide a specific implementation for Dog.

How Classes Relate to Prototypes

Even though we're using the class syntax, JavaScript is still using prototypes behind the scenes. Methods defined within a class are added to the class's prototype, which means that all instances of the class share the same method definitions, just as they would with traditional prototype-based inheritance.

Best Practice: Use Classes for Readability and Compatibility

In modern JavaScript development, classes are generally favored over direct manipulation of prototypes. Classes offer several advantages:

CHAPTER 12 OBJECTS AND ARRAYS

- **Improved Readability**: The syntax is more concise and similar to other languages with class-based inheritance, making it easier to understand.
- **Framework Compatibility**: Many JavaScript frameworks, including Angular, use classes by default for defining components, services, and models.
- **Maintainability**: Classes provide a clearer structure, making code easier to maintain and extend.

Advice: For most new projects and especially when working with frameworks, use classes instead of prototypes to ensure readability, maintainability, and compatibility with common front-end development practices.

EXERCISE 7: PROTOTYPAL INHERITANCE

Task: Create an object using `Object.create()` with a prototype object containing shared methods. Access the shared method from the new object.

Hint: Define the shared method in the prototype object.

Code for Reference:

```
let animal = {
  speak() {
    console.log("I am an animal");
  }
};

// Create a new object here
```

Summary

In this expanded chapter, we covered

- **Objects and Arrays**: How to work with structured data using properties, methods, and various array operations.

- **Prototypes and Prototypal Inheritance**: An understanding of JavaScript's foundational inheritance model.

- **Classes and Best Practices**: How ES6 classes offer a cleaner syntax for creating and inheriting objects. We recommend using classes as they align well with modern JavaScript frameworks and improve code readability.

By choosing classes, you will be well-prepared to work with popular libraries and frameworks like Angular and React, which rely on classes for core functionality. This approach reflects best practices in today's JavaScript ecosystem, helping new developers write code that's both effective and easy to collaborate on.

CHAPTER 12 OBJECTS AND ARRAYS

Full Solutions

SOLUTION TO EXERCISE 1: UNDERSTANDING OBJECTS

```
let car = {
  make: "Toyota",
  model: "Corolla",
  year: 2020
};

console.log(car.make); // Dot notation
console.log(car["model"]); // Bracket notation
```

SOLUTION TO EXERCISE 2: OBJECT LITERALS

```
let book = {
  title: "JavaScript Essentials",
  author: "John Doe",
  pages: 300
};
```

SOLUTION TO EXERCISE 3: FACTORY FUNCTIONS

```
function createProduct(name, price) {
  return {
    name,
    price,
    applyDiscount(discountPercentage) {
      this.price -= (this.price * discountPercentage) / 100;
    }
  };
}
```

```
// Create two product objects
const product1 = createProduct("Laptop", 1000);
const product2 = createProduct("Phone", 500);

// Apply discounts
product1.applyDiscount(10); // Reduce price by 10%
product2.applyDiscount(20); // Reduce price by 20%

console.log(product1.price); // Output: 900
console.log(product2.price); // Output: 400
```

SOLUTION TO EXERCISE 4: DYNAMIC PROPERTIES

```
let user = {};
let propertyName = "age";
user[propertyName] = 30;

console.log(user); // { age: 30 }
```

SOLUTION TO EXERCISE 5: CREATING ARRAYS WITH ARRAY.FROM()

```
let numbers = Array.from({ length: 5 }, (v, i) => i + 1);
console.log(numbers); // [1, 2, 3, 4, 5]
```

SOLUTION TO EXERCISE 6: USING FOREACH

```
let numbers = [1, 2, 3, 4, 5];

numbers.forEach(number => console.log(number));
```

CHAPTER 12 OBJECTS AND ARRAYS

SOLUTION TO EXERCISE 7: PROTOTYPAL INHERITANCE

```
let animal = {
  speak() {
    console.log("I am an animal");
  }
};
let dog = Object.create(animal);
dog.speak(); // I am an animal
```

CHAPTER 13

Error Handling

Objective

This chapter introduces the essential concept of error handling in JavaScript. Error handling ensures that code runs smoothly even when unexpected issues arise, enabling developers to manage and respond to errors effectively. By understanding JavaScript's error-handling syntax and using best practices, you'll be better equipped to write robust, reliable code. We'll explore techniques like `try`, `catch`, and `finally` statements, along with creating and throwing custom errors, which help enhance your code's resilience and improve the user experience.

Introduction to Error Handling

Errors are a natural part of programming. They can stem from a variety of sources, including user input, network issues, or unforeseen logical errors in code. In JavaScript, handling these errors gracefully is crucial to prevent an application from crashing and to ensure a smooth user experience.

JavaScript provides specific mechanisms to handle errors using `try`, `catch`, and `finally` statements. These statements enable developers to anticipate potential failures and handle them in a controlled manner, allowing programs to recover or fail gracefully.

CHAPTER 13   ERROR HANDLING

Types of Errors in JavaScript

1. **Syntax Errors**: Issues in the code syntax (e.g., missing brackets or typos)
2. **Runtime Errors**: Errors that occur during code execution (e.g., calling a method on an undefined object)
3. **Logical Errors**: Errors in the logic of the code that produce unexpected results

Example – Syntax vs. Runtime Error:

```
// Syntax Error
console.log("Hello World  // Missing closing quote

// Runtime Error
const obj = undefined;
console.log(obj.name); // Cannot read properties of undefined
```

Key Reasons for Error Handling:

- **User Experience**: Well-handled errors improve the user experience by preventing abrupt disruptions.
- **Debugging**: Handling errors can make debugging easier by allowing you to pinpoint exactly where and why an issue occurred.
- **Fault Tolerance**: Ensures the system continues to function even when errors occur.
- **Security**: By controlling what happens when an error occurs, error handling prevents sensitive information from being exposed.

CHAPTER 13   ERROR HANDLING

EXERCISE 1: SPOT THE SYNTAX ERROR

Task: Review the following code and identify the syntax error.

Hint: Look for missing or misplaced characters.

Code for Reference:

```
function greet(name) {
    console.log("Hello, " + name;
}
```

EXERCISE 2: DEBUGGING A RUNTIME ERROR

Task: The following code attempts to access a property of an undefined variable. Modify the code to fix the runtime error.

Hint: Ensure the variable is properly initialized before accessing its properties.

Code for Reference:

```
let person;
console.log(person.name);
```

EXERCISE 3: FIXING A LOGICAL ERROR

Task: The following code attempts to calculate the sum of numbers in an array. However, it contains a logical error. Identify and correct the error.

Hint: Review how the loop and array indices are handled.

Code for Reference:

```
function sumArray(arr) {
    let sum = 0;
    for (let i = 1; i <= arr.length; i++) {
```

```
      sum += arr[i];
    }
    return sum;
}
console.log(sumArray([1, 2, 3]));
```

try, catch, and finally Blocks

The try, catch, and finally blocks are the foundation of error handling in JavaScript. These statements enable you to isolate code that might throw an error and provide a response without halting the entire application.

Syntax:

```
try {
  // Code that might throw an error
} catch (error) {
  // Code that runs if an error is thrown
} finally {
  // Code that always runs, regardless of an error
}
```

- **try Block**: Contains code that may throw an error.
- **catch Block**: Executes if an error is thrown in the try block. It can access the error object, which provides information about what went wrong.
- **finally Block**: This block runs regardless of whether an error was thrown or not, making it useful for cleanup tasks.

CHAPTER 13   ERROR HANDLING

Syntax:

```
try {
  let result = riskyOperation();
  console.log(result);
} catch (error) {
  console.log("An error occurred:", error.message);
} finally {
  console.log("Execution complete.");
}
```

In this example, if **riskyOperation()** fails, the **catch** block handles the error, preventing the program from crashing. The **finally** block executes regardless of the outcome, making it suitable for tasks that must run, such as closing resources.

EXERCISE 4: HANDLING EXCEPTIONS

Task: Wrap the following code in a `try-catch` block to handle any potential exceptions. Log a custom error message if an error occurs.

Hint: Simulate an error by dividing a number by zero.

Code for Reference:

```
function divide(a, b) {
    return a / b;
}
console.log(divide(10, 0));
```

CHAPTER 13 ERROR HANDLING

Creating Custom Errors

Sometimes, the built-in error messages may not fully convey the specific issue within your code. JavaScript allows you to create custom error messages, making it easier to provide informative feedback for debugging and improving error responses.

Syntax:

```
throw new Error("Custom error message");
```

Example:

```
function divide(a, b) {
  if (b === 0) {
    throw new Error("Cannot divide by zero");
  }
  return a / b;
}
try {
  console.log(divide(4, 0));
} catch (error) {
  console.error(error.message); // Output: Cannot divide by zero
}
```

In this example, a custom error is thrown when attempting to divide by zero. Custom errors make debugging easier by providing meaningful messages.

CHAPTER 13   ERROR HANDLING

EXERCISE 5: THROWING CUSTOM ERRORS

Task: Create a function checkAge that throws a custom error if the input age is below 18. Use the `Error` class to define the error message.

Hint: Use `throw new Error("Custom message")` to throw an error.

Code for Reference:

```
function checkAge(age) {
    // Add your custom error handling here.
}
checkAge(15);
```

Using the Error Class

A better approach is to create your own class by extending the `Error` class.
   Example:

```
class DivideByZeroError extends Error {
  constructor(message) {
    super(message);
    this.name = "DivideByZeroError";
  }
}
try {
  throw new ValidationError("Cannot divide by zero");
} catch (error) {
  console.error(error.name); // Output: DivideByZeroError
  console.error(error.message); // Output: Cannot divide by zero.
}
```

391

The Error Object and Its Properties

When an error is thrown in JavaScript, an Error object is created, which includes several properties that provide insight into the error's nature. These properties are helpful for logging, debugging, and providing detailed error responses.

Common Error Properties:

- **message**: Describes what went wrong
- **name**: Specifies the type of error (e.g., ReferenceError, TypeError)
- **stack**: Contains the stack trace, showing where the error occurred

Example:

```
try {
  let undefinedFunction = null;
  undefinedFunction();
} catch (error) {
  console.log("Error Name:", error.name);       // Output: TypeError
  console.log("Error Message:", error.message); // Output: undefinedFunction is not a function
  console.log("Error Stack:", error.stack);     // Shows the full stack trace
}
```

Using the Error object allows for a structured approach to error handling and logging, helping developers identify and resolve issues faster.

CHAPTER 13　ERROR HANDLING

EXERCISE 6: INSPECTING THE ERROR OBJECT

Task: Use a `try-catch` block to intentionally generate an error. Inside the `catch` block, log the error's name and `message` properties to the console.

Hint: Use `throw new Error("Example error")` to generate an error.

Code for Reference:

```
try {
    // Throw an intentional error here.
} catch (error) {
    // Log the error name and message here.
}
```

Advanced Error Handling with ??= Operator for Fallbacks

Adding Methods to Objects

In some cases, you might want to set a fallback value only if a variable is `null` or `undefined`. The `??=` operator allows you to do this concisely, ensuring that essential variables have fallback values when missing.

Example:

```
let userPreference = null;
userPreference ??= "default setting";
console.log(userPreference); // Output: default setting
```

Here, if `userPreference` is `null` or `undefined`, it gets assigned the fallback value of `"default setting"`. This operator helps ensure key variables have default values, reducing the risk of dealing with null or undefined.

393

> ⚠ **Note** While ??= provides a fallback for null or undefined, it does not catch other types of errors, such as exceptions from an API response. If an API call fails due to a network issue or returns an unexpected data structure, additional error handling (e.g., try...catch or default values in API response handling) may be required.

EXERCISE 7: USING THE ??= OPERATOR

Task: Use the ??= operator to provide a default value for a variable that might be null or undefined.

Hint: Test the operator with variables that have initial values of null and undefined.

Code for Reference:

```
let username;
username ??= "DefaultUser";
console.log(username);
```

Error Handling with `async` and `await`

When working with asynchronous code in JavaScript, async and await make it easier to manage promises. However, handling errors in asynchronous functions requires a slightly different approach. In an async function, any error that would normally cause the function to reject is instead thrown as an exception, making it possible to handle with try/catch.

Using try/catch with async/await

To handle errors in `async` functions, you can use a `try/catch` block around the awaited code. This lets you catch any errors that occur during the asynchronous operation without requiring `.catch()` on every promise.

However, some promise rejections may still go unhandled if they occur outside the try...catch block. To prevent this, you can also set up global error handlers like window.onunhandledrejection in the browser or process.on('unhandledRejection', handler) in Node.js to catch and log unexpected rejections.

Example:

```
async function fetchData() {
  try {
    let response = await fetch("https://jsonplaceholder.
    typicode.com/posts");
    if (!response.ok) {
      throw new Error(`HTTP error! Status: ${response.
      status}`);
    }
    let data = await response.json();
    console.log(data);
  } catch (error) {
    console.error("An error occurred:", error.message);
  }
}
fetchData();
```

In this example, if the `fetch` request fails or returns a non-ok response, an error is thrown and handled in the `catch` block. This approach provides a clear and structured way to manage errors within asynchronous code.

CHAPTER 13 ERROR HANDLING

EXERCISE 8: HANDLING ERRORS IN ASYNC FUNCTIONS

Task: Create an async function `fetchData` that simulates fetching data from an API. Use a `try-catch` block to handle any errors.

Hint: Use `throw new Error` inside a `Promise` to simulate an API failure.

Code for Reference:

```
async function fetchData() {
    // Simulate API fetch with a potential error here.
}
fetchData();
```

Handling Multiple Asynchronous Calls

If you have multiple `await` statements in a single `try` block, any of them could throw an error, and they will all be handled by the same `catch` block. In cases where each asynchronous call requires its own error handling, you may need to nest `try/catch` blocks, though this can impact readability.

Example:

```
async function processData() {
  try {
    let data1 = await fetchData1();
    console.log("Data 1:", data1);
    try {
      let data2 = await fetchData2();
      console.log("Data 2:", data2);
    } catch (error) {
      console.error("Error fetching Data 2:", error.message);
    }
```

CHAPTER 13   ERROR HANDLING

```
    } catch (error) {
      console.error("Error fetching Data 1:", error.message);
    }
  }
}
processData();
```

   In this example, if `fetchData1` or `fetchData2` encounters an error, the respective `catch` block will handle it, allowing you to control error handling for each asynchronous call individually.
   Instead of nesting multiple try...catch blocks, you can use Promise.allSettled() to execute multiple asynchronous operations concurrently while capturing both resolved and rejected results. This method ensures that all promises complete, allowing you to handle successes and failures individually without stopping execution due to a single failure.

```
const fetchData = async () => {
  const results = await Promise.allSettled([
    fetch("/api/data1").then(res => res.json()),
    fetch("/api/data2").then(res => res.json()),
    fetch("/api/data3").then(res => res.json())
  ]);

  results.forEach((result, index) => {
    if (result.status === "fulfilled") {
      console.log(`API ${index + 1} succeeded:`, result.value);
    } else {
      console.error(`API ${index + 1} failed:`, result.reason);
    }
  });
};
fetchData();
```

397

By using Promise.allSettled(), you avoid unnecessary nesting and ensure that all requests are processed, even if some fail. This approach is particularly useful when working with multiple independent API calls or background tasks.

EXERCISE 9: MANAGING MULTIPLE PROMISES

Task: Use Promise.all to wait for multiple promises to resolve. Keep in mind that if one of the promises is rejected, the entire operation will fail, and the rejection will be immediately propagated. Handle errors appropriately to ensure the process doesn't break entirely.

Hint: Use try-catch or .catch() for error handling.

Code for Reference:

```
const promise1 = Promise.resolve(1);
const promise2 = Promise.reject("Error in promise2");
const promise3 = Promise.resolve(3);

// Use Promise.all here.
```

Global Error Handling

Global error handlers are a safety net for unhandled errors, providing a last line of defense when other mechanisms fail. However, they should **almost always** be used as a last resort. While they can catch errors that escape other error-handling mechanisms, relying on them too heavily can result in unintended application behaviors, making it harder to pinpoint the root cause of issues. Use them sparingly and ensure they don't obscure underlying problems that should be addressed directly.

Using window.onerror

Example:

```
window.onerror = function (message, source, lineno, colno, 
error) {
  console.error("Global Error Caught:");
  console.error("Message:", message);
  console.error("Source:", source);
  console.error("Line Number:", lineno);
  console.error("Column Number:", colno);
  console.error("Error Object:", error);
};
```

By logging all the parameters, you can gain a better understanding of the context of the error, such as where it occurred, what the specific error is, and any additional stack trace details. This approach helps in diagnosing and fixing issues more effectively.

Using process.on in Node.js

```
process.on("uncaughtException", (error) => {
  console.error("Uncaught Exception:", error.message);
});

process.on("unhandledRejection", (reason, promise) => {
  console.error("Unhandled Promise Rejection at:", promise, 
  "reason:", reason); });
```

Explanation:

- **uncaughtException:** This event is triggered when an error occurs in your application that is not caught by any try...catch block.

- **unhandledRejection:** This event is triggered when a promise is rejected but no .catch() handler is attached to it.

Both of these global events act as safety nets, but using them too much can mask underlying issues in your code. It's best to address errors at the point where they occur, but these handlers can help catch errors that are missed.

EXERCISE 10: HANDLING UNCAUGHT ERRORS IN NODE.JS

Task: Write a script that catches uncaught exceptions using `process.on`. Simulate an uncaught exception.

Hint: Use `throw` inside an asynchronous function to simulate the error.

Code for Reference:

```
process.on("uncaughtException", (err) => {
    console.error("Caught exception: ", err);
});

// Simulate an uncaught exception here.
```

Graceful Degradation vs. Failing Fast

- **Graceful Degradation**: Ensure the application continues to work with reduced functionality after an error.
- **Failing Fast**: Immediately terminate execution to prevent propagating corrupted states.

When to Use:

- Graceful degradation is ideal for user-facing applications.
- Failing fast is preferred for back-end services where data integrity is critical.

Summary

In this chapter, we've explored JavaScript's error-handling mechanisms to create resilient and robust applications. We started with `try`, `catch`, and `finally` statements, discussed creating custom error messages, and reviewed the `Error` object's useful properties. We covered the `??=` operator for providing fallback values and introduced handling asynchronous errors with `async` and `await`, which includes using `try/catch` to manage promise-based errors effectively.

By mastering these error-handling techniques, you're better equipped to write reliable JavaScript applications that manage unexpected issues gracefully, improving user experience and code reliability in both synchronous and asynchronous contexts.

Full Solutions

SOLUTION TO EXERCISE 1: SPOT THE SYNTAX ERROR

```
function greet(name) {
    console.log("Hello, " + name);
}
```

Explanation:

The issue was a missing closing parenthesis) in the `console.log` statement.

CHAPTER 13 ERROR HANDLING

SOLUTION TO EXERCISE 2: DEBUGGING A RUNTIME ERROR

```
let person = { name: "John" };
console.log(person.name);
```

Explanation:

The variable person was undefined. Initializing it as an object with a name property resolves the runtime error.

SOLUTION TO EXERCISE 3: FIXING A LOGICAL ERROR

```
function sumArray(arr) {
    let sum = 0;
    for (let i = 0; i < arr.length; i++) { // Changed `i = 1` to `i = 0` and `<=` to `<`
        sum += arr[i];
    }
    return sum;
}
console.log(sumArray([1, 2, 3])); // Output: 6
```

Explanation:

The loop was starting from the wrong index (1 instead of 0), and it was iterating out of bounds due to i <= arr.length.

SOLUTION TO EXERCISE 4: HANDLING EXCEPTIONS

```
function divide(a, b) {
    try {
        if (b === 0) {
            throw new Error("Division by zero is not
            allowed");
        }
        return a / b;
    } catch (error) {
        console.error(error.message);
    } finally {
        console.log("Operation complete");
    }
}
console.log(divide(10, 0)); // Logs the error message and
"Operation complete"
```

Explanation:

The `try-catch` block handles the division by zero case gracefully by throwing a custom error.

SOLUTION TO EXERCISE 5: THROWING CUSTOM ERRORS

```
function checkAge(age) {
    if (age < 18) {
        throw new Error("Age must be 18 or older");
    }
    console.log("Age is valid");
}
```

```
try {
    checkAge(15);
} catch (error) {
    console.error(error.message); // Output: "Age must be 18
                                  or older"
}
```

Explanation:

The function uses the throw statement to create a custom error when the input age is below 18.

SOLUTION TO EXERCISE 6: INSPECTING THE ERROR OBJECT

```
try {
    throw new Error("This is a test error");
} catch (error) {
    console.log("Error Name:", error.name); // Output:
    "Error Name: Error"
    console.log("Error Message:", error.message); // Output:
    "Error Message: This is a test error"
}
```

Explanation:

The Error object's name and message properties are accessed inside the catch block.

SOLUTION TO EXERCISE 7: USING THE ??= OPERATOR

```
let username;
username ??= "DefaultUser";
console.log(username); // Output: "DefaultUser"

let existingUser = "Alice";
existingUser ??= "DefaultUser";
console.log(existingUser); // Output: "Alice"
```

Explanation:

The ??= operator assigns a default value only when the variable is null or undefined.

SOLUTION TO EXERCISE 8: HANDLING ERRORS IN ASYNC FUNCTIONS

```
async function fetchData() {
    try {
        const data = await new Promise((resolve, reject) => {
            setTimeout(() => reject(new Error("API fetch
            failed")), 1000);
        });
        console.log(data);
    } catch (error) {
        console.error("Error fetching data:", error.message);
        // Output: "Error fetching data: API fetch failed"
    }
}
fetchData();
```

CHAPTER 13   ERROR HANDLING

Explanation:

The `try-catch` block ensures that errors in the asynchronous operation are handled gracefully.

SOLUTION TO EXERCISE 9: MANAGING MULTIPLE PROMISES

```
const promise1 = Promise.resolve(1);
const promise2 = Promise.reject("Error in promise2");
const promise3 = Promise.resolve(3);

async function handlePromises() {
    try {
        const results = await Promise.all([promise1,
        promise2, promise3]);
        console.log(results);
    } catch (error) {
        console.error("One of the promises failed:", error);
        // Output: "One of the promises failed: Error in
        promise2"
    }
}
handlePromises();
```

Explanation:

The `Promise.all` method fails if any of the promises reject. The `try-catch` block handles this scenario.

SOLUTION TO EXERCISE 10: HANDLING UNCAUGHT ERRORS IN NODE.JS

```
process.on("uncaughtException", (err) => {
    console.error("Caught exception: ", err.message);
    // Logs the uncaught exception message
});

throw new Error("This is an uncaught exception");
```

Explanation:

The process.on method in Node.js captures uncaught exceptions and prevents the application from crashing immediately.

CHAPTER 14

Working with ES6+ Syntax

Objective

In this chapter, we aim to provide a comprehensive understanding of the powerful ES6+ features that have revolutionized JavaScript development. These modern syntax enhancements simplify code, increase readability, and offer greater flexibility in addressing complex programming scenarios. Through detailed explanations and examples, we will explore

- **Template literals**, for creating dynamic and easily readable strings
- **Destructuring arrays and objects**, enabling intuitive data extraction and assignment
- **Spread and rest operators**, which streamline operations involving arrays, objects, and function arguments
- **Default parameters**, ensuring robust and fault-tolerant function definitions
- **Optional chaining and nullish coalescing**, simplifying safe property access and default value assignments

- **Iterators and generators**, providing custom iteration logic and lazy evaluation for complex datasets
- **Proxies and Reflect**, allowing developers to define custom behavior for fundamental operations

By the end of this chapter, you will not only be equipped to use these features but also understand their underlying mechanics, enabling you to write cleaner, more efficient, and maintainable JavaScript code.

Template Literals

Template literals revolutionize how strings are handled in JavaScript. Unlike traditional strings, which require cumbersome concatenation, template literals use backticks (`) to simplify string creation, interpolation, and multi-line text handling.

Multi-line Strings

One of the most notable advantages of template literals is the ease of working with multi-line strings. Before ES6, developers had to use newline characters (\n) and concatenation operators (+) to format text. This approach often made code cluttered and difficult to read. Template literals eliminate this problem, allowing multi-line strings to be created naturally, improving readability and maintainability.

Traditional strings required awkward concatenation for multi-line text:

```
const text = "Line 1\n" +
             "Line 2\n" +
             "Line 3";
```

With template literals, multi-line strings become straightforward:

```
const text = `Line 1
Line 2
Line 3`;
```

Interpolation

The ability to embed expressions within strings using ${} is another game-changer. Developers can dynamically include variables, calculations, and even function calls directly within the string. This is particularly useful in scenarios like dynamically generating HTML, crafting personalized user messages, or debugging complex output.

Example:

```
const name = "Alice";
const greeting = `Hello, ${name}!`;
console.log(greeting); // "Hello, Alice!"
```

Tagged Templates

Tagged templates extend template literals by allowing developers to process them with custom functions. This feature is commonly used for tasks like escaping HTML, internationalizing strings, or preprocessing template data before rendering. The syntax may seem advanced initially, but its flexibility proves invaluable in complex applications.

Example:

```
function tag(strings, ...values) {
  return strings[0] + values.map(value => value.toUpperCase()).
  join('');
}
```

```
const result = tag`Hello ${"world"} and ${"JavaScript"}`;
console.log(result); // "Hello WORLD and JAVASCRIPT"
```

Use Case: Tagged templates are ideal for escaping HTML or localizing content.

EXERCISE 1: CREATING DYNAMIC STRINGS WITH TEMPLATE LITERALS

Task: Create a multi-line string using template literals that includes interpolated values.

Hint: Include a variable like name and a calculation, such as age + 5.

Code for Reference:

```
const name = "Alice";

const age = 25;
// Use a template literal to create a multi-line string.
```

Limitations of Template Literals

While template literals offer significant advantages, they also come with some limitations:

1. **Cannot Be Used Inside JSON**
   Since JSON only supports double-quoted ("") and single-quoted ('') strings, **backticks (`) are not valid inside JSON files**. This means you cannot use template literals directly in JSON configurations.

   ✗ **Invalid JSON:**
   ```
   {
     "message": `Hello, World!`   // SyntaxError
   }
   ```

2. **Issues with Backticks in Some Scenarios**

    - If your string content includes backticks, you must **escape** them using a backslash (`` \` ``). Otherwise, JavaScript will misinterpret them.

    - This can lead to **unexpected syntax errors** when dynamically constructing strings.

    ✅ Here's a correct way to include a backtick inside a template literal:

    ```
    const message = `Here is a backtick: \``;
    console.log(message); // Output: Here is a backtick: `
    ```

3. **Performance Considerations**
   While template literals improve readability, they **may introduce minor performance overhead** compared with traditional string concatenation in certain cases, especially when dealing with heavy string operations inside loops.

4. **Strict Mode and Security Risks**
   If user-generated input is interpolated inside template literals without sanitization, it can introduce **security risks**, such as code injection vulnerabilities.

Best Practices

- **Use template literals only where necessary** – for simple strings, traditional string concatenation may suffice.

- **Be cautious when working with backticks** inside dynamic content or nested template literals.
- **Validate user input** before using interpolation to avoid security risks.

Destructuring Arrays and Objects

Destructuring is a powerful feature that simplifies the extraction of values from arrays and objects. It reduces boilerplate code, making assignments more concise and expressive.

Array Destructuring

Array destructuring is particularly useful in scenarios where the structure of the data is consistent. For example, when working with API responses, destructuring allows developers to extract specific values effortlessly. This feature is also invaluable in simplifying function arguments that receive arrays, such as coordinate points in graphics programming.

Example:

```
const colors = ["red", "green", "blue"];
const [firstColor, secondColor] = colors;
console.log(firstColor); // "red"
console.log(secondColor); // "green"
```

Object Destructuring

Object destructuring offers similar benefits for working with complex objects. Instead of manually extracting properties, destructuring allows developers to assign values to variables directly. This is particularly useful in React props, configuration objects, or when interacting with large datasets.

CHAPTER 14   WORKING WITH ES6+ SYNTAX

Example:

```
const user = {
  name: "Alice",
  age: 25
};

const { name, age } = user;

console.log(name); // "Alice"
console.log(age); // 25
```

Destructuring can also be used with function parameters, making it easier to access values from objects passed as arguments.

Nested Destructuring and Default Values

In real-world applications, data often comes in deeply nested structures. Destructuring supports nested patterns, enabling the extraction of deeply buried properties. By incorporating default values, developers can ensure that their code gracefully handles missing or undefined properties, reducing the risk of runtime errors.

Example:

```
const config = {
  server: {
    host: "localhost",
    port: 8080
  }
};

const { server: { host, port = 80 } } = config;
console.log(port); // 8080
```

415

Practical Example:

```
const { data, error } = await fetchData();
```

EXERCISE 2: EXTRACTING VALUES FROM ARRAYS AND OBJECTS

Task: Given an array of numbers and an object with nested properties, use destructuring to extract specific values.

Hint: Use array destructuring for the first two elements and object destructuring to get nested values.

Code for Reference:

```
const numbers = [1, 2, 3, 4];
const person = {
  name: "Bob",
  address: {
    city: "Paris",
    zip: 75001
  }
};
// Destructure numbers and person object here.
```

Spread and Rest Operators

The spread (...) and rest (...) operators are among the most versatile additions to JavaScript. While they share the same syntax, their functionality varies depending on context.

Spread Operator

The spread operator allows developers to expand arrays or objects into individual elements. It is a powerful tool for combining or copying data structures. For example, creating shallow copies of arrays or merging multiple arrays into one becomes straightforward. In object literals, it simplifies merging and cloning, which is essential in functional programming or when managing immutable states in frameworks like Redux.

Example:

```
const arr1 = [1, 2, 3];
const arr2 = [...arr1, 4, 5];
console.log(arr2); // [1, 2, 3, 4, 5]
```

In objects, the spread operator is used to create shallow copies or merge properties.

```
const user = {
  name: "Alice",
  age: 25
};
const updatedUser = { ...user, age: 26 };
console.log(updatedUser); // { name: "Alice", age: 26 }
```

Performance Considerations

While the spread operator is convenient, **using it with large arrays or objects can lead to performance issues**. Since it creates **shallow copies**, spreading a large object or array **duplicates its entire structure in memory**, which can be costly in performance-sensitive applications.

For example, spreading a **large object** may significantly increase memory usage:

```
const largeObj = { /* thousands of properties */ };
const copiedObj = { ...largeObj }; // Can be inefficient for
                                          large objects
```

Best Practices:

- Avoid using the spread operator unnecessarily for large objects or arrays.

- When working with large datasets, consider using **structured cloning** (structuredClone(obj)) or specialized libraries for deep copies.

- Be mindful of memory overhead when spreading deeply nested objects.

Rest Operator

The rest operator collects multiple elements into a single array or object. It is particularly useful in function arguments, allowing developers to handle an arbitrary number of inputs gracefully. This operator shines in scenarios where functions need to accept varying arguments, such as mathematical calculations or event handlers.

Example:

```
function sum(...numbers) {
  return numbers.reduce((total, num) => total + num, 0);
}
console.log(sum(1, 2, 3, 4)); // 10
```

CHAPTER 14   WORKING WITH ES6+ SYNTAX

EXERCISE 3: COMBINING ARRAYS AND OBJECTS

Task: Use the spread operator to merge two arrays and two objects. Then, use the rest operator to create a function that accepts a variable number of arguments and returns their sum.

Hint: Write two separate code snippets: one for the spread operator and one for the rest operator.

Code for Reference:

```
const arr1 = [1, 2, 3];
const arr2 = [4, 5, 6];
const obj1 = { a: 1 };
const obj2 = { b: 2 };
// Merge arrays and objects here.

// Function using rest operator
function sum(...nums) {
  // Calculate sum here.
}
```

Default Parameters

Default parameters address a long-standing challenge in JavaScript: handling function arguments that are undefined or missing. By providing default values, developers can ensure that their functions remain robust and avoid unnecessary checks for undefined.

CHAPTER 14 WORKING WITH ES6+ SYNTAX

Basic Defaults

Default parameters simplify code by eliminating the need for conditional assignments within the function body. They are especially helpful in utility functions where arguments often go unspecified.

Example:

```
function greet(name = "Guest") {
  console.log(`Hello, ${name}!`);
}
greet(); // "Hello, Guest!"
```

Dynamic Defaults

Dynamic defaults enable functions to compute default values at runtime, providing flexibility for scenarios like setting timestamps, generating unique identifiers, or initializing configuration options.

Example:

```
function createUser(timestamp = Date.now()) {
  console.log(`User created at ${timestamp}`);
}
```

> **EXERCISE 4: CALCULATING DISCOUNTS WITH DEFAULT PARAMETERS**
>
> **Task**: Write a function calculateTotal that accepts two arguments: price and discountRate. Set a default value of 0.1 for discountRate and calculate the total price after the discount.
>
> **Hint**: Use the formula price * (1 - discountRate) for the calculation.

Code for Reference:

```
function calculateTotal(price, discountRate = 0.1) {
  // Calculate total price after discount.
}
```

Optional Chaining

Optional chaining (?.) is a lifesaver when dealing with deeply nested objects or arrays. It prevents errors caused by accessing properties of null or undefined.

In large applications, especially those relying on API data, it's common to encounter deeply nested structures. Optional chaining reduces the need for verbose checks, making the code cleaner and less error-prone. By using this operator, developers can write code that anticipates missing data and handles it gracefully.

Example:

```
const user = {
  profile: {
    name: "Alice"
  }
};

console.log(user.profile?.name); // "Alice"
console.log(user.address?.city); // undefined
```

With optional chaining, JavaScript will return undefined if a property doesn't exist, instead of throwing an error.

CHAPTER 14   WORKING WITH ES6+ SYNTAX

Nullish Coalescing Operator (??)

The ?? operator provides a more accurate fallback mechanism compared with the traditional OR (||) operator. It ensures that only null or undefined triggers the fallback value, preserving other falsy values like 0 or ' '.

This operator is particularly useful in user interfaces, where inputs like 0 or an empty string might be valid but should not invoke default values.

Example:

```
const username = null;
const displayName = username ?? "Guest";
console.log(displayName); // "Guest"
```

EXERCISE 5: SAFE ACCESS AND DEFAULT VALUES

Task: Access a nested property of an object safely using optional chaining, and provide a fallback using the nullish coalescing operator.

Hint: Use ?. for safe access and ?? for fallback.

Code for Reference:

```
const user = {
  profile: {
    name: "Charlie"
  }
};
// Access user.profile.age safely with a fallback.
```

Enhanced Object Literals

JavaScript object literals received several enhancements in ES6, making them more concise and expressive.

Shorthand Property Names

By using shorthand syntax, developers can eliminate redundancy when property names and variables share the same name. This feature is prevalent in modern frameworks, where objects are frequently used to define state, props, or configurations.

Example:

```
const x = 10, y = 20;
const point = { x, y };
console.log(point); // { x: 10, y: 20 }
```

Computed Properties

Computed property names bring dynamism to object literals, allowing property keys to be evaluated at runtime. This is particularly useful for generating object structures based on dynamic inputs.

Example:

```
const prop = "color";
const obj = { [prop]: "blue" };
console.log(obj.color); // "blue"
```

Method Definitions

Methods can now be defined more succinctly within objects, improving readability and consistency with class syntax.

Example:

```
const obj = {
  greet() {
    console.log("Hello!");
```

```
    }
};
obj.greet(); // "Hello!"
```

Classes

JavaScript classes introduce a structured, object-oriented approach to building reusable components.

Basic Syntax

Classes simplify the definition of constructor functions and methods, making code easier to understand and maintain.

Example:

```
class Person {
  constructor(name) {
    this.name = name;
  }
  greet() {
    return `Hello, ${this.name}!`;
  }
}
```

Inheritance

Class inheritance allows developers to create hierarchies, promoting code reuse and extensibility.

Example:

```
class Employee extends Person {
  constructor(name, jobTitle) {
```

```
    super(name);
    this.jobTitle = jobTitle;
  }
}
```

Iterators and Generators

Iterators and generators provide fine-grained control over data processing, especially for sequences or streams.

Custom Iterators

A custom iterator in JavaScript is implemented by creating an object with a `next()` method that adheres to the iterator protocol. The iterator protocol defines a standard way to produce a sequence of values, one at a time, upon request. Additionally, you can define custom iteration behavior by implementing the `Symbol.iterator` property.

Basic Syntax

Here's the basic syntax for creating a custom iterator.

Example:

```
const customIterator = {
  // Required 'next' method
  next() {
    // Must return an object with 'value' and 'done' properties
    return {
      value: /* next value in sequence */,
      done: /* boolean indicating if iteration is complete */
    };
```

```
  }
};
// Usage example:
const iterator = customIterator[Symbol.iterator] ?
customIterator[Symbol.iterator]() : customIteratcr;

let result = iterator.next();
while (!result.done) {
  console.log(result.value); // Process the value
  result = iterator.next(); // Get the next value
}
```

Key Components

1. next() **Method**:

    - The next method returns an object with twc properties:

        - **value**: The next value in the sequence

        - **done**: A boolean indicating whether the iteration is complete (true) or not (false)

2. **Symbol.iterator Property (Optional for Iterable Objects)**:

    - If an object implements the Symbol.iterator method, it is considered iterable and can be used with the for...of loop or spread syntax.

Example: Custom Iterator Syntax in Practice

Let's define a simple custom iterator that generates a sequence of numbers:

```
const numberSequence = {
  current: 1,
  last: 5,

  next() {
    if (this.current <= this.last) {
      return { value: this.current++, done: false }; // Produce
      the next value
    } else {
      return { value: undefined, done: true }; // End of
      iteration
    }
  }
};

// Using the iterator manually
let result = numberSequence.next();
while (!result.done) {
  console.log(result.value); // Outputs: 1, 2, 3, 4, 5
  result = numberSequence.next();
}
```

Making It Iterable with `Symbol.iterator`

For objects to work seamlessly with `for...of` loops and other iterable contexts, you need to implement the `Symbol.iterator` property:

```
const iterableNumbers = {
  current: 1,
  last: 5,
```

```
    [Symbol.iterator]() {
      return {
        current: this.current,
        last: this.last,

        next() {
          if (this.current <= this.last) {
            return { value: this.current++, done: false };
          } else {
            return { value: undefined, done: true };
          }
        }
      };
    }
};
// Using the iterable with for...of
for (const num of iterableNumbers) {
  console.log(num); // Outputs: 1, 2, 3, 4, 5
}
```

Generators

Generators simplify working with asynchronous data by pausing and resuming execution. They're particularly useful for complex workflows or integrating with asynchronous APIs.

Basic Syntax of a Generator

Here's the general syntax for defining a generator:

```
function* generatorFunction() {
  yield value1; // Produces the first value
  yield value2; // Produces the second value
```

```
  // Additional logic...
  return finalValue; // Completes the generator
}
// Using the generator
const generator = generatorFunction();
console.log(generator.next()); // { value: value1, done: false }
console.log(generator.next()); // { value: value2, done: false }
console.log(generator.next()); // { value: finalValue, done: true }
```

Key Components

1. `function*` **Declaration**:
   - The * indicates a generator function.
   - Generators return an **iterator object** when called.

2. `yield` **Keyword**:
   - Pauses the generator function and outputs a value.
   - The generator remains paused until `.next()` is called again.

3. `next()` **Method**:
   - Resumes execution of the generator from where it was paused.
   - Returns an object with
     - **value**: The value produced by `yield`
     - **done**: A boolean indicating if the generator has completed

4. **return Statement**:
   - Ends the generator and optionally provides a final value.

Example: Simple Generator for a Number Sequence

```
function* numberSequence() {
  yield 1;
  yield 2;
  yield 3;
  return "Done!";
}

// Using the generator
const numbers = numberSequence();

console.log(numbers.next()); // { value: 1, done: false }
console.log(numbers.next()); // { value: 2, done: false }
console.log(numbers.next()); // { value: 3, done: false }
console.log(numbers.next()); // { value: "Done!", done: true }
```

Advanced Example: Infinite Sequence with Generators

Generators are ideal for creating infinite sequences because they don't calculate values up front:

```
function* infiniteSequence() {
  let i = 0;
  while (true) {
    yield i++;
  }
}
```

```
// Using the generator
const sequence = infiniteSequence();

console.log(sequence.next().value); // 0
console.log(sequence.next().value); // 1
console.log(sequence.next().value); // 2
// Keeps generating values indefinitely
```

Example: Custom Iterator with Pagination Using Generators

Generators simplify creating custom iterators, like paginating data:

```
function* paginateData(items, pageSize) {
  for (let i = 0; i < items.length; i += pageSize) {
    yield items.slice(i, i + pageSize); // Yield a page of data
  }
}

// Sample data
const dataset = ["Item 1", "Item 2", "Item 3", "Item 4", "Item 5", "Item 6"];

// Using the pagination generator
const pages = paginateData(dataset, 2);

console.log(pages.next().value); // [ 'Item 1', 'Item 2' ]
console.log(pages.next().value); // [ 'Item 3', 'Item 4' ]
console.log(pages.next().value); // [ 'Item 5', 'Item 6' ]
console.log(pages.next().done);  // true (no more pages)
```

Combining Generators and Iterables

Generators can be used to define iterable objects directly:

```
const iterableObject = {
  *[Symbol.iterator]() {
    yield "A";
    yield "B";
    yield "C";
  }
};
// Using the iterable object
for (const value of iterableObject) {
  console.log(value); // Outputs: A, B, C
}
```

Benefits of Generators

1. **Lazy Evaluation**:
   - Generators produce values only when needed, making them memory-efficient for large or infinite sequences.

2. **Simplified Custom Iterators**:
   - Generators significantly reduce the boilerplate code required to implement custom iterators.

3. **Pause and Resume**:
   - The ability to pause execution and maintain state simplifies handling asynchronous workflows and complex logic.

CHAPTER 14   WORKING WITH ES6+ SYNTAX

EXERCISE 6: CUSTOM ITERATION WITH GENERATORS

Task: Write a generator function that yields the first five Fibonacci numbers. Use the generator in a `for...of` loop.

Hint: Start with the Fibonacci formula, and use `yield` to generate each value.

Code for Reference:

```
function* fibonacci() {
  // Generate Fibonacci sequence.
}
```

Promises and Async/Await

Promises and async/await simplify asynchronous programming in JavaScript, making code more readable and maintainable. Promises help handle asynchronous operations by representing eventual completion or failure, while async/await provides a more synchronous-looking syntax for working with promises.

Callback Hell and Why Promises Are Better

Before Promises, handling multiple asynchronous operations required **nested callbacks**, leading to **callback hell**, which makes code difficult to read and maintain.

Example of Callback Hell:

```
function getUserData(userId, callback) {
  setTimeout(() => {
    console.log("User data fetched");
```

```
    callback(null, { id: userId, name: "Alice" });
  }, 1000);
}
function getOrders(user, callback) {
  setTimeout(() => {
    console.log("Orders fetched");
    callback(null, [{ orderId: 1, total: 100 }]);
  }, 1000);
}
getUserData(1, (err, user) => {
  if (err) return console.error(err);
  getOrders(user, (err, orders) => {
    if (err) return console.error(err);
    console.log("Final Data:", { user, orders });
  });
});
```

Handling Multiple Promises the Right Way

The same logic can be written in a cleaner way using **Promises**:

```
function getUserData(userId) {
  return new Promise((resolve) => {
    setTimeout(() => {
      console.log("User data fetched");
      resolve({ id: userId, name: "Alice" });
    }, 1000);
  });
}
function getOrders(user) {
  return new Promise((resolve) => {
```

```
    setTimeout(() => {
      console.log("Orders fetched");
      resolve([{ orderId: 1, total: 100 }]);
    }, 1000);
  });
}

// Using async/await for better readability
async function fetchData() {
  try {
    const user = await getUserData(1);
    const orders = await getOrders(user);
    console.log("Final Data:", { user, orders });
  } catch (error) {
    console.error(error);
  }
}
fetchData();
```

Chaining Promises

Promise chaining is effective for sequential operations, such as fetching and transforming API data.

Example:

```
fetchData()
  .then(data => processData(data))
  .then(result => console.log(result))
  .catch(err => console.error(err));
```

Async/Await

`async/await` provides a synchronous-like syntax for asynchronous code, simplifying error handling and improving maintainability.

Example:

```
async function fetchAndProcess() {
  try {
    const data = await fetchData();
    const result = await processData(data);
    console.log(result);
  } catch (err) {
    console.error(err);
  }
}
```

Do's and Don'ts of Promises and Async/Await

✓ Do	✗ Don't
Use async/await for readability when handling multiple asynchronous operations.	**Don't mix async/await with .then() and .catch() unnecessarily**, as it reduces clarity.
Always handle errors properly using try/catch for async/await and .catch() for Promises.	**Don't forget to handle rejected Promises**, as unhandled rejections can crash applications.
Use Promise.all() when multiple promises are independent and need to be resolved in parallel.	**Don't use await inside loops** like forEach(), as it executes sequentially instead of in parallel.

(*continued*)

CHAPTER 14   WORKING WITH ES6+ SYNTAX

✓ Do	✗ Don't
Use Promise.race() when only the fastest promise result matters (e.g., handling timeouts).	**Don't use await without understanding its blocking nature**, as it pauses execution until completion.
Use Promise.allSettled() when all promises should be processed regardless of success/failure.	**Don't rely on Promise.all() when one failure should not cancel other async operations.**
Ensure async functions return a Promise explicitly, especially when wrapping callbacks.	**Don't declare an async function without await inside**, unless returning a promise.
Use finally() for cleanup logic (e.g., closing a connection, hiding a loader).	**Don't mutate shared/global state inside async functions**, as it can lead to race conditions.

Sets and Maps

JavaScript provides Set and Map as efficient alternatives to traditional arrays and objects for storing unique values and key-value pairs, respectively.

Set: Unique Value Storage

A set is a collection of unique values, meaning duplicate entries are automatically removed. It is useful for filtering duplicate elements and performing set operations like union, intersection, and difference.

437

Example:

```
const mySet = new Set([1, 2, 3, 4, 5]);
console.log(mySet);  // Output: Set {1, 2, 3, 4, 5}

mySet.add(5);
mySet.delete(2);

console.log(mySet.has(3)); // Output: true
console.log(mySet); // Output: Set {1, 3, 4, 5}
```

Map: Efficient Key–Value Storage

A map is a collection of **key-value pairs** where keys can be of any type, including objects and functions. Unlike regular objects, Map maintains insertion order and provides better performance for frequent key-value lookups.

Example:

```
 const myMap = new Map();
myMap.set("name", "Alice");
myMap.set(42, "Answer");
console.log(myMap.get("name")); // Output: Alice
console.log(myMap.has(42)); // Output: true
myMap.delete(42);
console.log(myMap.size); // Output: 1
```

Performance Comparison: Map vs. Set vs. Object vs. Array

Operation	Map Complexity	Set Complexity	Object Complexity	Array Complexity
Insert	O(1)	O(1)	O(1) (average)	O(1) (push)
Search (has/get)	O(1)	O(1)	O(1) (average)	O(n)
Delete	O(1)	O(1)	O(1) (average)	O(n)
Iteration	O(n)	O(n)	O(n)	O(n)

Key Takeaways

- Map and Set **outperform objects and arrays** when frequent insertions, deletions, or lookups are required.

- Set is preferable for **storing unique values** and eliminating duplicates efficiently.

- Map is **faster than objects** for frequent key–value lookups and supports non-string keys.

- Arrays are **inefficient for lookups and deletions** unless indexed keys are used.

For high-performance applications dealing with large datasets, **prefer Map over objects** and **Set over arrays** when unique value storage is needed.

Proxy and Reflect

What Are Proxies?

A **proxy** in JavaScript acts as a wrapper for an object, allowing you to intercept and redefine fundamental operations on that object, such as property access, assignment, enumeration, function invocation, and more. Proxies are incredibly useful when you need fine-grained control over how an object behaves.

The syntax for creating a proxy is as follows:

```
const proxy = new Proxy(target, handler);
```

- **target**: The original object to proxy
- **handler**: An object that contains traps (intercepting functions) for the operations you want to customize

Common Use Cases for Proxies

1. **Validation**: Enforce rules on property values during assignment.
2. **Logging**: Monitor access and modifications to properties.
3. **Default Values**: Return a default value if a property does not exist.
4. **Dynamic Properties**: Compute properties dynamically based on certain conditions.
5. **Object Protection**: Prevent certain operations, like deleting properties.

Example: Property Validation

Here's how a proxy can be used to validate property values:

```
const user = {
  name: "John",
  age: 30
};

const validator = {
  set(target, property, value) {
    if (property === "age" && (typeof value !== "number" ||
    value <= 0)) {
      throw new Error("Age must be a positive number.");
    }
    target[property] = value;
    return true;
  }
};

const proxyUser = new Proxy(user, validator);

proxyUser.age = 25; // Works fine
console.log(proxyUser.age); // 25

proxyUser.age = -5; // Throws an error: Age must be a
                       positive number.
```

Reflect: A Companion to Proxy

The **Reflect** API complements proxies by providing methods for performing object operations in a way that is consistent with the language's internal methods. It simplifies tasks like accessing properties, calling functions, or defining properties.

CHAPTER 14   WORKING WITH ES6+ SYNTAX

Reflect methods are often used inside proxy handlers to delegate the original operation to the target object.

Here's an example combining **Proxy** and **Reflect** for clean delegation:

```
const user = {
  name: "Alice",
  age: 25
};

const handler = {
  get(target, property) {
    console.log(`Accessing property '${property}'`);
    return Reflect.get(target, property);
  },
  set(target, property, value) {
    console.log(`Setting property '${property}' to
    '${value}'`);
    return Reflect.set(target, property, value);
  }
};

const proxyUser = new Proxy(user, handler);

console.log(proxyUser.name); // Logs: Accessing property 'name'
| Returns: Alice
proxyUser.age = 30;          // Logs: Setting property
'age' to '30'
console.log(proxyUser.age);  // Logs: Accessing property 'age' |
Returns: 30
```

Practical Scenarios for Proxies and Reflect

1. **API Request Wrapping**: Intercept API calls to log, cache, or modify requests.
2. **Virtual Properties**: Implement virtual attributes that are computed dynamically.
3. **Internationalization (i18n)**: Automatically translate property values based on locale.
4. **Security Enforcement**: Restrict access to sensitive properties based on user roles.
5. **Immutable Data Structures**: Prevent modification of objects by intercepting assignment operations.

Example – Default Values for Undefined Properties:

A common use case is returning default values when a property doesn't exist:

```
const defaults = {
  name: "Anonymous",
  age: 18
};

const defaultHandler = {
  get(target, property) {
    return property in target ? target[property] : `Default: ${defaults[property] || "N/A"}`;
  }
};

const user = {};
const proxyUser = new Proxy(user, defaultHandler);
```

```
console.log(proxyUser.name); // Default: Anonymous
console.log(proxyUser.age);  // Default: 18
console.log(proxyUser.job);  // Default: N/A
```

Advantages of Using Proxy and Reflect

- **Enhanced Control**: Customize behavior for objects at a granular level.
- **Improved Debugging**: Log or modify interactions with objects in real time.
- **Dynamic Behavior**: Create objects that adapt to changing requirements.

Limitations

- **Performance**: Proxies introduce a slight overhead since every interaction goes through a handler.
- **Browser Compatibility**: Proxies are not supported in older environments like Internet Explorer.
- **Complexity**: Overuse can make code harder to read and maintain.

By understanding the **Proxy** and **Reflect** features, you can harness their power to create flexible, controlled, and dynamic object behaviors, opening up new possibilities for modern JavaScript applications.

CHAPTER 14 WORKING WITH ES6+ SYNTAX

EXERCISE 7: CUSTOM BEHAVIOR WITH PROXY

Task: Create a proxy for an object that logs every time a property is accessed or modified. Use the Reflect API to manage the actual property operations.

Hint: Use `get` and `set` traps in the proxy.

Code for Reference:

```
const target = { a: 1, b: 2 };
// Create a proxy for the target object.
```

Summary

In this chapter, we explored the powerful features introduced in ES6+ that have revolutionized JavaScript development. These features, designed to simplify and enhance coding efficiency, include **template literals** for dynamic string handling, **destructuring** to easily extract values from arrays and objects, and the versatile **spread and rest operators**. We discussed how **default parameters** can make functions more robust and how modern operators like **optional chaining** and **nullish coalescing** provide safer and more concise ways to access and assign values.

Each section highlighted the practical benefits of these features, with detailed explanations and hands-on examples demonstrating their usage. From reducing boilerplate code with destructuring to improving error resilience with optional chaining, these tools equip developers to write cleaner, more efficient, and maintainable code.

By mastering these features, developers can take full advantage of modern JavaScript's capabilities, improving their productivity and making their applications more robust and scalable.

CHAPTER 14   WORKING WITH ES6+ SYNTAX

Full Solutions

> **SOLUTION TO EXERCISE 1: CREATING DYNAMIC STRINGS WITH TEMPLATE LITERALS**

```
const name = "Alice";
const age = 25;

const greeting = `
  Hello, my name is ${name}.
  I will be ${age + 5} years old in 5 years.
`;

console.log(greeting);
```

> **SOLUTION TO EXERCISE 2: EXTRACTING VALUES FROM ARRAYS AND OBJECTS**

```
const numbers = [1, 2, 3, 4];
const person = { name: "Bob", address: { city: "Paris", zip: 75001 } };

// Array Destructuring
const [first, second] = numbers;
console.log(first, second); // 1, 2

// Object Destructuring
const { name, address: { city, zip } } = person;
console.log(name, city, zip); // Bob, Paris, 75001
```

CHAPTER 14   WORKING WITH ES6+ SYNTAX

SOLUTION TO EXERCISE 3: COMBINING ARRAYS AND OBJECTS

```
const arr1 = [1, 2, 3];
const arr2 = [4, 5, 6];
const obj1 = { a: 1 };
const obj2 = { b: 2 };

// Using the spread operator to merge arrays
const combinedArray = [...arr1, ...arr2];
console.log(combinedArray); // [1, 2, 3, 4, 5, 6]

// Using the spread operator to merge objects
const combinedObject = { ...obj1, ...obj2 };
console.log(combinedObject); // { a: 1, b: 2 }

// Function using the rest operator
function sum(...nums) {
  return nums.reduce((total, num) => total + num, 0);
}
console.log(sum(1, 2, 3, 4)); // 10
```

SOLUTION TO EXERCISE 4: CALCULATING DISCOUNTS WITH DEFAULT PARAMETERS

```
function calculateTotal(price, discountRate = 0.1) {
  const total = price * (1 - discountRate);
  return total;
}
```

```
console.log(calculateTotal(100)); // 90 (with default
discount)
console.log(calculateTotal(100, 0.2)); // 80 (with custom
discount)
```

SOLUTION TO EXERCISE 5: SAFE ACCESS AND DEFAULT VALUES

```
const user = { profile: { name: "Charlie" } };

const age = user?.profile?.age ?? 30; // Default to 30 if
age is undefined or null
console.log(age); // 30
```

SOLUTION TO EXERCISE 6: CUSTOM ITERATION WITH GENERATORS

```
function* fibonacci() {
  let a = 0, b = 1;
  while (true) {
    yield a;
    [a, b] = [b, a + b];
  }
}
const fibSeq = fibonacci();
for (let i = 0; i < 5; i++) {
  console.log(fibSeq.next().value); // 0, 1, 1, 2, 3
}
```

SOLUTION TO EXERCISE 7: CUSTOM BEHAVIOR WITH PROXY

```
const target = { a: 1, b: 2 };
const handler = {
  get: (target, prop) => {
    console.log(`Accessed property: ${prop}`);
    return prop in target ? target[prop] : 'Property
    not found';
  },
  set: (target, prop, value) => {
    console.log(`Setting property: ${prop} to ${value}`);
    target[prop] = value;
    return true;
  }
};

const proxy = new Proxy(target, handler);

console.log(proxy.a); // Accessed property: a, 1
proxy.b = 3; // Setting property: b to 3
console.log(proxy.b); // Accessed property: b, 3
console.log(proxy.c); // Accessed property: c, Property
                          not found
```

Index

A

add function, 337
addClickListener function, 340
Angular, 91, 143
Angular's signals, 108
applyMiddleware, 340
Argument function
    validation, 280–284
Arithmetic operators, 155
Array destructuring, 414
Array.prototype.at(), 77
Array.prototype.filter method, 122
Array.prototype.flat(), 65
Array.prototype.flatMap(), 66
Array.prototype.includes(), 51, 52
Array.prototype.indexOf(), 43
Arrays, 419, 447
    accessing elements, 364
    adding elements, 365
    creation
        using Array.from(), 363, 364, 383
        using Array.of(), 363
        using constructor, 362
        using literals, 362
    definition, 361
    destructuring, 270

ECMAScript 3, 33, 34
extracting values, 416, 446
forEach method, 366, 371, 383
for…of loop, 371
immutability, 161
map method, 336
methods, 35, 37–39
modifying elements, 364
multidimensional, 369
nested, 371
reasons, 361
removing elements, 365
returning values, 278, 279
search methods, 367
.slice(), 368, 369
sorting methods, 367, 368
traditional loops, 366
transformation methods, 367
Arrow functions, 46
    add function, 284
    benefits, 286
    and context, 293, 345
    definition, 283
    no parameters, 285
    return keyword, 284
    single parameter, 284, 285
    syntax, 284
    this keyword, 286–292

INDEX

Assignment operators, 156
Associativity, 157, 158
Async/await, 436
   advantages and disadvantages, 436, 437
   breakpoints, 141
   cleaner code, 55
   cognitive load, 54
   definition, 54, 55
   example, 15
   handling errors, 396, 406
   multiple asynchronous calls, 396–398
   try/catch block, 395
Asynchronous calls, 396–398
Asynchronous iteration, 62, 63
Asynchronous operations, 136
Asynchronous programming, 14, 16
Atom, 20

B

Babel, 114
Basic defaults, 420
BigInt, 69, 72, 73
Block scope, 295, 296
Block scoping, 35
Breakpoints
   action setting, 134, 135
   asynchronous code, 141
   code setting, 135, 136
   JavaScript execution, 132
   setting, 132
   types, 133

break statement
   defined, 241
   example, 241
   reasons, 243
   usage, 244

C

Caching systems, 77
Callback function, 38
Callback hell, 54, 55, 433
Callbacks, 340
Call stack
   debugging guide, 137, 138
   debugging issues, 136
   definition, 136
   execution flow diagram, 139
   LIFO, 136
   understanding in action, 137
   usage, 140
Cascading style sheets (CSS), 10
Catch block, 32, 33, 388, 389, 395
Chrome Developer tools (DevTools), 22, 23
Classes, 47
   advantages, 379
   constructor, 378
   definition, 378
   inheritance, 378, 424
   methods, 378
   object-oriented approach, 424
   object-oriented programming, 377

INDEX

private methods and
    fields, 81, 82
prototypes, 379
readability and
    compatibility, 379
syntax, 424
Closures
    in action, 327
    asynchronous code, 332–334
    bank account, 328, 329
    concept, 330
    data encapsulation, 331, 332
    definition, 326
    deposit method, 329
    dynamic function factories,
        334, 335
    encapsulation, 328
    inner function, 326
    lexical scope, 326, 327
    mechanism, 327
    outer function, 326
    output breakdown, 327, 328
    private variables, 328
    withdraw method, 330
Code editor, 21
    Atom, 20
    DevTools, 22, 23
    HTML template, 24, 25
    Node.js, 23
    online playgrounds, 25, 26
    Sublime Text, 20
    VS Code, 20, 21
    web browsers, 22
    WebStorm, 20

CodePen, 25, 29
Code readability, 154, 155, 169
Code splitting, 106
Comparison operators, 156
Compiler, 115, 116
Component-based
    architecture, 87
Computed property names,
    359, 423
Conditional breakpoints, 133
Conditional logic, 216, 258
config.apiUrl, 322
console.assert(), 132
console.error(), 132
console.info(), 132
console.log() method
    asynchronous code, 140
    best practices, 131
    real-time inspection, 131
console.warn(), 132
const
    behavior, 159
    immutability, 147, 159–162
    objects, 147
    performance implications
        actual performance
            improvement, 164
        immutability, 164–167
        intent developer, 164
        optimizations, 164
    reasons, 160
    scope, 147
    usage, 162
    use cases, 162

453

INDEX

Constructor functions, 355–357
Content management system (CMS), 89
Content security policy (CSP), 107
continue statement
    defined, 242
    example, 242
    reasons, 243
    usage, 244
Control flow
    design, 217
    if and else (*see* if and else statements)
    loops (*see* Loops)
    mechanisms, 253, 254
    switch statement, 218–221
counter.increment(), 319
counter.reset(), 320
createCounter function, 331
Cross-site scripting (XSS), 107
curriedAdd function, 307, 309
Currying, 315, 346
    benefits, 299, 300
    caution, 315
    cleaner code, 314
    closures, 307
    definition, 298, 306
    event handlers, 300
    example, 298
    functional programming libraries
        code execution, 306
        configuration settings, 304
        impure function, 304
        inner function, 305
        nested inner function, 305
        outer function, 305
        pure function, 303
    mathematical operations, 307–310
    memoization, 315
    memory impact, 315
    partial application, 314
    performance and memory, 313
        memoization, 311
        memory overhead, 312, 313
        partial application and reuse, 310
    performance considerations, 314
    performance-sensitive applications, 298
    reusability, 314
    use cases
        logEvent function, 300–303
Custom errors
    defined, 390
    syntax, 390
    throwing, 391, 404
    using class, 391, 392
Custom iterator
    components
        next() method, 426
        Symbol.iterator property, 426–428

pagination, 431
protocol, 425
syntax, 425, 426

D

Data encapsulation, 331, 332
Data structures, 165
Debugger statement, 141
Debugging
    asynchronous JavaScript
        breakpoints, 141
        console.log(), 140
    breakpoints, 132–133
    call stack, 136–140
    code stepping, 133–136
    console logging, 131–132
    debugger statement, 141
    DevTools, 129–130
    performance and memory, 142
    tools, 142, 143
Default parameters, 265, 345
    basic defaults, 420
    calculating discounts, 420, 447
    dynamic defaults, 420
Default values, 415, 448
Destructured parameters
    advantages, 270
    APIs responses, 272
    arrays, 270, 272
    benefits, 274, 275
    calculate function, 271, 272
    defined, 268
    extract properties, 269

extract values, 270
fetchUserData function, 273, 274
objects, 268
parameter list, 271
Destructuring
    array, 414
    assignment, 49, 50
    object, 414, 415
Developer Tools (DevTools)
    features, 130
    opening, 130
displayUser function, 269
divide function, 280
Document object model (DOM), 11–12, 85
DOM breakpoints, 133
do...while loop
    condition, 231
    defined, 230
    ensuring first execution, 232
    error prevention, 232
    example, 230
    real-world flexibility, 232
    syntax, 230
    user input validation, 231
Dynamic content, 85, 86
Dynamic defaults, 420
Dynamic function factories, 334, 335
Dynamic property assignment, 359, 360, 383
Dynamic updates without reloads, 86

INDEX

E

ECMAScript 3
  browser environment, 31
  regular expressions, 32
  string and array methods, 33, 34
  try/catch block, error handling, 32, 33
ECMAScript 4, 34, 35
ECMAScript 5 (ES5)
  array methods, 37–39
  bind() method, 44
  features, 35
  getter and setter methods, 41, 42
  indexOf(), 43
  JSON, 39, 41
  Object.create(), 42
  Object.defineProperty() and Object.defineProperties(), 42, 43
  use strict, 36, 37
ECMAScript 6, 116
  arrow functions, 46
  classes, 47
  class syntax, 116
  destructuring assignment, 49, 50
  let and const, 45
  modules, 48
  template literals, 48
ECMAScript 7
  exponentiation operator, 52, 53
  includes() method, 51, 52

ECMAScript 8
  async/await, 54–56
  features, 58
  Object.entries() and Object.values(), 56, 57
  smoother and intuitive development, 58
ECMAScript 9
  for-await-of loop, 62, 63
  functionality and usability, 59
  Promise.finally(), 60, 61
  regex, 63, 64
  rest and spread operators, 59, 60
ECMAScript 10
  code readability, 64
  flatMap() method, 66
  flat() method, 65
  JSON.stringify(), 68, 69
  Object.fromEntries() method, 68
  optional catch binding, 65
  trimStart() and trimEnd(), 67
ECMAScript 11
  BigInt, 72, 73
  edge cases, 69
  nullish coalescing operator, 70
  optional chaining, 70–72
ECMAScript 12
  at() method, 77
  logical assignment operators, 74
  numeric separators, 75
  Promise.allSettled(), 78, 79
  Promise.any(), 76

456

INDEX

replaceAll() method, 75, 76
WeakRefs and
    FinalizationRegistry, 77
ECMAScript 13
    error handling, 80
    numeric separator, 81
    private methods and
        fields, 81, 82
    record and tuple types, 82, 83
    Top-Level Await, 79, 80
Equality, 190, 203
    operators, 183
Error class
    creation, 391
    inspecting, 393, 404
    object and properties, 392
Error handling, 4, 55, 80
    async and await, 394–401, 406
    creating custom errors, 390–392
    global, 398–400
    graceful degradation *vs.* failing
        fast, 400
    mechanisms, 385
    reasons, 386
    and recovery, 229
    sources, 385
    try, catch and finally blocks, 32,
        33, 388, 389
    types, 386
    with ??= operator, 393, 394, 405
escapeHtml function, 107
ESLint, 104
ES6+ syntax
    classes, 424

    default parameters, 419–421
    destructuring, 414–416
    iterators and
        generators, 425–433
    nullish coalescing
        operator, 422
    object literals, 422–424
    optional chaining, 421
    promises and async/
        await, 433–436
    proxy and reflect, 440–445
    sets and maps, 437–439
    spread and rest
        operators, 416–419
    template literals, 410–414
Event-driven model, 86
Event-driven programming, 229
Event handlers, 13
Event handling, 13, 86
    and callbacks, 340
    this keyword, 291
Event listener breakpoints,
    133, 141
Exception handling, 389, 403
Exercises
    additional tools, 28, 29
    creating HTML file, 26, 27
    creating JavaScript file, 27
    organizing, 28
    running code, 28
    tips, 29
Exponentiation operator (**),
    52, 53
Express, 92

F

Factory function, 352, 356, 382
Factory *vs.* constructor functions, 352, 354, 355
Fallback systems, 76
fetchData function, 333
FinalizationRegistry, 77
Finally block, 388, 389
Firefox, 22
Floating-point numbers, 191, 192, 204
For-await-of loop, 62, 63
forEach loop
    benefits, 234
    cleaner code, 236
    data processing, 235, 236
    defined, 232
    example, 233, 234
    functional programming approach, 236
    improved readability, 236
    iteration details, 234
    limitations, 235
    real-world relevance, 236
    syntax, 233
forEach method, 366, 371
for loop
    advanced patterns, 225
    code optimization, 225
    condition, 222
    defined, 222
    efficiency with collections, 225
    example, 222, 224
    increment, 222
    initialization, 222
    iteration, 240, 259
    real-world use cases, 225
    structured iteration, 225
    syntax, 222
    use cases, 223
for...of loop, 371
    defined, 237
    direct access to values, 239
    error reduction, 240
    example, 237
    vs. forEach, 240
    iterating through string, 239
    modern JavaScript paradigm, 240
    scenarios, 238
    summing numbers in array, 238
    syntax, 237
    versatile iteration, 240
Frameworks
    back-end
        Express, 92
        NestJS, 92
    definition, 90
    front-end
        Angular, 91
        React, 91
        Vue.js, 91
Full-stack language, 14
Functional programming, 166
Function.prototype.bind(), 44
Functions
    arguments object, 267
    arrow (*see* Arrow functions)

benefits, 266, 267
composition, 341, 342
declaration, 261
default parameters, 265
definition, 261
destructured
  parameters, 268–275
destructuring, 279
expressions, 262
hoisting, 263
parameters, 263
real-world use case, 275
rest parameters, 265
returning multiple values, 279
  using arrays, 278, 279
  using object, 277
returning single values, 276, 279
validating arguments, 279–283
variable declarations, 264, 344
Function scope *vs.* block
  scope, 148–150

G

Garbage collection, 165
Generators
  asynchronous data, 428
  benefits, 432
  components
    function* declaration, 429
    next() method, 429
    return statement, 430
    yield keyword, 429
  custom iteration, 433, 448

custom iterator with
  pagination, 431
infinite sequences, 430, 431
and iterables, 432
number sequence, 430
syntax, 428
getMinMax function, 278
getStats function, 277
Getter Method, 41, 42
GitHub Copilot, 20
Global error handling
  defined, 398
  using process.on, in Node.js,
    399, 400
  using window.onerror, 399
Global scope, 293, 294
Global variable pollution,
  323–325
Global variables, 152, 153
Google Chrome, 22, 130
Graceful degradation *vs.* failing
  fast, 400
greet() function, 281, 294, 295

H

Higher-order functions (HOFs), 302
  abstracting repeated logic, 338
  creating middleware/plugins,
    339, 340
  custom, 337, 338
  custom utilities and
    composition, 341, 342
  defined, 335

INDEX

Higher-order functions
(HOFs) (cont.)
event handling and
callbacks, 340
map method, 336
working, 343, 346
Hypertext markup language
(HTML), 10

I

if and else statements
decision-making, 216
using else with if, 211
else if and multiple conditions,
212, 214
example, 210
foundational tools, 217
handling defaults with else,
211, 258
isLoggedIn, 210
making decisions, 210, 258
multiple conditions in single
check, 213, 214
readability and
maintainability, 216
syntax, 210
ternary operator, 214–215
Immediately invoked function
expression (IIFE)
avoiding global scope
pollution, 317
count variable, 319
definition, 316

encapsulation, 317, 318, 320
execution, 316, 318
execution context, 317
function definition, 316
global variable
pollution, 323–325
immediate invocation, 316
increment and reset
methods, 319
initializing
configurations, 320–322
stateful object, 320
syntax, 316
Immutability, 159
const keyword, 159
copying data structures, 165
functional programming, 166
garbage collection, 165
modifying variables, 163, 169
mutability, 167
Object.freeze(), 161, 162
objects and arrays, 161
optimization techniques,
166, 167
primitive types, 160
Implicit conversion, 191, 204
Implicit string, 190
indexOf() method, 51
Infinite loops, 227
Inheritance, 378, 424
innerFunction(), 297
Integrated Development
Environment (IDE), 20, 27
Interactivity, 85, 86

Interpolation, 411
Interpreted language, 5, 6, 10
Ion-button element, 101
Ionic, 100, 101
Iterator protocol, 425

J, K

Jasmine, 92
JavaScript
    AI and ML integration, 109, 110
    asynchronous
        programming, 14, 16
    in currying (*see* Currying)
    defined, 1
    DOM, 11–12
    ecosystem
        build tools, 103, 104
        linting and formatting,
            104, 105
        package management,
            102, 103
    events, 13
    front-end and back-end
        development, 14
    functions, 16
    interpreted language, 5, 6, 10
    mechanisms, 15
    mobile development, 98–102
    prototypal inheritance
        model, 47
    server-side, 88–90
    user interaction, 13
    Wasm, 108

WebAssembly with service
    workers, 109
web development, 9–11
zoneless frameworks, 108
JavaScriptCore, 10
JavaScript object notation (JSON),
    35, 39, 41
Jest, 92
JetBrains, 20
JSFiddle, 25, 29
JSON.parse() method, 39, 40
JSON.stringify(), 39, 40, 68, 69
Just-in-time (JIT), 4

L

Last-in, first-out (LIFO), 136
let
    no hoisting, 146
    scope, 146
Lexical comparison, 176
Lexical scope, 296, 297, 305,
    326, 327
Library
    definition, 90
    structural sharing, 166
    testing
        Jest, 92
        Mocha and Jasmine, 92
Line breakpoints, 133
Live server extension, 29
.localeCompare() method, 178
Locale-sensitive comparisons, 178
Local scope, 294, 295

INDEX

Lodash, 303, 304
logEvent function
    closures, 302
    console logging, 301
    errorLogger, 302
    example, 300
    HOFs, 302
    infoLogger, 302
    inner function, 301
    outer function, 301
    reusability, 303
    usage, 303
loggedAdd function, 338
logger function, 337, 339
Logical assignment operators, 74
Logical errors, 386
    fixing, 387, 402
Logical nullish assignment (??=) operator
    comparison to ||=, 251
    default values, 252
    example, 250
    null/undefined, 249
    real-world use case, 251
    scenario, 250
    syntax, 249
logTime function, 333
Long-term support (LTS), 23
Loops
    benefits, 245
    break and continue statements, 241–244
    controlling execution, 244
    controlling execution, 259
    do...while loop, 230–232
    for loop, 222–226
    forEach loop, 232–236
    for...of loop, 237–240
    real-world use cases, 246
    repetitive tasks, 221
    traditional, 366
    while loop, 226–229

M

Machine learning, 109
Map
    key-value storage, 438
    vs. set, 439
map() method, 37–39, 336
Math.ceil(), 181
Math.floor(), 181
Math.max(), 181
Math.min(), 181
Math operations, 180
Math.pow() function, 52
Math.random(), 181
Math.round(), 181
Memoization, 167, 311, 315
Memory overhead, 312, 313
Microsoft Edge, 22, 130
Middleware/plugins, 339, 340
Mobile development
    Ionic, 100, 101
    React Native, 98, 99
Mocha, 92

Modular codebases, 48
Module creation, 322
Modules, 48
Mozilla Firefox, 130
Multidimensional arrays, 369
Multi-line comments, 154
Multi-line strings, 173, 202, 410
Multiple JavaScript files, 28
multiplier function, 334

N

Named capture groups, 63
Negative indices, 77
Nested callbacks, 433
Nested destructuring, 415
Nested function calls, 136
Nesting ternary operators, 215
NestJS, 92
Node.js
   building REST APIs, 89
   handling file systems and
      databases, 89
   real-time applications, 89
   responsiveness and low
      latency, 89
   server-side code, 90
   server-side development, 14
   setting up, 23
   uncaught errors, 400
   using process.on, 399, 400
Not-a-Number (NaN), 192, 204
Nullish coalescing operator
   (??), 70, 422

assigning default values,
   252, 259
example, 248
falsy values, 249
null/undefined, 247
real-world use case, 248
syntax, 247
targeted approach, 246
Numbers
   conversion, 190
   falsy and truthy values
      assigning default values,
         198, 205
      comparison, 200, 207
      conditional checks,
         193, 194
      evaluation, 193
      examples, 196
      explicit type-checking, 194
      filtering, 197, 199, 205, 206
      null and undefined, 196
      objects, 199, 206
      use cases, 194, 195
      validating input, 198, 205
   finding maximum value,
      182, 203
   floating-point, 191
   floating-point
      arithmetic, 180
   math methods and
      rounding, 181, 182
   math operations, 180
   NaN type, 192
Numeric separators, 75, 81

463

INDEX

O

Object.create() method, 42, 351, 375–377
Object.defineProperties(), 42, 43
Object.defineProperty(), 42, 43, 153
Object destructuring, 414, 415
Object.entries(), 56, 57
Object.entries(obj), 370
Object.freeze(), 161, 162
Object.fromEntries() method, 68
Object.keys(obj), 370
Object literals, 417
    computed property names, 423
    method definitions, 423
    shorthand property names, 423
Object-oriented programming, 47
Objects, 419, 447
    accessors, 371
    adding methods, 358
    classes (ES6 Syntax), 357
    computed property names, 359
    constructor functions, 351, 355–357
    dynamic property assignment, 359
    extracting values, 416, 446
    factory function, 352
    factory *vs.* constructor functions, 352, 354, 355
    immutability, 161
    key–value pairs, 348
    literals, 349, 350, 382
    methods, 348
    Object.create() method, 351
    properties, 348, 370
    reasons, 348
    understanding, 349, 382
    use cases, 351
Object.values(), 56, 57
Object.values(obj), 370
Object *vs.* array, 439
Online code editors, 29
Online playgrounds, 25, 26
Operator precedence, 156, 157
Optimization techniques, 166, 167
Optional catch binding, 65
Optional chaining (?.), 70–72, 421
outerFunction(), 297
Output property, 104
Overwriting methods, 374

P, Q

Package management, 102, 103
Parentheses for clarity, 158
Pattern matching, 63
Pollyfills
    advantages, 122, 124
    Array.prototype.filter method, 122
    compatibility, 121
    core logic, 121
    definition, 120
    filter() method, 121
    usage, 123
    use cases, 121, 123

INDEX

validation, 121
Prettier, 104
Primitive types, 160
processOrder function, 282
Progressive web apps (PWAs)
    enhanced performance, 95
    installable and offline capable, 93
    offline capabilities, 93
    push notifications, 95
    responsive and platform-independent, 93
    SEO benefits, 95
    service workers, 94
Promise.allSettled(), 78, 79
Promise.any(), 76
Promise.finally(), 60, 61
Promises
    advantages and disadvantages, 436, 437
    asynchronous tasks, 60
    callback hell, 433
    chaining, 435
    ES6, 122
    multiple, 398, 406, 434
Prototypes
    chain and inheritance, 373–375
    classes, 379
    creating object, 372
    defined, 372
    inheritance, 380, 384
    Object.create(), 375–377
    usage, 377

Proxies
    advantages, 444
    custom behavior, 445, 449
    definition, 440
    limitations, 444
    practical scenarios, 443
    property validation, 441
    syntax, 440
    use cases, 440
Python, 4

R

Ramda, 303, 304
React, 91, 142
React Native, 98, 99, 101
Record, 82
Recursion, 136
Redux, 143, 417
Reflect
    advantages, 444
    definition, 441
    delegation, 442
    limitations, 444
    practical scenarios, 443
Regular expressions (regex), 32, 63, 64
Replit, 26, 29
Rest operator, 418
Rest parameters, 265, 267, 345
Rest/spread operators, 59, 60
Runtime errors, 386
    debugging, 387, 402

S

Safari, 130
Safe access, 448
Scope
    block, 295, 296
    defined, 293
    global, 293, 294
    lexical, 296, 297
    local, 294, 295
Search engine optimization (SEO), 23, 95
Search methods, 367
Security risks, 413
Security threats, 107
Server-side JavaScript, 88–90
Service workers, 94, 109
Set, unique value storage, 437
setConfig function, 305
Setter method, 41, 42
setTimeout function, 333
s (dotAll) flag, 63
Shallow copies *vs.* deep copies, 166
Shorthand property names, 423
Single JavaScript file, 28
Single-line comments, 154
Single-page applications (SPAs), 14, 91
    benefits, 87, 88
    frameworks, 87
    web development, 87
Sorting methods, 367, 368
Source-to-source compiler, 113
SpiderMonkey, 10
Spread operator, 417, 418
StackBlitz, 26
Strict mode
    activation, 36
    error, 36
    example, 36
    security, 37
    undeclared variable assignment, 36
String, 33, 34
String interpolation, 49
String literals, 172
String.prototype.replaceAll(), 75, 76
String.prototype.trimEnd(), 67
String.prototype.trimStart(), 67
Strings, 171
    capitalizing first letter, 179, 203
    comparisons
        case sensitivity, 177
        endsWith(), 178
        includes(), 178
        lexical comparison, 176
        locale-sensitive, 178
        special characters, 177
        startsWith(), 178
    implicit, 190
    manipulation, 179, 202
    methods
        indexOf() and includes(), 175
        length, 175
        slice() and substring(), 176
        toUpperCase() and toLowerCase(), 175
        trim(), 175

Structured cloning, 418
Sublime Text, 20
Switch statement
    case blocks, 218
    definition, 218
    example, 218
    fall-through behavior, 219
    vs. if...else, 220, 221
    intentional fall-through, 220
    for multiple cases, 221, 258
    syntax, 218
Symbol.iterator method, 426–428
Syntax
    code readability, 3
    debugging, 5
    definition, 2
    errors, 5, 386, 387, 401
    goals, 4
    interpreted execution, 6
    invalid assignment operator, 3
    keyword results, 2
    logic connection, 5, 6
    re-parsing, 4
    rules, 3
    transition, 4
    variable, 2

T

Tagged templates, 411
Tail call optimization (TCO), 314
Template literals, 48, 172
    best practices, 413, 414
    dynamic strings, 412, 446
    ES6, 172
    interpolation, 411
    limitations, 412, 413
    multi-line strings, 410
    single and double quotes, 174
    tagged, 173
    tagged templates, 411
    usage, 172, 174, 202
Template strings (*see* Template literals)
Temporal dead zone, 150
TensorFlow.js, 109, 110
Ternary operator
    advantage, 215
    defined, 214
    example, 214
    nesting, 215
    syntax, 214
    usage, 215
this keyword
    arrow functions, 288
    .bind() method, 289, 290
    .call() and .apply() method, 290
    constructors/classes, 290, 291
    event handlers, 291
    execution context, 287
    methods, 287
    regular function, 288
    scenarios, 287
toFixed(), 182
Top-Level Await, 79, 80
toPrecision(), 182
Transformation methods, 367

INDEX

Transpilers
    Babel, 114
    benefits, 114
    class syntax, 117, 118
    vs. compilers, 115, 116
    definition, 113
    ES6, 116
    real-world usage, 118–120
    TypeScript compiler, 114
    working, 114
Transpilers *vs.* polyfills
    best practices, 127
    challenges, 126
    features, 124
    functionality, 125
    tools, 126, 128
Tree-shaking, 106
Try block, 32, 33, 388, 389, 395
Tuple, 82
Type coercion
    best practices, 186, 187
    definition, 183
    equality, 183
    object comparisons, 184, 185
    == operator, 187–189
    sorting data, 185
    truthy and falsy values, 185
    user input validation, 184
typeof operator, 200
typeof null operator, 200, 201, 208
TypeScript, 6, 20

U

Uncaught errors handling, 400, 407
UncaughtException, 399
Undefined variables, 150, 151
Unexpected token, 5
UnhandledRejection, 400
User interface (UI), 12
User login system, 216
Utility functions, 420

V

var, 45
    function scope *vs.* block scope, 148–150
    global variables and window object, 152, 153
    hoisting, 146
    redeclaration and accidental overwritten, 151, 152
    scope, 146
    spotting issues, 152, 168
    undefined variables, 150, 151
Variables
    data storage, 145
    declarations, 148, 168
    declaring const, 147
    declaring let, 146
    declaring var, 146
Visual Studio Code (VS Code), 20, 21
Vite, 103
Vue.js, 91

W

WeakRefs, 77
WebAssembly (Wasm), 108, 109
Web browsers, 22
Web development, 9–11
    challenges
        browser compatibility, 106
        performance issues, 106
        security risks, 107
    dynamic content and
        interactivity, 85, 86
    frameworks and libraries,
        90–93
    PWAs, 93–95
    real-time applications, 96–98
    server-side JavaScript, 88–90
    SPAs, 87, 88
Webpack, 103, 104
WebSockets, 96–98
WebStorm, 20
while loop
    condition, 226
    defined, 226
    dynamic conditions, 229
    error handling and
        recovery, 229
    event-driven programming, 229
    example, 226, 227
    flexibility in logic, 229
    infinite loops, 227
    syntax, 226
    use cases, 227
    user input, 228
Window object, 152, 153

X, Y

XHR/fetch breakpoints, 133

Z

Zoneless frameworks, 108
Zone system, 108

Printed in the United States
by Baker & Taylor Publisher Services